CHRISTIANS UNDER THE HAMMER & SICKLE

CHRISTIANS UNDER THE HAMMER & SICKLE

WINRICH SCHEFFBUCH

TRANSLATED FROM THE GERMAN BY MARK A. NOLL

ZONDERVAN
PUBLISHING HOUSE   OF THE ZONDERVAN CORPORATION
GRAND RAPIDS, MICHIGAN 49506

CONTENTS

CHRISTIANS UNDER THE HAMMER & SICKLE

1

EVANGELICAL CHRISTIANS IN RUSSIA

IN THE SOVIET UNION today there are more evangelical Christians than most people think. It is estimated that about five million people participate in Protestant worship services regularly. Thirty thousand preachers, most of whom hold other employment, serve in the proclamation of the Gospel.

The most important group of Protestant churches and fellowships, a group embracing various denominations, has become well-known under the name Evangelical Christians and Baptists. The once numerous Lutheran congregations of German settlers on the Volga River and in the southern Ukraine were destroyed in Stalin's purges. As far as we know, the large numbers of German Lutherans still are not permitted more than a few congregations. Lutheran church groups can be organized at this present time only in the Soviet republics of Latvia and Estonia. In Siberia and Central Asia, except for seventeen tightly regulated churches which the state tolerates, hundreds of Lutheran congregations are able to have only a clandestine existence.

Observers describe the Evangelical Christians and Baptists as the "most active Christian church in the Soviet Union." The confederation functions as an umbrella for different groups of evangelical Christians which arose out of the revivals of the last century and for the League of Russian Baptists which has existed since 1884. Under pressure from the government Pentecostals, Adventists, and Mennonites also have had to join the confederation of Evangelical Christians and Baptists.

Although the government of the Soviet Union makes propaganda out of the religious freedom in the country, half of the Protestant congregations are denied official recognition. The authorities do presently tolerate a portion of these congregations, but it is their intention

9

to systematically extinguish the rest. Even among the officially permitted congregations — in the Soviet Union they are called "registered" congregations — the situation varies greatly according to local conditions. In general, however, it can be said that in spite of occasionally oppressive controls imposed by the government, evangelical congregations in the Soviet Union are growing. Above all, a strikingly large number of young people participate in their meetings.

The Russian Orthodox writer, Levitin Krassnov, wrote to Pope Paul VI early in 1968 concerning the current church revival in Russia:

"Today's young people in Russia are a restless young people. They are boiling inside, and they are passionately seeking new ways. In connection with this mood a thoroughgoing religious breakthrough is common for a considerable number of young men and women. It is not an exaggeration to say that the power and intensity of the religious breakthrough by these young people are not inferior to the burning zeal of the early Christians. In Moscow there is a growing number of instances in which the sons of Communists, even of old Chekists, are baptized. When we consider these young men and women, who came in as strangers to the church and who just a few years ago did not have even the faintest notion of religion, when we observe these young men and women, whose turning to religion usually occasions bitter strife and stormy conflict with their families (sometimes it even results in a total separation) — then the words of the gospel of John 3:8 come spontaneously to mind: 'The wind blows where it wills, and you hear the sound of it, but you do not know whence it comes or whither it goes; so it is with every one who is born of the Spirit.'

". . . We have cited examples of conversions to Christianity in the Russian Orthodox Church. But the Baptists can pride themselves on an even greater number of conversions. In every case, however, the conversions take place among those young people who were previously unchurched. . . ."

There are many signs which sketch the broad scale of the current awakening in the Soviet Union. The hunger for biblical preaching of the Gospel may also have been the reason that in the last twelve years the state has tried at least to halt the growth of the evangelical congregations by increased persecution and repression. It is clear that such attempts, in spite of inhuman measures, have up to now been in vain in most cases.

How in fact did it come about that evangelical congregations developed in Russia?

The Beginnings

The evangelical movement in Russia is young. Its actual history spans only a little more than 100 years. A few roots stretch back farther, but these were only intimations of things to come.

Beginning in 1820, Johannes Gossner worked in Petersburg as a pastor. He wrote the following concerning the great possibilities for biblical preaching in Russia: "It is a fertile soil; a great, wide field; an open door; yes, a great door which opens as the entrance to almost an entire continent." He led Bible classes week by week in a palace on the Marskaya, one of the magnificent streets in the old Russian capital. The former ballroom of the palace which he had rented and its more than 1,000 seats often were filled to overflowing.

After only five years of ministering to countless souls Gossner was forced to leave the Russian empire, for during the closing years of the reign of Czar Alexander I, whose accession to the throne had offered remarkable promise for Christian missions, the government relapsed into the use of totalitarian measures. Under the oppressive absolute power of Alexander's successor, Nicholas I, freedom of conscience — and also freedom for Protestant teaching — was unthinkable. The omnipresent state police ruled the land.

Other missionary efforts also left no outwardly visible effects. Years before, August Hermann Francke had sought contact with Czar Peter the Great. He hoped, far-sightedly, for a biblical Reformation of the Russian Orthodox Church. He did succeed in engaging a few of his students as tutors and pastors in Russia, but other doors were barred.

Later Zinzendorf sent his missionary embassaries to the East. They were to push forward to China in fulfillment of the Count's bold missionary strategy. But these plans were thwarted by the long years which his missionaries had to spend in prisons. The visible results of these missionary efforts were small, yet no one can say that all which has vanished before our eyes has also been in vain before God.

Scottish missionaries labored in Astrakhan at the mouth of the Volga River on the north shore of the Caspian Sea. The Basel mission had a station with Count Zaremba in the Caucasian Mountains, but these missions gained access only to the non-Russian peoples who lived in these areas.

When a new czar came to the throne, the situation changed dramatically. Czar Alexander II succeeded in liberalizing the system of government. For example, the Russian peasants were freed from serfdom in 1861. The government resolved to combat illiteracy, and a great spiritual hunger grew from this.

The Bible Movement

A Russian Bible Society had been founded in Petersburg as early as the beginning of the nineteenth century under Czar Alexander I. Prince Galatsin undertook its leadership. Besides a good Russian translation of the New Testament, testaments were also printed in the Tartar and Kalmuck languages.

The distribution of the Bible was greatly expanded fifty years later through the efforts of the Scot, Melville. Bible colporteurs carried the full Bible, printed by the London Bible Society, from village to village. Between 1869 and 1892 the circulation of the Bible increased thirty times. Seventy thousand Bibles a year were sold. The fact that the Russian Orthodox Church had fully recognized the translation was an important factor in the success of this effort.

The Bible movement became the foundation of the evangelical revival which followed. Although the Russian Orthodox state church permitted the circulation of the Bible, it did not always look kindly on this activity. For example, Jakov Delyakovich Delyakov was not only a Bible seller but at the same time a preacher and zealous missionary in southern Russia. In order to keep his identity hidden from the police, who persecuted him often enough as it was, he disguised himself as a peddler. As he sold his wares in the market places, he waited only for a propitious moment to display his Bibles. In order to preach he let himself be invited into private homes.

The "Hourlies"

At the beginning of the nineteenth century many settlers had emigrated to Russia from southern Germany. Although Alexander I had invited them, the actual reason for their migration lay deeper. These Christians suffered under the rationalistic theology of their church leaders as expressed in teaching, preaching, and the hymnal. From their homeland they brought the "hour" with them to Russia. This form of meeting, including exposition of the Bible by members of the congregation, is a characteristic service of Pietism.

At that time pastors concerned about missions kept the emigrant congregations from leading only parochial, withdrawn lives. Under pastors Bonekemper and Wüst, revivals began amidst the German congregations, and from that time on the Ukranian farmhands, who hired themselves out at harvest time to the Germans, were regarded as more than just a supply of cheap labor. They came along to the "hours"; the Word of God and the strong impression of testimonies from the farmers themselves did their work; and many Ukranians came to faith this way.

The conversion of the mill-master Ivan Ryaboshapka was of great importance. He had purchased a Bible in Odessa. A German blacksmith noticed that Ryaboshapka was searching for the truth and led him to biblical rebirth. Ryaboshapka became a "Strannik," or traveling preacher. He called people together in houses and at the annual fairs. They streamed from all around to hear him, and he read to them from the Bible. Strong assemblies arose. The scornful talk of the neighbors who rejected his message led to the name, the "hourlies."

Persecution From the Beginning

The Russian Orthodox Church, particularly its priests, was too little grounded in the Bible to be able to approve of this revival movement. Out of fear of the activity of the members of their own congregations, they shut themselves off from the new forms of communion. Conflicts also arose concerning the honoring of images, for the members of the "hour" rejected all images, without compromise.

When in rural areas someone became "believing," it was noticed immediately. It was characteristic of the Russian Christians that there was no gap between belief and life, doctrine and practice. When a Russian was converted, drunkenness stopped. At work and at home, personal industry and cleanliness became the rule.

Such lives, now changed into new persons, drew the hatred and envy of neighbors. Police action followed when such changes in behavior were reported. The Russian Orthodox Church was so closely linked to the state that criticism of the church was regarded as treason against the state.

Brutal measures followed. Many families were deported. The leaders of the revival movement were sentenced to forced labor in Siberian mines. Children were taken away from their parents to be "educated" in monasteries. The writer Count Leo Tolstoy struggled, finally with success, against these cruelties.

There was no change in this pattern until 1905. At that time Czar Nicholas II resolved to liberalize his domestic policies. By means of a toleration edict he permitted members of the "hour" to form a few congregations. Some of these Christians stood in the Baptist tradition through their connections with Germany. The others took the designation "Gospel Movement" and called themselves "Christians According to the Gospel," and later "Evangelical Christians." Thousands of imprisoned people were freed because of the toleration edict. Countless people who had been exiled were permitted to return to their homes.

For all that, there was then in czarist Russia still no full freedom for these congregations which had so recently arisen. The imperial governors ruled their provinces with undiminished power. Police surveillance continued in force against awakened Christians. In defiance of all opposition the movement grew in the two branches, Evangelical Christians and Baptists.

A Bible Hour in the Prince's Castle

In addition to the Ukraine, where even today a considerable portion of all evangelical Christians in the Soviet Union live, the capital city Petersburg (modern Leningrad) became a second center of the awakening. If it was principally the common man in the south of Russia who was touched by the biblical preaching of the missionaries, the Petersburg revival had definite aristocratic features.

In 1874 the English Lord Radstock stayed for several months in this city on the Neva. In the palace of his hostess he conducted evangelistic lectures from the Bible which held the nobility of the city enthralled.

The nobility was much aware of how decayed and flawed its own style of life was, and thus many were looking for the truth. The testimony of this English lord was so simple, strong, and biblically deep that they listened to him gladly and with great openness. Many of the nobility heard for the first time in their lives that there was certainty of salvation in faith.

Lord Radstock belonged to the "Open Brethren," who rejected almost every ecclesiastical organization and were much more earnest in missionary service and surrender to Christ.

The Petersburg revival movement came to be well known beyond the borders of the city. The faith was lived openly as a visible testimony. Class distinctions faded. It is reported that scoffers made sport over the smell of the stable in the drawing rooms of the believing counts, for it was well known in the city that there in the lordly halls the nobility knelt daily to pray with coachmen and stableboys.

Influential nobles belonged to the Bible groups: Colonel Pashkov, aide-de-camp of the Czar and also one of the wealthiest land owners of the day; Count Korff, court marshall of the Czar; Princess Lieven, the widow of the Czar's Chief Master of Protocol; and trade minister Count Bobrinsky.

The procurator of the Most Holy Synod, the supervising council of the Russian Orthodox Church, assumed the responsibility for suppressing this revival movement with great severity. In 1884 a conference of the "hourlies" of southern Russia with the revival groups of the Petersburg nobility, financed by Pashkov, was dispersed by the terror of a police raid. The farming brothers came under arrest. Shortly thereafter Pashkov and Korff were exiled from the land. Others lost their official positions, yet none of them bowed to the demand to cease their evangelistic activity.

Lenin's Tactical War Against the Churches

To Lenin, "religion was a kind of intoxicating spirit in which the slaves of capital drowned their human nature and the claims for an existence tolerably appropriate for mankind."

In spite of this opinion, modern Evangelical Christians and Baptists in their present distress look back to Lenin's official decree on religion with longing, and in historical retrospect the period from 1918 to 1929 dominated by Lenin is viewed as the "golden decade" of the Evangelical Christians and Baptists and as a period of freedom for belief and conscience.

How can that be explained?

The separation of the churches from the power of the czars in the revolution of 1917 was a catastrophe only for the Russian Orthodox state church. For the Protestant congregations it meant, first of all, the end of a period of persecution. The leading preachers of the Baptists returned home again from Siberian exile.

For the furtherance of its goals Communism acted with tactical acumen — if also at the expense of its logical unity — and it carried on its battle against religion only moderately at first. Lenin knew how strongly the people were rooted in religion. He struck hard, to be sure, at the Russian Orthodox Church by confiscating church property, by abolishing government support for the church, and by separating church and school, but he indulged religious feelings by postponing the ideological battle against religion itself. For this reason the Protestant congregations at first were not directly menaced by Lenin's measures.

The Constitution of 1918 signaled a broadening of possibilities for the Evangelical Christians and the Baptists. This document, in conformity with Lenin's decree, granted to atheists and Christians alike the same right of defending their beliefs in public.

The unwieldy debating tactics of the atheistic groups could not seriously endanger the Protestant congregations. To the contrary, the Evangelical Christians with their aristocratic and intellectual background seized their chance to develop an alternative to Communism in this unexpected freedom, and they thrived in situations of religious and political contention. In this activity they appealed then, as they do today, to the right of laboring as missionaries in public — however much that appeal was in vain then as now.

Point Nine of Lenin's decree reads as follows: "Citizens can teach — that is, study — their religion privately." When, however, evangelical Christians refer to that today, they are told: "Every religious impression which is exercised upon those of tender years must be punished as a crime in accordance with the sense of common law." And such an "impression" is taken for granted when a mother teaches her child to pray.

Total War Against Religion

If there were, comparatively speaking, only rare trials and prison sentences for the Evangelical Christians and the Baptists before 1929, this was changed shockingly after that date. The year 1929 saw a change in the law. Christians no longer had a right to confess their faith publicly; only atheists now had this right. A "law concerning the religious cults" was promulgated to accomplish this. The possibilities for a congregation to function were almost entirely restricted by its sixty-eight articles. Any testifying outside of the worship service was forbidden. This covered cultural, evangelistic, and missionary activities as well as all kinds of assemblies for children, youth, women, and for prayer.

It was the end of the "golden decade."

A dreadful persecution began. Thousands of preachers were deported to Siberia, but only a very few returned. It is probably no longer possible to ascertain fully what the congregations suffered in connection with Stalin's purges.

The extent of the destruction of congregational life can be surmised from an examination of the Russian Orthodox Church. Of 77,776 churches in 1917, only about 500 remained in 1939.

In this persecution all denominations and religions were affected equally.

The Establishment of the Church Confederation

As early as 1937 a census of the people showed clearly that the attempt to destroy the churches had not had the success which had been expected. In the census, and in spite of the unequivocal position of the government, 70% of the rural population and 50% of the urban population called themselves believers. In 1939 with the start of World War II the government had to mobilize all its power for defense. The laws concerning religion remained on the books but were no longer enforced as extensively as was legally possible.

Many prisoners were released upon their promise to work with the government. But of the 5,000 Protestant places of assembly only a third were opened. These were granted "registration," which was equivalent to a limited official toleration. The other congregations were denied this.

The communistic leadership may have had an important reason for granting this toleration: that is, to sanction the establishment of an "All-Russian Confederation of Evangelical Christian and Baptist Churches" in which the two main branches of the Russian revival movement could be joined together.

For during Stalin's great persecution it was seen clearly how difficult it was to wipe out independent and autonomous local congregations. They can exist without official structures. Thus it is understandable that with the relaxation of all-out persecution of Christians, the "All-Russian Confederation of Evangelical Christians and Baptists," which arose in 1944, received restricted official backing.

The planned goal of the Communist Party to eventually destroy all religion in the USSR was not abandoned with this new development. It was important for the state and its religious policy, already directed clearly at the destruction of Christian congregations, to have at its disposal a centralized church organization through which it could spread its influence to even the most distant Christian congregation. It could bind the confederation's board of governors to the state regulations by loyalty oaths and in this way reduce it to a tool of its policies.

To be sure, most congregations themselves had worked for a merger; an attempt dating from 1920 was conclusively frustrated in 1929 with the change in the constitution. Nevertheless, a not inconsiderable number of the congregations in 1944 looked at the merger with great skepticism. They were hostile to any centralized church leadership, and thus the germ of dissension in the "All-Russian Confederation" was present even at its establishment.

The negative criticism gained stature, moreover, when in 1960 it became generally clear how the state put the leadership of the confederation — called the All-Union Council — under pressure in order to curb the congregations which were active in missionary work. Since then, outsiders retain the impression that the state has made the All-Union Council its servant against the Council's own will and that it has done this by granting special privileges. The actual official pressure under which the All-Union Council labors today, however, can be surmised only from afar. We must therefore resist casual defamations of the All-Union Council.

Khrushchev's Method

At the height of the Khrushchev era, that is, after 1958, a comprehensive battle against religious groups was begun again by the party and the state. Many congregations were dissolved through administrative channels. As a result of the necessity to register congregations, undesirable ministers could be removed easily and replaced by "reliable people." At the same time gathering for worship services in private accommodations was forbidden.

The All-Union Council of Evangelical Christians and Baptists in Moscow also must have been under severe official pressure at this time, but the actual events will have to remain unknown. We ought not forget in all this that the men of this board possessed the unlimited trust of the totality of the Evangelical Christians and Baptists. That the All-Union Council finally allowed itself to be forced to "voluntarily" accept official demands shows only that it must have been faced with sinister alternatives.

Whatever the origins of this action were, the All-Union Council set forth the following provisions in a *New Statute* for the "All-Russian Confederation" and in a *Letter of Instructions* for elders:

Baptisms of young people under 18 years of age are to be discontinued;

Baptisms of individuals between 18 and 30 years of age are to be reduced to a minimum;

Assemblies of preachers are forbidden;

Courses for the training of choir leaders are forbidden;

Congregational collections for the support of those in material need
(e.g., those families whose fathers are imprisoned) are forbidden;
  Excursions of believing youth are not allowed; and
  Elders must proceed against "unhealthy" missionary activity.

The Resistance of the "Initsiativniki"

Under A. F. Prokofiev, who had already suffered several severe
penalties, and G. K. Kryuchkov an "Initiative Group for the Calling
of an Assembly" arose. In accordance with the way that Evangelical
Christian and Baptist congregations understood the Bible, this was
the prescribed way to put to the test those centralized demands which
had been forced upon the ecclesiastical leadership in Moscow.

It was indicative of the situation which existed that the All-Union
Council did not acknowledge the request of the Initiative Group.
What could it have answered in this dilemma? There can be no doubt
that the restrictive regulations promulgated by the Moscow All-Union
Council had been forced upon it by the state, which must have been a
heartache for the responsible leaders in Moscow.

The General Secretary of the Evangelical Christians and Baptists,
A. V. Karev, stated the reason for his and the All-Union Council's
actions in 1966: "One cannot and may not ignore the laws in our
work. To do so would only lead us down a blind alley." And in
another place in the same statement he said: "Our whole brotherhood
is in the hands of the Most High, and at His time and hour He will
fulfill His divine plan, be the circumstances what they may."

Because, in the opinion of the "Initsiativniki," these sentiments
contradicted the biblical witness, they leveled serious charges against
the All-Union Council. They spoke of a Satanic leading and of regulations directly contrary to the commands of God. With this decision,
continued the "Initsiativniki," the leadership of the All-Union Council
had thrown itself under the laws of men — which was not to be denied
— and with that it had departed from the teaching of the Lord. In
June, 1962, the "Initsiativniki" excommunicated leading members of
the All-Union Council. In September, 1965, after all efforts at a reconciliation had finally come to naught, they organized themselves into an
independent church with the "Council of Churches of Evangelical
Christians and Baptists" as its board of directors. Thus from this point
it is necessary to distinguish between the two boards of directors: the
Moscow All-Union Council of Evangelical Christians and Baptists (registered) and the Council of Churches of Evangelical Christians and

Baptists (independent). The charges against the All-Union Council can be summarized as follows:

(1) The independence of congregations is not observed.

(2) Missionary service as the principal task is obstructed.

(3) Proclamation of the Gospel to children and young people is discontinued.

(4) The separation of church and state according to Lenin's decree is not maintained.

Frustrated Efforts at Mediation

In spite of the outstretched hand of the All-Union Council, there could be no reconciliation. The "Initsiativniki" (The Council of Churches) demanded from the All-Russian Confederation, particularly from its board of directors, public repentance and withdrawal of the objectionable statutes. The All-Union Council on its part was ready to bend somewhat in repentance because of the quarrel, but it could not comply with all the demands of the Council of Churches.

The congregations that gathered into the Council of Churches have no confidence in the present All-Union Council since they see in it a tool of the state. That weighs all the more heavily since both sides acknowledge a doctrinal unity of belief. The Council of Churches, it is necessary to note, never makes ideological criticism of the social system in the Soviet Union. It emphasizes rather its loyal behavior toward the state and has proven this by repeated petitions for official registration.

Thus the controversial issue between the two groups of Evangelical Christians and Baptists (ECBs) has emerged clearly. The group gathered about the Council of Churches is convinced that it has the task to bind the state to its original actions in Lenin's decree and to the Conventions for Human Rights to which the Soviet Union is also a signatory. By doing this it feels that it can remain obedient to the Gospel. On the other side, the All-Union Council handed itself over to dependence upon the state, which allows it sometimes more, sometimes less, freedom to follow the way of obedience to the Gospel.

No Quarrel in Front of Unbelievers

The schism within the Evangelical Christians and Baptists (ECBs) can be nothing but a good thing for atheism, for many rumors emerged which spread fabricated charges stirring up one group against the other.

From an inspection of court records gleaned from judicial proceedings against the independent ECBs, the striking fact emerges that the believers always refuse to discuss the reasons for the rupture in front of non-Christians. This testifies to a spiritual discipline and to a solidarity which in the last analysis still exists within God's single body.

For example, here is the testimony of Yu. I. Kimmel, who was called to testify against F. V. Makhovitski, an elder, on 25-28 November, 1966, in Leningrad: "Oh, Citizen Judge, what we could say to each other! Every trade has its own pattern. The mechanic cannot understand a physician, nor the physician a mechanic. They can only shrug their shoulders. Give us permission for the conference and then we will clear things up. But what could we settle here with each other?"

The independent ECBs ("Initsiativniki") reproach the All-Union Council for having opposed the convening of the conference which they demanded to discuss the existing state regulations. The consequence of this refusal is said to have been that hundreds of leading brothers of the independent congregations were arrested, sentenced, and imprisoned because they had come out for the conference.

More Freedom As a Tactical Expedient

As a result of the separation of the Initiative Group, the All-Union Council was handed arguments which could be used to obtain a relaxation of regulations from the official "Council for the Affairs of Religious Cults." To this governing board the need to bring developments under control once more and to obstruct a final schism, which would have driven an active part of the ECBs into an ungovernable, underground church, must have been compelling.

So it was that in 1963 the *Letter of Instructions* for elders, which had led to separation, was retracted. The independence of local congregations from the All-Union Council was given greater stress in new statutes of 1963 and 1966. Decision-making authority was — in accordance with the wishes of the Initiative Group — transferred to a congress which was to meet every three years. The independence of local congregations was confirmed.

The independent ECBs wrote this in their newspaper, *Fraternal Leaflet*, January, 1970, concerning the split: "We do not want to provoke each other or be antagonistic to one another, but to do the tasks with which God has commissioned us. If God provides the circumstances for us to come together, we desire to make use of them."

But at the Moscow congress of the Confederation of Evangelical Christians and Baptists in December, 1969, no representatives of the Initiative Group took part since they had not been given the right to vote.

New Persecutions

Even though individual segments of the laws could be changed, it did not mean that the state intended to return the old independence. The Confederation's leadership, the All-Union Council, remained under the direct influence of the state even if outwardly it was no longer as obvious. It must also be mentioned in regard to the agitation for freedom by the independent ECBs that in light of the totalitarian governmental policies of the Soviet Union, the demand for an unregulated area of life engendered a distrust by the government toward its citizens which is almost unimaginable for us.

The All-Union Council was able to recall its own restrictive instructions precisely because a governmental decree of 12 December 1962 had, in the meantime, promulgated even harsher restrictions. From that point forward, preachers were forbidden to tend their congregations outside of their own homes. Beyond this no more religious gatherings of any kind were allowed in private dwellings without official permission.

These regulations went beyond the Stalinist ordinances of 1929 by a considerable margin. An all-out persecution of religious bodies is now possible at any time. The legal foundation is in place. Only the "favorable" moment is yet unknown.

To the present time these prohibitions are enforced differently in the various administrative districts, and the situation varies in any one place from time to time.

After the fall of Khrushchev the battle against all religions was eased for a short time. The independent ECBs used this period from the fall of 1965 to the spring of 1966 to increase their missionary activity. This led to a great number of arrests and trials. It was reported that tightened legal measures, leading to three-year prison terms for repeatedly organizing or directing so-called disallowed religious events, as well as higher fines, thwarted this group's wider activity. Sentences of five years in prison camps followed by five years in exile were later pronounced in many cases.

While this was going on, the All-Union Council obtained even greater privileges. In 1968 they were able to print a hymnal and an edition of the Bible as well as a correspondence course for the training of pastors — all in very small editions, to be sure. Behind this permission may well have rested the desire to make the independent Initiative Group appear insignificant by comparison with the All-Russian Confederation of ECBs and to eliminate its influence.

It is possible that the Moscow All-Union Council was convinced that evidence of its good conduct would disarm official restrictions. One can only speculate as to the disadvantages which such a policy also entails in light of the overall struggle which the government so clearly directed against the church. The goal of Communism, fixed from first to last, was articulated in 1963 by the Ideological Commission of the Central Committee of the Communist Party in the Soviet Union: "The Party has set itself the following task: to completely liberate the consciousness of Soviet Man from the intellectual residue of the old regime, including its religious prejudices. Religious ideology under whatever aspect and in all forms is out of place in our society."

Throughout the struggle dividing the ECBs, the merit of the Initiative Group has been to make crystal clear the fact that a congregation cannot free itself from the missionary mandate of Jesus by virtue of its own opinions. To the Initiative Group surrender of missions is tantamount to surrender of the faith.

Thus in the Protestant churches of Russia martyrdom for Jesus' sake has been experienced almost continuously for one hundred years. The experiences of Russian believers set a serious question before us. We are suddenly no longer merely indifferent spectators. Self-examination is demanded, since the life or death of our churches and the power or weakness of our service to God depends upon our response to this question.

2

MARTYRDOM TODAY

MARTYRDOM — NOT THE WORD, but the reality, is alien to us.

Yet to one who lives according to the words of Jesus, martyrdom cannot be alien. Jesus spoke of it. He said that only that person who is prepared to pledge his life to its end for Him can be His disciple. Jesus also said that His disciples would have the offensive burden of the cross laid on their backs.

No one follows Jesus who is not prepared for martyrdom.

And yet we live completely differently today. We do not consider the fact that life with Jesus could have its price. We have excluded martyrdom from our thoughts. We desire to live in faith without suffering. As if they could ever be divided!

Many marvel at the martyrdom of brave Christians, but are not willing to place their lives on the line. They only flee in the face of suffering.

It is certainly a possibility that our gratitude for freedom, which we express so often, is only an effort to hide this flight from personal suffering. With thanks we today recall the freedom that we have. But what if all the talk of freedom were only the expression of fear that this freedom might someday come to an end! What if in reality we were not at all prepared to live today even with the hatred of an enemy of the Gospel! If this is so, then our life of faith is crippled by cowardice. Our faith will be bottled up by narrow limitations. We will always grasp at merely earthly security. If this is so, our lives will be without fruit since we will never give ourselves completely into Jesus' hand. With this attitude we could never conquer the world and its fear.

A detour can be made around martyrdom. Self-deception can exist in Christian faith and reduce imitation of Christ to nothing. When

24

this is done, it does not cost much to be a Christian. To do this an individual needs only to silence the Word, the one scandalous Word which he does not want to hear, the Word which judges all things and which creates new life, the Word of Jesus and His divine authority. For the witness of Jesus always demands total commitment.

It can be no less.

We are today inclined to mouth many pious phrases which cost us nothing. It is empty rhetoric which fades away. But Jesus' words do not pass away. They are spirit and life. They will last forever.

Whoever is struck by the words of Jesus must speak. He must proclaim these words and the Lord who honors them. He must pass them on freely just as he has received them. He stands under the authority of this Word. It is more important to him than his own life. Everything that belongs to this world will pass away, but these words of Jesus will not pass away before they are fulfilled. Therefore witnesses, standing under the authority of their Lord and captured by this Word, are willing to give up their lives. They can distinguish the valid from the valueless. The Word of Jesus is worth their life to them.

Many people are disturbed today by one aspect of this dedication. Can a person be so sure about it all? Is it possible to step out so forthrightly? In the uncertain groping and searching for truth that is characteristic of our day the martyr is provocatively effective as a witness to the truth. In those Christian churches in which everyone is free to search for salvation after his own fashion, the intolerant martyr will be an offense. For martyrs, as those who confess the one sure Word, are people without compromise. So it is that in our day the martyr is assaulted not only by the scorn of the Gospel's enemies but often he also is cast off by his brothers in the faith.

But there is martyrdom even in our day. And by these witnesses we are thrust up against the Word of Jesus. They want to tell us this: this Word will exist even if we deny it. The truth must be confessed. Because the martyrs know this greatest thing, they can surrender the smaller thing, in this case their lives — for the sake of the one Word.

It can be no less. One cannot be a witness to Jesus any other way. And nothing should hold our attention in the lives of the martyrs except the Word alone which they speak.

If only Christ be glorified!

In the Shadow of the Cross

The following poem is taken from the fifty-six page special edition of the hand-reproduced newspaper, the *Messenger of Salvation* (no. 19), which the independent Evangelical Christians and Baptists (ECBs) of the USSR published in celebration of their 100th anniversary in 1968.

To the church:
Dear sad and faithful mother of so many children!
I will never weary of singing to you.
You are never forgotten when my heart is joyful.
No one can compare with you,
with you life is easy and good, I am free!
And does not the spirit of heaven shine from your face on me?

Your name lives on from generation to generation.
You do not exist to enjoy the world's pleasure.
You were born in martyrdom,
in martyrdom you bring your children into the world.
Your tender concern is great profit
for orphans and widows and those who have no share in the
    world's wealth.
You have opened your arms wide
to the outcasts, the fallen, the confused.
You have founded a great family
and no one can name its number.
To many who were far away you became as one close by,
gracious mother of more children than anyone has ever had.

There is love in my heart as I think of you night and day
with deep and moving emotion.
I do not despair, for your love
is worth tears and burdens and woe.
When I look at you, I think:
how much have you had to weep,
how many holy tears have you shed,
how many sorrowful nights have you watched through,
how many times have you led your best sons and daughters
doubled over with pain to death,
to be grist for wild and hungry beasts!
And your agonizing groans were heard
in the dungeons at the time
of the hangmen who served the "holy" Inquisition.

Time and again you have had to seek hiding anew,
first in the catacombs, later in forests from the police.
Even now it is no different, you are afflicted and wander from
   place to place.
You are scorned as the vilest criminal, and today you seek shelter
from the attacks of humane and cultured people, and from their
   agents.
Because you do good deeds and are so pure,
your name is given over to shame.
And the children of your house, witnesses of the living God,
suffer in the torment of bondage.
But you bear the names of those tried in their faithfulness
close to your zealously loving heart
and do not forget them in eternity:
Andrew, John, and Peter; James and Paul —
apostles who followed Christ — and many like them afterwards.
Jan Hus is in this company — and today in our time:
Brother Baratov, did not we see him just yesterday?
You have not forgotten even the most recent martyrs:
Brother Odintsov, Timoshenko, and that one slain so painfully,
   Khmara
from the distant Altai, Station Kulunda.

How many walk there, at your side,
close to your thorny way.
The crowd of pharisees and corruptible spectators
watch and listen; day and night they watch carefully
to see if you will weaken under the burden of your cross
and perhaps give it all up, or at least renounce some detail
of that which Jesus has commanded to be done.
Your suffering does not concern them, it does not touch them —
your sorrow is distant and foreign to them.
They will arrange a settlement and make their peace.
They will repent with enmity in the heart — this will remain there
   and smolder away.
You will not find the peace which you seek for your soul with
   these triflers.
You would fall asleep for good under their guilt-ridden, human
   protection.

No, you are not alone and forsaken.
The heavens are spread over you and are your tent
for protection. They open over you without limit.
You are standing firm as a rock in a sea of passion and guilt.
Like a lighthouse you shine in a sea of evil
for the protection and rescue of the lost.
You are frightening and threatening
as troops under a banner in battle.
Your place on earth is with holy altars,
your vocation among the brides —
for you are the bride of the King of Kings.

Dear mother, not much longer, not much longer now
do you have to pilgrimmage and wander and suffer.
Soon the Lord will receive you in His marvelous dwellings
   as His true love.
Hold what you have, your unsullied conscience;
you are hidden under the care and shadow of the cross,
bearer of sorrows, child-rich church of the Lord.

(Translated from Russian to German
by Irmgard Stoldt)

The Congregation in Brest Refuses to Be Wiped Out

Brest is called the western gate of White Russia. The location of this city on the Polish border — as a station on an important rail line and lying astride the great highway connecting Berlin, Warsaw, and Moscow — gives it this important position.

A report came from this city of the martyrdom of evangelical Christians. The suffering began when the congregation of Evangelical Christians and Baptists (ECBs) was forbidden to meet together for services within the city limits. In spite of this, the congregation at Brest was unable to forsake the preached Word of God. They gave themselves to the martyrdom which was laid upon them.

We must first recall the situation in 1959: Khrushchev had begun strenuously to suppress churches and religious groups.

It is a misconception to conceive of the domestic policies of Khrushchev as merely a relaxation of the communistic ideology practiced for so many years. The de-Stalinization which the Premier proclaimed in 1956 at the Twentieth Party Congress in Moscow had as its goal the creation of a new man, the Soviet Man. This meant in a few essential areas, such as education and the economy, that party pressure would be increased. And for Khrushchev the fulfillment of this goal was connected indissolvably with the battle against "religious remnants."

It is in this sense that the Communists' chief ideologist, Ilyichev, in a lecture before the Ideological Commission of the Central Committee of the Party, November, 1963, labeled the concessions which Stalin had granted to the church during the Second World War as "deviations from Leninist laws."

Even as Ilyichev was condemning Stalin's "gentleness" toward the churches, renewed opposition to these same churches was already in full swing.

Within three years 10,000 Russian Orthodox churches alone were closed. Thus, for example, of 400 churches which had previously existed in the administrative area of Odessa, only 90 were now still open. And earlier only a small remnant of the total number of churches had been reopened in the wake of Stalin's persecution. In other districts the ratios were similar.

The congregations of ECBs were also attacked by these new and oppressive measures. The executive power injected itself directly into the battle against religion. Under massive pressure over 800 Protestant congregations were simply dissolved through administrative channels in the Ukraine alone. Thousands of elders and preachers were removed from their positions. Others, often incompetent members of the congregation, were put in their places. The suspicion would not be allayed that in this process people who would serve the state as reliable informants were called into places of leadership by the authorities. In any case this suspicion was aired bluntly in the circles of independent ECBs.

It was at this time, with the dissolution of congregations, that the hour had come for many churches to make a public profession.

We can reconstruct how it occurred in Brest from a report of a communistic newspaper in Minsk. *Soviet White Russia* carried this story on 12 May 1963 in connection with the sentencing of two leaders of the ECBs in Brest to five years in prison and two other preachers to four years:

"In 1960 the congregation of ECBs in Brest merged with the con-

gregation of Vulka-Podgorodskaya [which was also in the Brest district].
But only 100 of a total of 380 believers were prepared to go to Vulka.
The rest, incited by their preachers Matveyuk, Shepetunko, Kotovich,
and Fedorchuk, began to organize secret meetings in private homes of
the city."

For these activities the four ministers were forced to submit to severe
prison sentences. In the religious laws of 1929 it had been established
that the request of twenty members of a congregation would be suffi-
cient to obtain official sanction for the formation of a congregation. Yet
in Brest, by order of the authorities, 380 Christians had to transfer their
worship services to a village lying apart from this well-known and often-
visited city.

The All-Union Council of ECBs in Moscow must have received
information concerning these shameful violations of the law, but their
hands were tied. They had to be content to be thankful that even
worse things could still be prevented.

However, the Christians in Brest refused to let themselves be robbed
of their worship services. As in early Christian times they gathered
here and there in houses. Arrest and severe prison sentences were the
consequence for congregational leaders responsible for these meetings.
Nevertheless, the forbidden congregation of ECBs in Brest could not
be wiped out.

For the 100th anniversary celebration of the ECBs in the Soviet
Union the leaders of the illegal congregation in Brest organized a
festival worship service. Since no building could be obtained by the
congregation, which had in the meantime grown to 500 members, they
assembled in a forest clearing near the village of Plosko. This open
step was designed as a testimony of their faith. A great banner, visible
from afar, was stretched between the trees: "And remember all the
way which the Lord has led you!" Young people with accordians
accompanied the opening songs. Old and young had gathered around
a festively decorated pulpit at the forest's shaded edge.

This was in no sense a provocation. Not a single word was spoken
against the authorities. The people were full of thanksgiving that the
congregation continued to exist and had even grown. They praised
God.

As a response to this service their two leaders, Trofim K. Feidak,
59 years old, and Vladimir Vilchenski, 37, and the father of four
children, were sentenced on 17 April 1968 to five years each in a labor
camp. The court cited these reasons for the severe sentences: the

worship service in the forest clearing had been a disturbance of public peace. In addition, children were "seduced" into participating at this worship service. Two young people were baptized, although they were not yet 18 years old as the laws concerning religion prescribed. The last charge dealt with a refusal to give testimony — the two congregational leaders of the unregistered congregations in Brest had refused during their trial to list the names and addresses of other Christians.

These two ministers were sent to a prison camp in Orsha, an important White Russian city in the Dnieper River Valley. Protests against their inhuman sentences had at least partial success. The two congregational leaders from Brest were granted amnesty after serving half their sentences.

Congregations Tested by Ten Years of Suffering

The Council of Churches of the independent ECBs, that is, the group of independent congregations, publish privately (*Samisdat*) a newspaper, the *Fraternal Leaflet*. It carries news about the congregations. In the Soviet Union writers who may not print their books officially also frequently publish privately. *Samisdat* means "secret private publishing." The term, "underground newspaper," sounds too much like political conspiracy. The *Fraternal Leaflet* is simply a straightforward little sheet for edification. Duplicated by the simplest means, it constitutes an important link among the individual suffering congregations. Besides this, a second newspaper is also published, the *Messenger of Salvation*. This paper tries above all to be the spiritual voice of the persecuted. Written sermons take up a large portion of its copy. These papers are indispensable for equipping ministers for their work.

Distribution of the *Fraternal Leaflet* and the *Messenger of Salvation* has been the occasion for arrest and sentencing time after time. But there is still no other method which the congregations can use than that of secret publishing. The only Baptist newspaper officially permitted in the Soviet Union, the *Fraternal Herald*, produced by the officially recognized All-Union Council in Moscow, is allowed to appear only in such small editions that every congregation may receive only one copy. And that only once every two months.

The July-August, 1971, number of the illegal *Fraternal Leaflet* of the persecuted ECBs was designed as an anniversary issue. It recalled the founding of the Action Group which later became known as the "Initsiativniki." Here is the text:

"The Council of Churches greets you all with its whole heart on the tenth anniversary of the spiritual awakening of our brotherhood.

"It was the year 1961. The brotherhood was upset by severe persecution. Religious freedom was crudely suppressed. Activity by the unregistered bodies was completely forbidden. All throughout the land there were mass arrests and the confiscation of houses used by believers for meetings. Even registered groups were dispersed by the hundred. During the first half of 1961, 300 such congregations were closed. The All-Union Council of ECBs calculated that at that rate of closure, all congregations would have been shut down in two and one-half to three years. . . .

"In early 1961 as the darkness appeared particularly impenetrable, the leaders of the unregistered group in Uzlovaya (Tula district) were the first popular assembly to pose the question about the necessity of forming an Action Group, under the control of the leaders of the registered bodies, in order to call all believers to prayer and a common defense of the truth, and to call for an All-Union Congress of the ECBs. . . .

"As is well known, the All-Union Council of ECBs could not see its way clear to work together with this Action Group. And for this reason the division occurred.

"It is impossible to even describe what blessings and transformations the Lord has sent to the entire brotherhood in the last ten years. His deeds cannot be comprehended with words.

"In 1966 we asked for 10,000 Bibles, 5,000 hymn books, and other spiritual literature, which was reported to have been produced in a government owned print shop, but this request was not granted. As a result of that refusal our brotherhood has its own publication society.

"The Council of Churches refused to conduct business in any other way except in conformity with the law and with full acknowledgement of the authorities; but since it never received an answer to its legitimate request, it had the right to conduct business independently.

"Thus the Lord brought us into a way of ever increasing independence in which He has sent us incomparably more than we could ask or think (Eph. 3:20).

"Our pathway may be hard and thorny, but in the face of suffering we have joy in abundance, for we are saved, and before us goes the One who has walked this way once before and who knows where the promised harbor is. Stand firm, church of Christ!

"Fellowships which had earlier been dispersed have renewed their worship services.

"The illegal, un-evangelical restrictions and prohibitions which had been introduced by collaborators of the All-Union Council of the ECBs were revoked.

"The spirit of the Most High has filled the hearts of His children with great power and with a .mind prepared for sacrifice. They have brought to the altar of the living church not only the fruit of their service and of their toil but their very lives, blood, and tears . . . and we praise God for these sacrifices. We can only remember with thanksgiving the manner in which the brotherhood gave about two and one-half million rubles (ca. $2,500,000) during this period to those families who had suffered for the sake of the Lord's name.

"Nothing but great joy can exist when considering the work of the publishing firm, *The Christian*, which has given the brotherhood over 40,000 New Testaments, hymn books, and other religious materials . . . [they are referring to books printed secretly in Russia — ed.].

"Those sturdy messengers, the *Fraternal Leaflet* and the *Messenger of Salvation*, brought joy and encouragement to our congregations and our homes. In spite of difficulties and the sadness of families separated from each other, even relatives of imprisoned ones went about their tasks.

"Our poets have sung of Christ and His church.

"N. P. Khrapov, who spent twenty-six years in chains, wrote the poem, 'Hail, Bright Hosts of Christ,' which has become a song well-loved by believers. . . .

" 'Summon thy might, O God; show thy strength, O God, thou who has wrought for us . . .' (Ps. 68:28).

"Christians of Calvary, follow your Teacher; eternal joy and glory with Christ await you there.

" 'Let us rejoice and exult and give him the glory' (Rev. 19:7)."

Young Prisoners

It is striking that many young people are found in the lists of those imprisoned for the sake of the Word of God. This shows clearly that even after fifty years of atheistic propaganda and a most massive suppression of Christian faith, Soviet young people are searching for God.

From a list which was drawn up in 1970 by the Council of Relatives of Imprisoned Evanglical Christians and Baptists, we have extracted the following individual cases:

Vladimir P. Sinchenko was arrested as an 18-year-old on 21 October 1968 and was sentenced in 1969 to three years in a prison camp. He came from the congregation of the ECBs in the Ukranian city Kharkov, the sixth largest city in the USSR.

Vladimir V. Bytin was also only in his 19th year when he was sentenced to a year in a prison camp for the sake of his faith in December, 1969. He belongs to the evangelical congregation in Briansk, a city which lies in the middle of the Kiefer forests on the Disna River in the black earth region west of Moscow.

Yevgeny K. Rodoslavov. In the second Odessa trial of 1968 Rodoslavov, a 19-year-old Christian, together with other members of the Odessa congregation, was sentenced to a total of ten years in a labor camp and exile. His term expires on 19 October 1978.

Nadezhda I. Nikitina was 21 years old when she was sentenced on 21 February 1969 to three years in a labor camp on account of her faith. She came from Elektrostal in the vicinity of Moscow and was sent to the camp at Noginsk.

Rosa N. Durmanova, 25 years old, from Gorky east of Moscow, was sentenced on 16 July 1970 to one and a half years in a prison camp. She came from a non-Christian family and was put in prison in Gorky.

Lidia I. Belykh was arraigned on 5 September 1969 for her activity as an evangelical Christian. This 25-year-old was sentenced to two years in a labor camp. She began her sentence in Lgov which lies in the vicinity of Riazan on the Oka River south of Moscow.

Alina M. Sviridyuk came from Ordzhonikidze, the capital of the North Ossetian Republic in the Caucasian Mountains north of Tiflis, a rugged mountain region. After the First World War the New Testament was translated into the Ossetic language by the missionary society "Light in the East," still located at that time in Wernigerode. Half of the rough mountain folk of the Ossets belonged to the Russian Orthodox Church, the other half of the clan to the Islamic faith. Fearful blood feuds prevailed among the Ossets even into the days after the Russian Revolution. But then living and active congregations of Evangelical Christians arose in this area. The men laid aside the "kinshale," their long daggers, when they were converted and carried, as they said, "swords which give men life." These were the Bibles which they carried constantly.

Alina Sviridyuk was sentenced to two years in a prison camp on 21 October 1969 as a member of the evangelical congregation of the North Ossetian capital. She was taken to Yavass in the Moldavian Republic, and was 28 years old at the time of her sentencing.

There is additional evidence for the spiritual vitality of the Ossetian congregations in the fact that a year ago an edition of the Ossetic New Testament numbering several thousand copies was secretly printed at an unknown location in the Soviet Union.

Pavel I. Runov, age 19, of Gorky, followed his father into the prison camp. He was sentenced on 15 July 1970 to one and one-half years because of his evangelical faith.

Galina I. Makushchenko was sentenced on 18 February 1968 to two years in a labor camp because of her faith. She was then 18 years old.

Lidia A. Bolgova from Rostov on the Don River was sentenced, at age 23, to a year in a prison camp. The sentence was pronounced on 27 May 1966.

Anatoli N. Balatski was 32 years old when he was sentenced in May, 1966, to four years in a labor camp.

Galina K. Pali from Shakhty near Rostov was likewise sentenced in May, 1966, to three years in a prison camp. She was then 26 years old.

Nina P. Nikolaeva, 25 years old, was sentenced on 7 June 1966 to three years in a labor camp.

They Will Never Again Be Free

The Council of Relatives of Imprisoned Evangelical Christians and Baptists released the following document in 1970:

" '. . . Some were tortured, refusing to accept release . . .' (Heb. 11:35).

"Nikolai Kuzmich Khmara, born 1922. He was sentenced in 1963 to three years imprisonment for preaching the Word. On 9 January 1964 he was tortured to death in the prison at Barnaul. Residence: Barnaul region, Kulunda. Wife: Maria Khmara, four children.

"Ivan Alekseievich Alfonin, born 1926. Elder of the ECBs in Uzlovaya, he was sentenced on 30 May 1967 to three years in a labor camp for preaching the Word. He died in a labor camp in the Tula region on 22 November 1969. Residence: Tula region, Uzlovaya, Maiskiy. Wife: Anna Stepanovna, nine children.

"Nikolai Samoylovich Kucherenko, born 1895. He was exposed to constant interrogation for his belief while in custody for questioning and died 22 July 1962 in the city of Nikolayev. Residence: Ukranian SSR, 174 Lenina Avenue, Nikolayev. Wife: Marfa Aleksevna.

"Peter Ivanovich Lanbin, born 1909. He was sentenced in 1966 to three years in a labor camp for his faith and died in the camp on 16 November 1967. Residence: Novosibirsk, district Sovietski. Wife: Matriena Fyodorovna.

"Lavrenti Ivanovich Rizhenko, born 1886. He was sentenced to four years in a labor camp and died in prison in 1963. Residence: Cherkessk, Krasnodar region.

"Otto Petrovich Viebe, born 1905. He spent fourteen years in a labor camp. On 23 January 1963 he was sentenced anew to four years in a labor camp with severe restrictions. He succumbed in prison on 30 January 1964. Residence: Karaganda 15, Kazakhstan SSR. Wife: Elisabeth Wilhelma.

" 'Greater love has no man than this that a man lay down his life for his friends' (John 15:13)."

Imprisonment in the Face of Death

In 1970 the Council of Relatives of Imprisoned ECBs passed out lists for intercessory prayer. On the sheet were entered the names of old or very sick Christians who were subject to repeated long prison terms.

The information sheet was entitled: "Here are people sentenced to death in prison."

"Christ is my life and dying my gain" (Phil. 1:21).

". . . Of whom the world was not worthy — wandering over deserts and mountains, and in dens and caves of the earth" (Heb. 11:38).

What will be waiting for these Christians if they survive their prison terms? Will they be brought again before the tribunals?

Alexei F. Iskovskikh is 81 years old. In his congregation in Dedovsk in the vicinity of Moscow he had held the office of elder. He has already suffered a total of twelve years in prison on account of his faith.

On 6 August 1968 he was sentenced for the fourth time to a three-year term in a penal camp. He is deathly ill. His wife, Maria, lives in Dedovsk. She reports that her husband is held imprisoned in Yaroslavl, a city in the central region of the country on the Volga River.

Nikolai P. Khrapov comes from Tashkent, the capital of Uzbekistan, the Republic in the south of the Soviet Union bordering Afghanistan. When he was 21 years old, Khrapov came to faith in Jesus Christ.

Born in 1914, he knew — in light of the horrors of Stalin's persecution
—what this faith commitment would bring him by way of suffering for
Jesus' sake. He was accordingly sentenced immediately to twelve years
imprisonment. He survived this long period of captivity, but shortly
thereafter he was sentenced again, this time to twenty-five years, for
his faith. After he had served a portion of this sentence, he was
released in the aftermath of de-Stalinization and was free. In 1960 he
was sentenced for the third time, and this sentence called for seven
years in prison. In 1964 he was again released. Of the thirty-two years
that Khrapov had been a Christian, he had spent twenty-two in prisons
and camps. On 18 May 1966 Khrapov was sentenced to five years in a
restricted prison camp with strenuous enforcement. The native-born
Rusisan was transferred to the camp at Bukhara, an oasis in the merci-
less Uzbekian desert, where years before a despotic emir had secured
his prisoners in ghastly underground cells. Even if today the external
circumstances may be somewhat more humane in the camps, the fate
of the Christian Khrapov would be an inhuman one if his life were
not lived in obedience to Jesus and endured in the hope of the faith.

Sergei T. Golev, elder of the church of Evangelical Christians in
Riazan and member of the Council of Churches, is 77 years old. In
1970 he spent his twentieth year in prison. His unbending faith
accounts for this. In obedience to the commands of God he can
countenance no compromise. On 13 July 1969 he was sentenced for
the fourth time by a Soviet court, this time to three years in a labor
camp with strict regulations. He was brought to the prison at Riazan.
He suffers from severe diabetes.

Ivan O. Runov was sentenced on 20 July 1970 for the fifth time to
a three-year prison term. In the same prison camp at Gorky into which
the 73-year-old was brought, his son, Pavel I. Runov, 19, was also imprisoned. Father Runov, an elder of a church of ECBs in Gorky, has
spent a total of twenty-two years of his life in prison for the sake of
his faith.

Dimitri St. Rogozhin was appointed as an elder of the congregation
of ECBs in Rostov on the Don. In this industrial city in the middle of
a fruitful grain growing region of the northern Caucasians, the then
69-year-old Rogozhin was arrested and on 13 September 1969 was
sentenced to three years in a severe prison camp. It was his third
sentencing for the sake of his faith. He was put in a labor camp in
Shakhty, not far from Rostov.

Vassili D. Zhovmituk is also one of the elders of the evangelical congregation of Rostov on the Don. He is suffering his fifteenth year in prison now, sentenced on account of his faith. Time after time, as in his case, the courts appeal to the "laws separating the church from the state and the school from the church" in their judgments. Instruction of children as well as witnessing to the faith before those who believe differently are designated as "crimes" by these laws. The 78-year-old elder was sentenced on 7 July 1970 to two years in a strict labor camp. Out of consideration for his age and his health he was placed in prison in Rostov.

Georgi T. Ossipov suffers grievously from tuberculosis. In spite of this he is held in prison. He comes from the Caucus region, from the city of Piatigorsk. In the Caucasians there had been a great Baptist awakening during the last century, and the first mass baptism of Baptists took place at Tiflis in 1867. Ossipov is also an elder of a congregation of ECBs. On 17 October 1969 he was sentenced for the second time in a proceedings at law. This time he received a sentence of four years in a labor camp with tightened regulations. He was located, at 74 years of age, in the camp of the Rakpass settlement in the Komi ASSR, a land of tundra and swamps which is bordered by the Ural Mountains on the east. There high in the north of the USSR the coal mines of Vorkuta are also found, and these are still notorious for many prisoners of war.

Semen T. Rasumov was sentenced on 5 October 1966 to five years in a labor camp under severe regulations. His home is Pashkovskiy in the land of the northern Caucasians, more precisely in the Krasnodar district on the Azov Sea. It was there as well that the now 70-year-old man was placed in a prison camp. He is now in Olginskaya in the district of Promorska Akhtarsk.

Homes Confiscated and Destroyed

The confiscation of houses used for meetings has turned out to be an effective means for the state to restrict active congregations. Tourist groups who travel through the Soviet Union are told by the trained travel guides that every religious body can rent a place of worship from the authorities. It is only necessary that twenty members of a congregation pledge themselves in writing to observe the laws concerning religion.

The following events, representative of those that have been documented, tell a clear tale of how these religious laws are actually used by the authorities.

The cancellation of officially registered places for assembly has an even more damaging effect since Khrushchev's legal decree of 1963 stated that religious meetings in private dwellings require (in principle) official approval. With this law, the total throttling of congregational life is possible without a trial, solely through administrative channels.

Most sentences to multiple-year prison terms result when evangelical congregations — captive to the Word of God — gather together in homes, or even in the open, for worship services in spite of the prohibitions of the authorities.

The Council of Relatives of Imprisoned ECBs' in 1970 released reports concerning the following arbitrary acts.

Tula. In the city of Tula, lying perhaps 120 miles south of Moscow, the court of the city took action against the house of an Evangelical Christian believer. On 2 September 1970 the home of Nikolai I. Vladykin (14 Krasnodontsev Street) was confiscated. Bible and prayer hours of the ECBs had taken place in this house. The 45-year-old Vladykin was sentenced on 20 February 1971, to ten and one-half months in a labor camp. But he was able to gain his freedom by a twenty-one day hunger strike.

The authorities of the city are said to have acted with open opposition to the independent ECBs. It was, in fact, in Tula that the Action Group of the independent ECBs was founded in 1961. Vladykin's house was said to have served as the headquarters of the brotherhood of the persecuted Council of Churches. All the propagandistic efforts of atheism had not succeeded in allowing the state to fulfill its goal of destroying these strongly confessional groups. The government itself does not seem to expect much success from these propaganda measures. For if it had real confidence in its propaganda, it would not have needed to take such inhuman measures.

Novosibirsk. In this Siberian city, the house which belongs to Maria A. Samsonov (Dzerzhinski district, Posselkovi 30a) was confiscated by the court on 6 July 1970. The complaint was that gatherings of the ECBs were held in this house. At the entrance of the house a notice was posted with this inscription: "Camp No. 5 of the Second Foodstuff Collective." No one was admitted into the house after this.

Podolsk. Here in the central region near Moscow the house of Vera V. Kuznetsov (38/42 Lagernoy) was seized on 1 September 1964 because Bible meetings of the ECBs had also taken place in this private residence. Other meeting places were not available in spite of every effort to obtain them. While Mrs. Kuznetsov was attending a hearing, another party took up residence in the house.

Dedovsk and Kharkov. The Romachuk house (Kharkov, Uzhotova 2) was confiscated by the city, and a library was placed in the house. As early as 1961 the private dwelling of Vassili Y. Smirnov (11 Pushkinskoy) was confiscated because prayer meetings of the ECBs were held also in this residence.

Leningrad. P. P. Lukas of Leningrad (K 30, 35 Sanevka) returned to his home after the completion of his prison sentence. He acted in accordance with the precept: "As for me and my house, we will serve the Lord." To this end he made his home available to the Evangelical Christians for prayer meetings. For this a fine of 700 rubles was assessed (about $700).

Barnaul. The following was reported from the important Siberian industrial city of Barnaul, a vital center in the Altai Mountains about 120 miles south of Novosibirsk:

"On 17 May 1966, the personal home of Eduard Hauf (22 Strelochnomu Street), in which regular worship serviecs were held, was completely destroyed. While Eduard Hauf was at work, agents of the militia and a group of security police came to his house. They knocked in the doors and windows with iron bars and took the crying children and the grandmother in a car to another lodging. When Hauf came home the house was completely destroyed. Wrecking equipment and bulldozers stood upon the ruins of his house."

Shchetova. On 22 August 1965, in Shchetova (Vorochilovgradskoy, 2 Buryenogo Street), the property of the married couple, Georgia I. and Maria I. Yefanova, was devastated. Both were numbered among the believers of the ECBs. On Sunday, August 22, they had invited their friends of like faith to a common worship service. There were perhaps 100 believers there. During the meeting the director of the local school, Adamchuk, and the chairman of the village council, Rodchika, came as representatives of the government and twice attempted to break up the worship service. They threatened severe measures. A certain Mrs. Garbeni who introduced herself as a chairman of the committee declared: "A crime will be committed today against you but no one will bear the responsibility for it." After the worship service, around 9 P.M., a band of youths appeared. There were about sixty of them under the leadership of Adamchuk, who had told them earlier: "Take what you can, and destroy whatever comes into your hand." The damage claim which resulted from the destruction amounted to 2,000 rubles (ca. $2,000). The public prosecutor said to Mr. and Mrs. Yefanova: "A judicial inquiry would not be worth anything."

Martyrdom Is to Be Kept Quiet

On 1 December 1970 the official authorities took action and arrested Lidia M. Vins. The complaint was her activity as president of the Council of Relatives of Imprisoned ECBs. She had made sure that the fate of the sentenced evangelical Christians was not shrouded in silence. She gathered news and sent letters to the government. She summoned the congregations to prayer. She could not forget those who had been judged on account of their faith. She remained true to them and kept them in memory.

The nature of Mrs. Vins' activity can best be grasped by observing the story of her life.

Mrs. Vins comes from extreme east Siberia. She was born in Blagoveshchensk, the capital of the Amur province which borders China. In 1923 she married the respected Baptist preacher, Peter Vins, who had shortly before concluded his theological education in the United States. He was arrested in 1930 as a congregational leader and sentenced to three years in a prison camp. He was sent to Solikamsk, the salt city on the Kama River in the Urals. From that point he was forced to march another 180 miles farther north with a band of prisoners into the prison camp.

When Peter Vins had served this sentence, he was forced to go into exile with his wife and his son Georgi, who had been born in 1928. They lived together in the distant steppes near Biysk, at the foot of the Altai Mountains in the vicinity of the Mongolian border.

In 1936, in the midst of Stalin's persecution of Christians, Peter Vins was arrested in Omsk by the state security police because he had preached the Word of God in that place. After his prison term he was placed under police supervision.

In 1937, just shortly after his release from prison, he was sentenced to ten years in a prison camp by the infamous "Troika," again for preaching the Word of God. He was forbidden to exchange letters with members of his family. Around Christmas, 1943, Peter Vins died of hunger in a camp in the vicinity of Magadan on the eastern border of Siberia.

Almost twenty years from the day of his death, on 21 December 1963 Peter Vins was absolved by a post-mortem order of the court in Omsk.

In 1938 Lidia Vins' brother, Peter Michailovich Sharikov, was arrested in Blagoveshchensk on the Amur River and slain in horrible tortures.

Vera Timofeievna Sharikov, Lidia's sister-in-law, was arrested in 1939 on account of her faith and was held for seventeen years in the camps of Magadan on the Okhotsk Sea, across from the Kamchatka peninsula. Her father also was sentenced to five years in a prison camp.

In these years between 1930 and 1940, thousands of evangelical Christians were tortured to death. Georgi Vins wrote to the court counsel in Kiev on 10 December 1970 that he could list the names of twenty people from the Omsk congregation who were murdered during this persecution because they were Christians.

Mrs. Lidia Vins joined the Council of Relatives of Imprisoned ECBs when her son, Georgi, was sentenced for the first time to a three-year prison term as General Secretary of the Council of Churches, the board of the independent ECBs. Georgi had completed training in industrial management and as a technician after World War II. He worked in Kiev, the Ukranian capital so rich in tradition, as a construction engineer in the Kalinina works. He also was active in his spare time as a preacher in the Baptist congregation.

Mrs. Lidia Vins, without any warning, was arrested in Kiev in December, 1970. It was around 10 P.M. She was taking care of her grandchildren in the house at 11B Shoshenko Street. Her daughter-in-law was not at home. The authorities knew how ill Mrs. Vins was so they even brought a doctor along to the arrest. The children cried helplessly, and one of them was sick. One of the officials said: "We'll have to take the children too." The oldest of the grandchildren, Natasha, desired of her own accord to accompany her grandmother, come what may. But the other weeping children held her back. Mrs. Vins was led away immediately by the police.

The trial was held on 8, 9 February 1971 in Kiev. The very ill Lidia Vins, 64 years old, was sentenced to three years in a prison camp. In the course of the proceedings Mrs. Vins pointed out the injustice done in the trial in that only those persons were allowed to testify who were active in harassing evangelical Christians in the Soviet Union. None of the persecuted Christians were allowed to testify. She said: "Whatever the sentence will be, for me it means the death sentence, for my circumstances are unbearable." In a report of October, 1971, we were notified that Mrs. Vins' health was very bad. In spite of diabetes, as well as high blood pressure and chronic stomach ulcers, it was reported that she had to go to work, leaning on someone's arm. The camp medical orderlies would not even free her from work for a short time.

To carry out this trial against Mrs. Vins must have weighed heavily on the Soviet sense of justice. Mrs. Vins confessed openly and fearlessly, even in her appeal to the Supreme Court, that she had written letters to relatives of the imprisoned with specific assertions about the persecutions. She demanded that the facts be investigated. In her letters, she went on, she had only presented matters of fact. It was hypocritical to accuse and sentence her for defamation of the state and infringement of the laws. The court, she continued, had the duty to investigate the facts. One could not simply prohibit news about actual events.

And then she enumerated these facts once more: 791 Christians had been under arrest for ten to fifteen days. Fines totalling 96,500 rubles (about $100,000) were imposed. Four thousand evangelical Christians had been interrogated. Since 1961, 524 Christians had been sentenced to multiple-year prison terms. Because of this, 1,000 children had been indirectly affected. All this, she went on, had occurred within the last nine years. "I ask the court to understand my motives in these letters, which were written to relatives and which presented only facts."

Mrs. Vins can be understood correctly only if she is seen in all her activity as supporting "stillness in the land." That is, nowhere did she ever attack the social order of the state. But she felt compelled to call for intercession for the imprisoned, since she knew herself how difficult it is to bear loneliness in suffering for Jesus' sake. Her son, Georgi, General Secretary of the Council of Churches, has now been sentenced for the third time.

3

FOR CHRIST'S SAKE

"Radi Christa," say the Russian believers — for Christ's sake.

Because it is for Christ's sake, they do not grow weary in suffering. Their bodies may quail before pain, they may be delivered to the whim of men who hate them fanatically, no relief may be in sight — and yet things can be suddenly bright in the sinister darkness where oppressed Christians are when they realize it is all happening for Christ's sake.

Believers discover this truth when they are stripped of their freedom, when their families are destroyed, when in great loneliness they fall prey to serious doubts, and when their bodies are weakened by long stretches in prison. They do not rely on that which has been taken from them. On the contrary, they understand that everything must be taken from them — for Christ's sake. Everything in their lives could be smashed to tatters, and that without exception.

Paul is of this opinion when he says: "For [Christ's] sake . . . we are regarded like sheep to be slaughtered" (Rom. 8:36). And: "For while we live we are always being given up to death for Jesus' sake." But we do not dwell upon the distress in our lives. God is not one who merely destroys. He desires "that the life of Jesus may be manifested in our mortal flesh" (2 Cor. 4:11).

Life itself hides in the uncanny process of death. And the victory over suffering is found in suffering. The key lies in this affirmation: for Christ's sake! That broadens the scope of earthly life beyond measure. Everything is measured against the background of eternity. And it is the tears, the sorrows, the dread — borne specifically for Christ's sake — which produce that encompassing hope that so outstrips the hope of the world. Or in Paul's words: "For this slight momentary affliction is preparing for us an eternal weight of glory

44

beyond all comparison, because we look not to the things that are seen but to the things that are unseen; for the things that are seen are transient, but the things that are unseen are eternal" (2 Cor. 4:17, 18).

Therefore, those who believe — for Christ's sake — must speak differently of their lives. They can have no association with injustice. They may not bury themselves in their dashed hopes. Their thoughts must be brought to bear on Jesus, who desires to make all things new.

This goes on in ordinary daily life. The following scene has been repeated often in the terrible hunger camps of the Soviet Union: former German SS officers will be dragging themselves on their last legs to work. A Russian girl will succeed in approaching this group of comfortless men straggling to their labor. Her heart will have been full of bitterness, almost of hatred, for she had suffered indescribably in the war. And then she will stand there and press a piece of bread into the hand of one of the passing enemy officers. And with this she will loudly say: "Radi Christa!" — for Christ's sake. That will mean more to her than the satisfaction of one who is starving. For the narrowness of her wounded life, the walls of hate and bitterness, have been penetrated. She has found her way to the new openness given by Christ.

How can a person suddenly spring from hate to the love of Jesus? Intellectual knowledge of the new life which Jesus gives is not able to take away anything from our despair. But it's different when an individual grasps this with his whole being! The Easter choir of the Russian Orthodox Church sings these words in the night of resurrection: "Let us embrace and kiss one another and, in the power of the resurrection, let us forgive those who hate us."

For Christ's sake! Christians certainly have much distress, suffering, loneliness, and oppression. Yet in spite of all this, these people sing the song of great joy exultingly. In the midst of the battle they sing songs of Jesus, who, they know, has borne all sufferings and is still the victor. Their eyes — for Christ's sake — are not fixed upon oppressive suffering. Suffering will pass away. Their eyes have long since been turned to Jesus' new creation.

In suffering, believing Christians break through the last barriers which our visible world can build. Often heavy burdens press upon their lives, and yet they claim that all has become new, even though all is outwardly the same. They weep, but these are not tears of self-pity and of wretchedness; they are tears of joy: "Jesus lives — He is truly raised from the dead."

So it was reported to us also of the apostles in the New Testament.

There were few things said about their suffering at that time. Perhaps today we would have written stirring stories about this, for example, about the terrible whippings they endured; and how the blood flowed over their backs. We would have been so deeply moved that we certainly would have counted the welts. But in the New Testament such matters are mentioned casually. Cudgel, sorrow, hate — regardless of how much pain they wrought — are no longer themes for Christians. There are, you see, more important things to talk about — namely, what Jesus did in and through these wounded, fragile men.

"They left the presence of the council, rejoicing that they were counted worthy to suffer [pain and reproach] for the name" (Acts 5:41). The essential basis of their happiness was that they were beaten for Christ's sake. It was manifest repeatedly in those terrible times of torture that they did not trust in themselves, for their endurance was not without limit. But they did know the might of Jesus, who had promised His all-conquering power to those who had reached the limit of their own strength.

When the authorities forced Professor Traugott Hahn to go through prison corridors with the waste bucket before his execution in 1919, Bishop Platon, his Russian Orthodox fellow-prisoner, whispered to him while he did this degrading task: "Radi Christa!" — for Christ's sake.

A stinking slop pail became the occasion for a full experience of new life with Jesus. For that believer cruel prison walls gave way before this vision. The sinister character of loneliness and the hopelessness of imprisonment were overcome by the knowledge that it was done for Christ's sake. A fragile, mortal man was deemed worthy to reflect the glory, the love, and the invincibility of Jesus in the comfortless corridors of a prison. A man, broken inwardly and outwardly, was nevertheless able to live out a clear affirmation of the way of the cross in imitation of Jesus. The waste bucket was thus no longer carried against his will, but willingly — for Christ's sake. The believer joined the community of passion with Jesus.

Many Christians today find it difficult to let their faith take hold of such a confident hope so far beyond the borders of the visible world. We are all confronted, in any case, with the polemics of a Feuerbach or a Marx, who picture such believing trust as a laughing stock or cheap consolation. As if comfort could ever be cheap! And yet they have greatly influenced Christian thinking. Christians are anxious and afraid to live with the uncomplicated joy of Jesus' new world. Many people are of the opinion that such trust is flight from contemporary trials.

Yet, on the other hand, is faith truly established where one can only speak out about the expectations of this life? Is it still faith when the struggle for happiness, possessions, and consumption becomes the determining factor in salvation? What does hope become at the moment of death, when all things visible from this world are torn from one's hand?

For Christ's sake! Only this is able to give the courage to believe the reality of this world. For this reason Christians perceive the need of the fallen creation with greater depth than Marx or Feuerbach. Sober, without idealistic or ideological trappings, we can bear for Christ's sake the suffering of this creation that bleeds from so many wounds. We see it no longer as a world that threatens us and fills us with fear. It is in reality merely raw material for Jesus' new creation.

Only faith that lives for the promise of Jesus can stand this tension. It comforts the tears, the suffering, the loneliness, the injustice, and the hatred of the world, and with patience it directs attention to the new heaven and the new earth where righteousness dwells. This does not lead to inactivity but in fact taps numerous sources of new energy. Martyrdom for Christ's sake is that which bears the challenge of the contemporary world. The power to endure this tension grows out of faith in Jesus' Easter victory. God has already spoken His new word of creation in this world of death: "Let this be!" And the resurrected Jesus promised surely: "I make all things new!" (Rev. 21:5). The world can no longer remain as it is. And even if, because of suffering, I experience the world today as a threat to my life, I nevertheless know by faith that this threat is transitory and limited by time; I know with the certainty of faith that Jesus' new creation will come.

The triumph of Jesus has broken up the death watch of this dying creation. And because He has accomplished that, there is strife which the new life of faith experiences as temptation. The place of security stands over against the insecurity of the outward life. Our faith stands opposed to our experience day by day.

How then can believers suffer abuse and oppression so willingly from other men? It is because they know the reality of the situation: "If you are reproached for the name of Christ, you are blessed, because the spirit of glory and of God rests upon you" (1 Peter 4:14).

For Christ's sake! Christians are no longer numbed by the prospect of death. They have seen the vision of indestructible life. For even in death we rejoice in the triumph of Jesus. That which will pass away *should* pass away. Let us give it up. Jesus has already conquered the world. And He carries us through it as well.

Persecutors Called to Repentance

It is February, 1967. In Solikamsk, a city in the Ural Mountains, a truck stands in front of the train station. A band of prisoners take their places on the open trailer. The goal is Chepechanka.

The thermometer reads −40°.

As the truck travels northward over icy roads into the mountains, the prisoners are silent. They must use all their energy to endure the cold and the sharply cutting wind. It is 150 miles to the prison camp in which they will spend the next several years.

One of the prisoners, 39-year-old Georgi Vins, ponders. More than thirty years before his father had marched on this same road. Georgi had not even been two years old then as his mother said good-by to her husband, Peter Vins. And they did not know at that time if they would ever see each other again. But Georgi's father had spoken a word which brought peace to his mother: "Radi Christa!" — for Christ's sake! Other memories of events years later come to this prisoner in the cold truck. He sees again the treeless steppes and the round Mongolian faces of the people of the Altai Mountains. At that time he did not understand what exile meant for his father. And then, when he was eight years old, his father said good-by to him for the last time. They suspected and feared the worst when the secret police found the place where his father, Peter Vins, had taught the small congregation from the Bible. By that time they were in Omsk in the Siberian steppes on the other side of the Urals. In this city of parks and flowers. . . .

Georgi Vins was General Secretary of the independent Council of Churches of ECBs. His sentence had been pronounced during the night of 1 December 1966 in Moscow. He had been forced to take the blame for the demonstration of 500 Baptist delegates in front of the Central Committee building, when actually congregations which had sought registration for years and were unable to receive it, were responsible for the demonstration.

From the Chepechanka camp Georgi Vins was taken to the Anyusha camp. The name sounds deceptively poetic. A special treatment for the prominent but obstinate churchman began here. Anyusha lay in the vicinity of the coal city Kizel in the Urals, perhaps 45 miles away.

The supervisors in this camp took great pains with the Baptist leader. After a few months, near the end of 1967, he was found to have a double hernia due to the severity of his forced labor. Then special officials from the secret police came to him. They would begin their work of indoctrination as he returned completely exhausted from work. They were very polite. His wife could visit him now. But the room where they met was well equipped with hidden microphones. Vins said once that he had been put in Camp Anyusha only because it was more conveniently situated to the railroad. Indeed several secret officials came repeatedly to visit him, primarily from Perm but also from Kiev. He knew two of them by name. They came on 19 September 1968 to enlist him as an agent for the secret service. They were from the KGB, the Soviet secret police, Col. Latki and Major Smirnov, both of Perm. But Vins rejected their offer.

Vins found it difficult in prison only when he was threatened by the arrest of his mother. The authorities were agitated when she sent petitions to the government for the release of her son. When Vins was put under even harsher pressure, he began the hunger strike. He held out for ten days. From then on he was left in peace, but the hunger strike brought him to the border of death by making him severely ill. He wrote concerning the hunger strike: "It would have been better to die in the camp than to become unfaithful to God and a traitor."

Georgi Vins described the facts of the stages of his suffering in a letter to the persecutors at the time of his mother's arrest in Kiev on 1 December 1970. That which Vins wrote was, however, no letter of political protest. Throughout this letter, as also in his other letters, Vins shows a patriotic respect for God-given authority. He does not even seek, as one would expect, release from suffering. He knows all too well the church's way of the cross. He even expresses this in the letter to his persecutors. But injustice must be called by name. Vins refers to God's judgment on the last day, a theme found repeatedly in the protest letters of the Baptists. The persecuted struggle for a total conversion of their persecutors, and for this they are glad to bear much suffering. Their thoughts are turned constantly to spiritual fruit. It is rare when this spiritual fruit does not appear, at least so far as foreign observers can tell. Yet considering the severity of suffering, who could make a final judgment of this?

Thus Georgi Vins in his letter of 12 December 1970 contended for right and truth, not for his personal freedom. His remarks have the same tone as Jesus' when in His night of passion He called the servant who had struck Him to account: "If I have spoken wrongly, bear witness to the wrong; but if I have spoken rightly, why do you strike me?" (John 18:23).

We will quote the following lines from the five-page letter which Georgi Vins wrote to the government in December, 1970:

"You have been told of Christians tortured to death, of children torn from their parents, of worship services dispersed, of houses where meetings were held confiscated or destroyed, of homes searched, of the interrogation of small children, of young people who are not permitted to attend high school because of their faith, of evil calumny in the press, of the continued persecution of the Council of Churches. . . .

"With the arrest of my mother the persecution has now also attacked the Council of Relatives of the Imprisoned because it had the courage to tell you about all the injustices which are going on. And not everything, by a long way, has been revealed yet.

"It is my task as a son of the imprisoned one and as a Christian to write that openly to you. . . .

"The chairman of the Council for Religious Cults, Mr. Puzin, also confirmed the facts of persecution cited above when he said before the Party Meeting of 5 August 1965: 'It has been customary for some time for the government to proceed against believers with harsh measures, as when houses are confiscated, prayer houses are not allowed to register, worship services are dispersed by the militia, private homes and meeting houses are searched. . . .'

"By this Puzin has admitted the persecution of Christians in our country.

"The entire responsibility for the imprisonment of my mother and of many believers, for her life, and for everything which is associated with the persecution lies on you, Leonid Ilyich Brezhnev, on you, Nicolai Viktorovich Podgorny, on you, Alexei Nikolaevich Kosygin, and on the general state prosecutor of the USSR, Rudenko, who in 1946 represented our land at the Nuremberg trial and judged severely those who had done these same things to believers and to the church.

"I am taking the opportunity to quote from the protocol of the Nuremberg trial. In the section, 'Persecution and Annihilation of Jews and Christians,' it is written: 'The Gestapo appointed specialists in church matters to whom instructions were given so that they could work toward the conclusive annihilation of the church . . .' The principal means of persecution and annihilation were the concentration camps . . .' (*Nuremberg Trial*, Book 7, pp. 17f.)

"How can similar persecutions exist now in our land?

". . . I ask nothing of you . . . . I am only fulfilling my duty as a Christian and drawing your attention to that responsibility which you bear personally before Almighty God for all that which has been done and is still going on. . . .

"I do not desire to be your accuser, with my father and mother, in the coming judgment of God.

"Feelings of contempt, revenge, and scorn have no place in me, as in general they have no place in all the members of the ECB churches.

"Christ has taught me to forgive all those who hate us and persecute us . . . . I have long since forgiven everything to the men who as long ago as my childhood robbed me of the love of my father. Even now as I receive the news about my mother's arrest I harbor no thoughts of revenge against her persecutors. I would like to also urge my children to feel the same way if their father should be taken from them.

"I am deeply distressed at the terrible acts of the persecutor, for the grace of God can some day end even for them. . . .

"The only thing that I wish you to do is this: repent sincerely before the Lord!"

They Accept Their Sentences

In Odessa, the city on the northwest coast of the Black Sea which has retained the image of an old czarist city in its downtown area, a trial was held for five men and two women on 2-7 February 1967. The accused belonged to the congregation of ECBs in Peressyp, a suburb of Odessa.

In 1958 their meeting house had been confiscated by the authorities responsible for religious affairs and transferred shortly thereafter to a poultry collective for use as a clubhouse. In spite of this the congregation had lived on because they were able to meet here and there in houses.

Since atheistic propaganda, official reprisals, and scientific thinking had not succeeded in overcoming Christian faith, the attempt was made in Odessa to force those evangelical congregations approved by the state to act as accusers at the trials. It is a sinister and oppressing thought that a group of Christians could be abused in such a traitorous way by enemies of the faith for the battle against their own brothers in the faith.

Considering the malicious nature of the church struggle in the Soviet Union, the suspicion never dies that such accusations of the independent congregations by the registered congregations are only the product of lies designed to break up the community of Christians. Where the end justifies the means, it is clear that such a method would be the strongest weapon for dissolving the essential unity of evangelical Christians.

It is true, unfortunately, that this unity of evangelical Christians has been disrupted for ten years.

In the Odessa trial the agents of the state caused Odessa's registered Baptist congregation to play a role. It was striking, though, that not one member of the registered congregation had to appear before the court as a witness. Did this result from official complacency? Or was the reason rather that in the moment of crisis the registered congregations refused to be abused for the accusation of their brothers in the faith?

As long as freedom of speech does not exist in the Soviet Union, we will not know for certain the reason for this silence.

The accused, of whom five were sentenced to three years in a prison camp, indicated in their final statements that they too desired to have the option of going into prison camps for Jesus' sake. Here are some of their comments:

Grigori G. Borushko, 29: ". . . Citizen Judge! Because of my religious convictions I was excluded from the Medical Institute. . . . Yet even now when there is a first-aid situation, they threaten to call on me. . . . If someone does take my freedom away from me, no one can take from me the right to suffer for my Christ. Whoever will carry the cross once will be crucified again and again. . . .

"You destine us for suffering. Yet God also destines us for it. Suffering is the life-nerve of Christianity. The church lives so long as it suffers; for Christ suffered and has offered suffering to us. . . . We await the promise of a new heaven and a new earth in which righteousness dwells."

Nikolai P. Shevchenko, 53: "In 1958 our prayer house was taken away from the congregation, and in the cold winter of that year believers gathered in front of the wall of their church building under the open sky. . . . And now I am guilty of having been a leader of an unregistered congregation. Yes indeed. I am not one of those shepherds who forsakes his flock and flees when he sees danger. Whatever may happen now to me, I am ready to fulfill the charge which is entrusted to me by the church."

Vassili T. Timchak, 37: "I am before you today under accusation as a Christian. Yes, I believe in God. The Word of God says, however, that we should not only believe in Him, but that we should also suffer for Christ. I am fortunate that I have the opportunity to fulfill these words of Christ. One thing I know, that He will never leave me. Christ Himself underwent suffering and He never forsakes those who follow Him. . . ."

Svetlana P. Solovyova, 26: "I do not ask the court for mercy since it is an earthly court. I am ready to accept its penalty for me with joy. Whatever way I must go, I will be true to the Lord. But I must say to you, Citizen Judge, that no czar and no judge goes unpunished for unjust judgments. I want you to think about that. Today is the acceptable time, today is the day of salvation, tomorrow your life will no longer be in your own hand."

Yakov N. Krivoi, 65: "Truth is like the sun. One cannot cover it with the hand. Twenty years ago I was sentenced to a ten-year term for the same crimes for which I stand today before the court. . . . Twenty years later I was absolved. . . . The whole trial has shown even now how unfounded the charges are which were raised against me. According to the laws of our country, I have committed no crime whatsoever, neither against society nor against the state. If, however, I suffer as a Christian, I am ready to have chains laid upon me. I have already been a believer for forty years. None of your methods will indoctrinate me, and none of your threats whatsoever will break me."

"A Preacher With Burning Zeal!"

In 1966 Michail Ivanovich Khorev — born in 1931, a resident of Kishinev, 28 Minsk Street, Apartment 30 — was sentenced to two and one-half years in a penal camp. He was arrested 19 May 1966, in the Central Committee building in Moscow as he sought to inquire after the whereabouts of a delegation of ECBs who two days before had been arrested at the Central Committee building. At his trial Khorev was reproached for the wide extent of his preaching activity. Excerpts from the speech of the state prosecuting attorney indicate the extent of the secret meetings held by ECBs.

"Citizen Judge! Freedom of belief, as the expert witness has already testified, is not intended to mean that believers are to be completely unrestricted. . . . The demand by believers for the right to educate children in the religious spirit contradicts the interests of the Soviet state. . . .

"Judged according to the law, Khorev systematically violated the law from 1961 to 1966 as one of the organizers for this group. He has organized and directed meetings, a fact the accused has confirmed by his own testimony. He has said that it would be easier to name the places where he has not been and has not preached than those where he has.

"It is beside the point that he considers his activity legal.

"On 1 August 1965 Khorev together with Bondarenko organized a baptismal service in Rovno. On the way to the river they sang psalms. The accused himself does not deny that he has been a preacher with burning zeal. The statements of witness Shilo confirm that they set out for the river with a brass band. Agents of the police were forced to accompany them. If the escorting police conducted themselves humanely, in order not to imperial the simple believers — 2,000 people were gathered together — that did not mean that no violations of the law regarding cults were observed.

"On 5 September 1965, they organized a gathering in the vicinity of Station DVRS (Kiev) in the woods, sang psalms, and preached. . . .

"All this forces one to think that these people hold nothing sacred. Soviet Men demonstrate on May 1 in order to exhibit joyfully their power and strength. But these gather at that time to pray for something that does not exist. This is an offense to the feelings of Soviet Men. . . ."

Ineffective Assaults

In the petition to the government of 10 March 1969, which was signed by Vins, Khropova, and Vilchinskaya on behalf of the parents of those imprisoned and sentenced in the USSR for the sake of God's Word, it was stated:

"In Chelyabinsk on Christmas day twelve believers were taken away by the police. Fines of 600 rubles were levied and they were beaten. Do you think that Christians will stop believing because of such treatment? Do you believe that a country is well ordered where such things go on?

"In the statement of the Chelyabinsk congregation the conclusion read: 'We are prepared to suffer and to do without everything, even life itself, but we will not denounce our conviction and teaching of Christ.'

"Evangelical Christians and Baptists in camps and prisons have no Bibles. We have already written many times about this unacceptable practice of withholding from believers that most vital thing, their spiritual nourishment. This deprivation only confirms the fact that they have been sentenced because of their faith. The Bible is appreciated by the whole world. But you put the Bible on secret and public indexes as a banned book and forbid its reading. . . .

"The attempts of past years indicate that to battle physically against faith in God accomplishes nothing. . . .'"

Forced Cure for Belief in God

"The life of our brother is in danger!" That was the conclusion of an urgent circular letter to all believing ECBs in the USSR. Twenty-four members of the congregation in Borodichi put their signatures to the following notice of 26 March 1970:

"Ivan Vassilyevich Lasuta, after a secret trial, has been assigned for 'treatment' to the district psychiatric hospital. Someone perhaps had remembered that nine years ago, while he was still an atheist, he had had a severe nervous breakdown which the doctors were not able to treat. That he later became healthy and could perform a highly qualified work was due to an act of God. He became a living testimony and proclaimed the grace of God.

"Only after a lengthy inquiry was his mother able to find out that her fully healthy son has been placed with the mentally ill. After he had been handed over to the authorities, this statement came from his place of employment: 'I. V. Lasuta performed as a highly qualified specialist during his time of work here and always met his work quotas at a rate of 110 to 120%. He was disciplined and upright in the conduct of his life.'

"No one from his neighborhood had observed any damage to his health from his former nervous breakdown. Nonetheless, the doctors began an insulin treatment. I. V. Lasuta asked the doctors several times: 'What would happen if I renounced my belief in God? If I no longer went to meetings and stopped praying, what would you do with me?'

" 'If that happened,' the doctors would say, 'we would release you immediately to go home.'

"On another occasion the doctor in charge asked him after a dose of insulin: 'Now, Lasuta, do you still persist in believing in God?' Since the answer was firm and definite, he said: 'We will cure you yet of your fanaticism.'

"Under the influence of new medicine his health has deteriorated so much that Lasuta has become totally bed-ridden and cannot move himself without help. God be praised that his spirit has not broken. With a deep joy he has said: 'If the Lord permits it, I am ready even to die for His name. Yet I will not deny Him.'

"His relatives also have this assurance as they close their appeal: 'We believe that the Lord will yet call many to be His children, even through these sufferings and privations. Therefore, we appeal to you to think about our beloved brother in your prayers and to ask the Lord to give our brother strength to remain faithful to the end.'

"The physical life of this brother is in danger. Once again those responsible for the well-being of the citizens have wrapped themselves in silence even though they have been asked to investigate the case."

Fifteen Fines for One Pensioner

The press attaché of the Soviet legation in Bonn felt himself obliged to publish an article on "Religion and Church in the USSR" in the magazine *Soviet Union Today* (no. 23/24, 1968). In it Yuri Alexandrov offered the following thoughts:

"Our constitution guarantees to all citizens freedom of conscience. All believers can practice their activities of religious worship without hindrances, all unbelievers can freely defend their atheistic world view. . . .

"If there were even a single word of truth in the reports constantly emerging during the last fifty years concerning persecution of Christians in the USSR, no one in the Soviet Union would go to church any more, no one would be baptized and married, and the church bells would have been silent long ago. Yet the churches stand open to all believers, religious people baptize their children, their marriages are blessed in church, and the ringing of bells can be heard on every Sunday and holy day throughout the entire country. . . ."

Such statements are simply for propaganda. One must look deeper: what does the day by day harassment of Christians look like?

We reproduce the petition of Semen Pechinnikov for this reason, since his is not a matter of a sensational prison term. It is rather the constant, grinding punishment by authorities who desire that no more worship services be held. And when one compares the income of the pensioner with the amount of the fines, one realizes how this harassment must demolish the livelihood of the 71-year-old Christian.

The following order for a fine was sent to him:

"Resolution #47. 10 May 1971. The Commission of Administrative

Officials of Viatskie-Polyany, which consists of five members, has worked through the public reports on citizen Pechinnikov, Semen Semenovich, born 1899, without work, pensioned (income 42 rubles), place of residence: Viatskie-Polyany, 2 ul.P. These make it clear that he . . . has violated the ordinance, PVS SSSR, of 18 March 1966. He conducted worship services and also organized them. Besides that he has refused to register the church. The Commission imposes a penalty of 50 rubles on citizen Pechinnikov. The fine must be paid at the bank within two weeks. Chairman of the Administrative Commission: Kuchmov; members: Malyekin, Yeshov, Darnitsin."

Pechinnikov, who lives in the Kiev region northeast of Moscow, turned to the government with a petition. In it he writes:

"I, a citizen of this land, must be able to live under the protection of the Soviet constitution without prejudice on account of my religious convictions. I am 71 years old, a pensioner, and receive 41 rubles and 90 kopecks pension. I have a 28-year-old son. Since he is an invalid of the first class, he lives at my expense. He receives 16 rubles as a pension. His mother is also a pensioner. She receives 48 rubles and 85 kopecks.

"The governmental authorities of Viatskie-Polyany treat me consistently as a sacrifice to their ridicule. And not only me, but also my son who must always be carried since he cannot walk by himself. I am enclosing a photo.

"When we celebrated Easter recently, the local authorities wanted to hinder us. They photographed us during the worship service and shouted, 'Stop this meeting! Stop your praying!' The children were frightened since someone had told them that the police would take them away.

"After these incidents I was fined again. Resolution #47 of 10 May 1971 is enclosed. In the course of only three years I have been fined fifteen times with levies of 50 rubles each time. This now totals 750 rubles (about $750). One is forced to inquire as to the means with which we are supposed to live.

"I am charged because, it is said, I am (1) a law breaker. But I fought once for the communistic Soviet government during the Civil War in the 28th Asian Division. . . . (2) I am reproached as a leader of the congregation of ECBs because I refuse to register our congregation. But our congregation has already turned to the authorities for that very purpose so many times. All were in vain. . . ."

4

SUFFERING REVEALED

Martyrdom can be forgotten, simply out of carelessness, as unimportant things slip from your mind.

Or it can happen consciously through an aesthetic avoidance of that which is painful. A "strong" church never shows pain in its activity before the world as do scorned Christians who have been made into laughing-stocks!

"The periods of persecution for the sake of the Gospel now at last are behind us." These were the words of the cultured theologian Friedrich Schleiermacher which expressed his joy at the self-respecting church of his day. The marriage between Christianity on the one hand, and culture, state, and society on the other, seemed to be a happy one. That was in 1833.

In Schleiermacher's day it had been a long time since preaching the Gospel had been accompanied by scorn and strife. Schleiermacher was pleased by the feeling that he had helped create a situation in which the Gospel of his time had been made suitable for fashionable drawing rooms. He certainly evidenced no awareness of the suffering undergone by Henhoefer, Blumhardt, and Gossner.

Some groups today have even more "progressive" ideas.

Why should modern Christians in an enlightened age also have to suffer? It is unheard of. The embarrassment created by the fact of suffering is significant.

Suffering congregations — what importance could they still have! We see the suffering "third world" every day on television. A gigantic effort is directed toward it. As a consequence we also desire to be a church for the world, to shape politics and change society. Adults must be trained and children educated. Peace must be sought and the hungry fed. And who would desire to call the urgency of these tasks into question?

In this situation it is uncanny, however, that we do not perceive the temptation for that church which seeks to make its mark on this gigantic constellation of problems. A modern, attractive, influential twentieth-century church can perhaps be built by a superhuman effort. It is another question entirely whether a Christian congregation can succeed in doing this or even should succeed. One cannot escape the fact, even after every effort has been exerted, that such an attempt veils the original biblical goal of Jesus' body, or replaces it entirely with a purely earthly plan of salvation, with world peace and social justice; but at this point an energy-killing work is in fact required to justify theologically the critical nature of this change for the congregation of Jesus.

Christians today should pitch in everywhere: in politics and culture, business and science. The tasks are immense; regardless of the con-temporary ideology which is fashionable at any one time — whether it is nationalism, humanism, liberalism, idealism, rationalism, socialism — there are always hands stretched out for help. Time and again in the history of the church Christianity has been tempted to let itself be captivated by these outstretched hands inviting the church to act as co-laborers. And when this happens, any understanding for the suffering church, for a persecution on Jesus' behalf, is lost. Is it really only misunderstanding when Christians are hated and persecuted? Is the cause of such enmity really just human ineptitude? Or can all this bad feeling be reckoned — as many claim boldly today — as simply the fruits of failure and sin by preceding generations?

Let us be clear about this: there is no degeneration in the fact that Christians work in support of earthly programs to help people. No one would want to contend seriously that Christians should refrain from all co-operation with worldly powers and movements! To seek "the best for the city" is also a command of the faith. Christians will cer-tainly want to ponder the good and honorable things in the world.

But there is definitely a falling away when the church purchases the leap to recognized status in modern society at a high price, when it pays with silence and forgetfulness, when it simply no longer speaks of that which, according to the words of Jesus, separates it from the world. To do this is to overlook the gulf between God's call and the world's idea of salvation. It is to lose, in open engagement with the affairs of this life, its unique possession, its spiritual mandate. It is to be so enthusiastic about its adaptability to contemporary thought — where no one will dispute that even a Christian is touched by the characteristics of his age — that it is tempted to regard the very effort to keep up to date as its misison. But this is not the church's mission. It cannot be its mission since the call to conversion, the challenge to biblical rebirth, no longer touches the whole man but merely the deficiencies of his behavior as they are determined by society's unfulfilled ethical imperative. And this is to fill the gulf which divides the body of Jesus from the society of the world.

Thus in all ages the danger has been near at hand that the churches who sensed their responsibility to the world would confuse biblical salvation with worldly programs of redemption, would roll up their sleeves and go to work, and in so doing fall into a Babylonian captivity to the powers of this world.

Time and again the report of Christians martyred for their faith has deeply shocked a church wrapped up in its own programs and so apparently free from harassment. People were at sea in this century when they heard of Christian persecutions in Armenia, Celebes, in Mexico and Communist Spain. The suffering of the Baltic martyrs, the struggle of the confessing church in Germany's Third Reich, and the oppression of Christians in East Germany have certainly affected our church, so happily secured on every side, at the deepest level.

Many have probably perceived all this as merely tragic individual incidents. Many Christians certainly felt nothing more than sympathy or even political passion when these things were reported. But there were also those who recognized the voice of God to their own congregations in the persecutions which occurred.

It is the Bible which gives us this essential spiritual understanding of martyrdom. For the fact that the body of Jesus suffers is not a tragic misfortune but a promise. In suffering the vine is pruned so that it can bring forth more fruit (John 15:6). In suffering Jesus leads His congregation back to its original calling.

But the tragedy of a busy Christianity so active in many areas is that it no longer recognizes this spiritual sense of martyrdom. It believes that it is strong and that it is doing God's work; it thinks that its self-confidence is the courage of faith and does not bother to ascertain if its activity is perhaps just a diversion or even the pure idolatry of self-affirmation. What is a church to do now, esteemed and respected in many quarters and regarding its task as putting the twentieth century firmly to right, when confronted with Christians who are beaten for the sake of their testimony? The world will not be impressed with suffering and scorned Christians! If they at the very least would suffer for spectacular acts of political liberation, that could be understood. If only they were guerrillas! Deeds which change our world are in demand today. But suffering for the Word of God — what can that possibly mean?

And so today martyrdom is hushed up — because it is embarrassing.

The church that is free of harassment knows only one necessity, the problem of co-operation. It needs people of rank, culture, and education and also of influence, power, and plenty of money — but no martyrs. What could it even begin to do with them?

In many places one cannot conceive of the church as anything but a church recognized and supported by ruling powers. But it is precisely these ruling powers which assault the suffering congregation. And with its suffering, the dying of its members, it touches the life-nerve of the unrestricted churches. For it sings the praises of a better security than the power blocks of this world. It knows of more reliable assurance than financial backing. The question is whether the unmolested church really knows yet what it means to live from the Word of God, from the Bible. The suffering congregation takes its life from it — daily. And does it know that all activities and deeds make sense only in light of the triumph of Jesus? The suffering church knows this, for the victory of Jesus is the only one they have.

The departure of people from the unmolested churches has made them aware of the fragility of their "greatness" more rapidly and with harsher clarity than the suffering of brothers and sisters. This is only an indication of how firmly they stand in the undertow of their own activities. With such a set of priorities and goals it is imperative for the established churches not only to hush up the suffering body but to prevent it from speaking at all. The suffering servants of Jesus are branded as psychopathic outsiders, fanatics, and sectarians who do not realize what age they are living in. It is not just their enemies who do this but also Christians who, consequently, are estranged from the spiritual law of the imitation of Jesus.

We Must Speak of Jesus: A letter of Aida Skripnikova to an atheist. New Year's Eve, 1961.

On the Nevski Prospect, the bustling main street of Leningrad with its many buildings so rich in tradition, a 19-year-old girl is distributing handwritten New Year's cards. They contain a few verses which she has written herself under the title: "Seek God while you can find him!" While she is distributing the cards she is arrested.

Aida Skripnikova is her name. A short time before her arrest she had become a convert. A thorough atheistic education in a state home was behind her. Born on 1 September 1942, she grew up as an orphan. Her father was shot because, for religious reasons, he refused military service in a combat role.

This educated lab assistant remained in custody only a short time. She was warned severely and then released. A year later she was informed that her presence in Leningrad was "not desired." On 4 July 1962, Aida Skripnikova was attacked in the Communist youth newspaper *Smena.* The atheistic propagandist, V. Kuzin, had entitled his article: "Don't Be a Corpse Among the Living!"

The young Christian responded to this challenge. But her reply was not printed by the magazine. With friends she duplicated it, and it was passed privately to others. It contained the following passages (in extracts):

"Imagine for yourself that we had agreed to race. And suddenly you bound my legs and you yourself ran like crazy to the finish line. 'Hurrah! I have won,' you cry. . . . I have the courage to say to you that you acted dishonestly and propose to you an honorable race: take the bonds off my legs! Give me freedom, and then we will see who wins. But then you answer: 'Release your bonds? Give you freedom? But that is an attack on my freedom. . . .'

"What would an impartial referee say to that? Certainly he could say, 'Kuzin is worried about defeat. . . .'

"That's right, isn't it? It is a fear of defeat which motivates you, Comrade Kuzin, and your comrades to sordid and oppressive actions, to resort to force. Your arguments are like a house of cards which falls apart at the slightest breeze. You consider that all is in order because that house of cards is protected from the blowing of the spirit of truth by a great heap of decrees, laws, and circular letters.

"Do you still remember? When I had read your article, I said to you: 'You have written that without reference to the facts.' You laughed at me and answered: 'Well, if you want to go to jail, why certainly go ahead.' You, as a convinced atheist, have not tried to show me that I am wrong. If you are of the opinion that people do not believe in God solely and strictly because of your superior reason and your superior scientific knowledge, why is it that you are afraid when a sorely befuddled person like myself talks with intellectuals? Why sentence me to a prison term for that?

"Unbelievers have the right to visit each other and to gather together whenever they desire. But this human right has been taken away from us although all are alike before the law. . . .

"If you, Comrade Kuzin, feel like spending your time in the company of your neighbors, you do not have to fear that in so doing you violate the law. You can gather together at any time and do whatever you please: talk together, read, sing. And why may we not visit each other? What law forbids us from doing that? Why are we not permitted to pray? Why may we not read the Bible where we want to read it? We are only allowed to talk about God in the prayer house. You would certainly not be pleased if you were permitted to talk about the theater only in the theater or about a book only in the library.

"This is the way we also speak about Jesus, wherever and whenever we meet, because He alone is the substance of our life.

"You call our modest meetings with friends illegal, but Christ the Lord gave us the legal right to assemble when He said: 'Where two or three are gathered in my name, there am I in the midst of them' (Matt. 18:20).

" 'Call on the Lord everywhere!' Christ did not say, 'Pray where one allows you to.' No, He said 'everywhere,' and consequently even in that place where it is not allowed!

"You arrange congresses, lectures, public meetings; you have thousands of agitators at your disposal, but you shake with terror when a few people gather for prayer.

" 'No one forbids you to believe in God,' you write. I am not completely sure that you will still say that tomorrow. It could be that soon even simple prayer will be regarded as a terrible crime.

"We have no guarantee that you will not shut our prayer house down even tomorrow. Certainly you can shut it down, but in so doing you cannot destroy the church of Jesus Christ. 'You all are the temple of the living God,' say the Scriptures.

"You write, 'No one forbids you to believe in God.' We, however, do not believe in God because you so nobly permit it. We will believe in God even if you forbid it. We are not Christians because we are guaranteed this in the constitution of the Soviet Union under freedom of belief, but because Jesus Christ has died for us on Calvary. . . .

"You do not like the fact that we distribute religious letters. Just imagine that a fire had broken out. You would sound the alarm. But if there were no alarm bell, you would grab hold of any old bucket, even if it were full of holes. In spite of the holes you would fill it up. No one could blame you in this instance that you had used an old, useless pail.

"If you would permit us to publish a mass-circulation newspaper which could be bought at any newspaper stand as desired, I will assure you that we will stop distributing religious letters.

"If you do not like the fact that we hold prayer meetings in private homes, then permit us to read the Bible in church. Allow us then to organize little meetings for young people in the church! Allow us then to be able to gather in our church when we desire!

"It is false when you say that we 'have just recently been seized by the urgent need to hold prayer meetings in homes.' It is false to say, 'just recently.'

"When I was still very small, people often would come to our house in order to read the Bible and pray. They met together although they had to reckon with a brutal persecution (1947). They even met after that night when several people were arrested. After they had spent between eight and ten years in prison, these people began again to meet where they could read the Bible and pray. We also gather in meetings and you can do nothing about that.

"You claim that we demand that 'atheistic journals be forbidden to promote anti-religious propaganda. . . .' We have never asked for that. . . . For when anti-religious propaganda is propagated, it is easier for us to refute your empty contentions. . . .

"Your rationalization — that to give believers freedom would be an attack on the freedom of conscience of the working classes — is absurd. If one put a Christian newspaper, for example *The Young Christian* or *Joyful News*, in a newspaper stand next to *Komsomolskaya Pravda*, how could that assault the freedom of any person? Only those people would buy our newspapers who wanted to.

"You write: 'We atheists are certainly not opposed to eternal life. Only it must be here on earth and not in another world. Immortality for us does not lie on the same plane as your religion, where one sits in the so-called heavenly halls without working, munches gingerbread, and watches with interest the greater part of mankind tormented in the blazing of hell-fire!'

"I do not know what 'religion' offers. But God's Word says this: 'The kingdom of God does not mean food and drink but righteousness and peace and joy in the Holy Spirit' (Rom. 14:17).

"You say: 'Man is immortal through his work.' Even the fact that you talk about immortality shows that, in spite of your atheism, it is a wretched thing for you to imagine that you could be forgotten forever. . . .

"In your opinion there is 'no more honorable, higher, or beautiful goal in the world than to build Communism and to live in it.' And you ask me if I am ready to serve this goal.

"No, Comrade Kuzin, I do not want to serve this goal for I do not see it as splendid or brilliant. The society which you are building will never be a just society since you yourself are unjust. I am convinced in my inner being that where there is no truth there will also be no happiness. It is the goal of my life to serve the truth.

"My father refused military service. You call that a crime. He declined combative service, and for this he lost his life. He died in order not to have to kill. If everyone were ready to die rather than to kill, there would be no more wars. Christ said: 'You shall not kill!' You scoff at this command. If only men would remember this command! But many today have forgotten it altogether, and others mock it. That is the only reason why the sword of war hangs over the world now.

" 'Your father,' you say, 'declined to take arms to defend you.' You say, 'defend.' I know Baptists who did bear arms in order to defend their children, their homeland.

"But today in this land, in the land they defended, they are despised. They are not trusted. They are forbidden to gather for prayer. A great flood of vulgarity is poured out upon them. And they must allow it to be said: 'We have no place for you in our beautiful world! We will indoctrinate you yet! We will isolate you yet! We will punish you!'

"You write that one cannot count the crimes of all religions, including the Baptist faith, which have been committed against mankind and especially against science.

"Jan Hus was burned by men who called themselves Christians. He said: 'Lord Jesus Christ! I am ready to bear joyfully a gruesome and horrible death for the sake of Your pure Gospel and for preaching Your holy Word. Forgive all my enemies. I implore You for that. . . . For the most important goal of all my preaching, my teaching, writing, and all other service was to rescue men from sin. And now I am placed before the Roman Curia to account for my preaching of the Gospel.'

"But you would not concede today that Jan Hus was burned as a preacher of the Gospel. And this is understandable, for you still persecute people because, when you come right down to it, they preach the Gospel. And if you would now admit that Jan Hus was executed for preaching the Gospel, you would judge your own position by this admission.

"If Jan Hus were alive in our day, in this land, he would be put in jail. . . .

"Here is the last point to which I would like to draw your attention. You are agitated over the fact that God killed all men with the exception of Noah's family. Yet the ark was constructed over a period of 120 years. Men were able to hear Noah say during that long period: 'Come in! Take heed for your deliverance! Repent!' Finally the ark was completely built. And even then the doors remained open for six days. Anyone who wanted to could have gone in. But the people did not want to. They were destroyed. The simple reason was that they did not want to let themselves be saved. You have already heard the cry of God many times: 'Turn back before it is too late! Turn back and inherit eternal life!'

"Just as the ark was offered to men in those days as a means to be saved, so Christ is given to us today. But you do not desire to receive Christ. You do not long to accept eternal life. God is offering this life to you, but you are rejecting the opportunity. Whom will you accuse at the judgment day of God? Who will bear the penalty for your fallen life? Do you want to do that yourself? Salvation had already been offered to you many times, but you did not want to come 'into the ark.'

"Still today, however, you can alter your destiny. Before it is too late, COME TO CHRIST!'"

More Than the World Can Offer: Aida Skripnikova fought for inner freedom.

In 1964 Aida Skripnikova was expelled from Leningrad. She received no immigration permit for other cities, so she stayed with Christians in various places in order not to be arrested as an undesirable "without fixed residence." After six months, she was permitted to return to Leningrad.

Yet shortly thereafter she was again arrested. A tourist had given her a Bible, and she was once again warned sternly and released.

In 1965 she was forced to spend a year in a work camp. Her membership in an unregistered Baptist congregation was given as the reason for the sentence. In judicial language it was expressed like this: "trafficking with obscurantists and religious fanatics."

When she was arrested once again on Good Friday, 1968, the authorities at the same time confiscated issues of the duplicated magazines, *Messenger of Salvation* and the *Fraternal Leaflet*, which came from circles of the independent ECBs. Moreover, her personal notes and the trial transcripts of other Christians were also confiscated. This time Aida was sentenced to three years in a work camp.

The direct course which this young Christian has steered in her life is striking. She said herself on one occasion that it would be easy for her to be free. All she had to do was to relax her uncompromising observance of the commands of God. She was of the opinion that every Christian is easily moved to fall away from God when such a relaxation occurs.

To keep from this she followed the missionary command of Jesus without slackening. Her conscience is bound to Jesus' Word and does not seek to reshape it according to her own ideas. She bore even her period of imprisonment with this same spirit of obedience. She expressed her convictions like this at one time:

"We draw persecution upon ourselves because we hold fast to Christ. We hold to Him because He will always hold to us. And that means more to us than those privileges which subjection to this world could gain for us. The world is ready to make peace with a church which renders more obedience to the words of the world than to the Lord. But to do that is to lose the blessing of the Lord!"

Life Loses All Sense Without God: A letter of Aida Skripnikova to a Christian.

In the wide expanse of forests and steppes which extends across the Mordovian Republic some 300 miles southeast of Moscow are found prison camps with a notoriety dating from earlier times. It was here that Aida was to serve her three-year sentence in accordance with the judicial decree of 10 April 1968. It was on Good Friday when she was arrested for the fourth time by the state police in Leningrad. She wrote from the prison camp:

"21 January 1970. 'Therefore, since we are justified by faith, we have peace with God through our Lord Jesus Christ. Through him we have obtained access to this grace in which we stand, and we rejoice in our hope of sharing the glory of God' (Rom. 5:1, 2).

"Faith is in life a clear light,
a guiding star! It is well with him for whom this light never goes out.

"Dear brothers in Christ! I greet you in the love of Jesus Christ!

"I received your letter today and I thank you for it. I would gladly answer your letter this very day, but unfortunately my time is restricted at present, and so it is not possible for me to write as much as I would like.

"You would like to know how I am feeling under conditions here. Above all I must say to you that I am sincerely thankful to God from my whole heart for this course of events. On this journey I can learn much and receive special blessings. I have sensed with special clarity the love of God, His leading, His keeping, and His protection. I must often hear unbelievers say: 'Look here, we have a secure life, we are happy — and what do you have? Aren't you fed up with going around in such clothes and living under such conditions?' I answer that I am happy and that my happiness is much more constant than theirs because it is not dependent upon outward conditions. They do not understand me and say that I must consider these three years of my life as lost. Although I have had genuinely difficult days and although being deprived of freedom is in itself very difficult, I have never regretted it, and I have never considered that I should not have done that for which I have been imprisoned.

"Yes, I have great longing for freedom, for home, and for friends, but I cannot turn away from the Lord to obtain these things since He gives gifts of incomparable value. Life loses all sense without God. I said in court that it is of inestimable worth for me to be a child of God, and for me freedom cannot purchase the price of disloyalty to the Lord. Now after a year and a half, I repeat that same thing and can add to it that the yoke of Christ is gentle and His burden is light (Matt. 11:30).

"A brother in his last speech before the court repeated the

thoughts of Martin Luther: 'This I believe, and I do not have the power to renounce it.' That's it precisely — I do not have the power, for we well know that nothing is worse in the world than life without God, especially for those who have once known God. They perceive the emptiness of heart with greater clarity than men who have never known God. I cannot imagine a life without God, I do not want such a life. I have been told many times: 'You may believe in God, but act differently,' in other words — 'believe in God, but do not follow His commands.' It is true that freedom can be retained under such an arrangement. And the devil appeals to us much more frequently to 'deny God's commands' than to 'deny God.' But that is one and the same thing. When a believer was told before the court that he could believe in God but that he should live according to the Bible only when he got to heaven and not right now, he replied: 'If I do not live according to the Bible while on earth, I will never be in heaven.'

"I would like to close my letter with a verse of a song . . . [which treated the joy in Christ which no one can take away].

"Give my most hearty greetings to all friends.

"Your sister in Christ, Aida."

After her release this slender, brown-eyed Russian girl was asked by friends what she experienced as the most difficult trial during her time in prison. After some delay she said:

"A most difficult thing was to be separated from friends. Besides that, it was difficult to be isolated from the outside world and never able to go anywhere. But the hardest thing of all was to live without a gospel. After I had been in prison for a while, I asked for a Bible, but they did not give me one. An imprisoned Christian girl brought me a gospel of Mark. When the guards discovered that I had a gospel, they were concerned. A search began in the camp. They searched thoroughly through everything twice, the second time they found it. For this I was confined ten days and nights in cold solitary confinement.

"A couple of weeks after this incident I was fortunate in my imprisonment to obtain the entire New Testament. I succeeded in keeping this book almost to the day of my release. The guards carried out numerous searches, but the Lord helped me each time so that I sensed in advance when a search would take place and could hide the precious book. Many of my fellow prisoners helped me to hide the book although they were not Christians. Shortly before my release they took away all the notes that I had made during my time there. Everything that I had written during the three years was lost.

"Although the conditions in confinement were all very severe, hope also lived in prison. I had no anxiety, my spirit was not weighed down with fear. I was able to live the three years with the words of Matthew 11:30 before my eyes: '. . . for my yoke is easy and my burden is light.' Although I knew this passage of Scripture well before my arrest, I could only in prison understand how reliable and true it was. The burden of a Christian is in fact easy to bear. I had a profound sense of this many times during the imprisonment. During my time there I had an excellent Friend, the risen Lord Jesus Christ. I had the same experience in prison as a sister who wrote from her cell that Christ shares His grace and peace with those in prison so that they can be steadfast regardless of the burdens that are laid upon them. We are not alone and abandoned, not even in prison . . .

Many greetings and packages were sent to the prison for me. One time someone told me that I had received ten packages from Norway but they could not give them to me since I had not as yet reformed my attitude. I do not know who sent these packages, but I would like to express my thanks to each one who prayed for me and for my brothers and sisters who shared my fate. Once when I was shown a package and was told that it contained chocolate and other good things, I felt that I did not even need the contents. The fact that my friends were looking after me was a far greater blessing.

"I did not suppose that all these remembrances were just for me, but rather also for all of us in need. It is a most wonderful thing that nothing can separate believers from each other. All who belong to the Lord are one body wherever and under whatever conditions they may be. Some have thought that Christians in closed lands were cut off from contact with the other parts of the body of Jesus. It is a great joy for us, in light of this feeling, to experience concretely the visible spiritual relationship with Christians who live in other parts of the world. Through these we have hope in prison. I would like to express our great love to those who were concerned and prayed for us.

"The task of intercession does not cease when someone is released from prison. We need sustained intercession. I would hope that all Christians could join together in prayer for each other. We should pray that our faith might not suffer calamities of any kind because of external circumstances."

After Release From Prison

For Aida Skripnikova release from prison was not the path to complete freedom. Until she "definitely improves" she must report regularly to the police at a specific place of exile. She herself reported:

"I was freed from the labor camp on April 12. We were not given our freedom at the site of the camp but were first brought to another place. There we underwent a two-week period of different kinds of testing. There they said to me that they considered me someone who had learned absolutely nothing from my sentence. They therefore did not even give me a pass as the other prisoners received. I got merely a paper which certified that I had been released from prison after serving my full sentence. The place in which I must live now is a fairly large city east of Moscow. Only when I had arrived there could I receive my pass. I am confined to my quarters after 9 P.M. Twice a week I must report to the local police that I am still in the city. Without police permission I may not travel outside of the city. I am bound to this arrangement for six months. If I have not improved after that time, the arrangement can be extended for another half year. I do not know what will happen after that. If I do not follow the regulations, they can arrest me again at any time. Such severe regulations are usually imposed only on criminals, murderers, and rowdies. Apparently they number me with these."

While still in prison before her release officials read the observations which Aida had made in her notebook. One of them asked her: "Don't you see that these people who bring Bibles to the Soviet Union are only trying to destroy us?"

To this Aida replied firmly: "If we had Bibles in Russia and the people in Sweden had none, I would be the first one ready to take the Bible there."

5

THE WORD OF GOD SUSTAINS THEM

A CHRISTIAN SHOULD NOT have illusions about what it means to follow Christ. Jesus prophesied clearly: "Behold, I send you out as sheep in the midst of wolves" (Matt. 10:16). It takes but a moment for hungry wolves to rip a sheep to pieces. It may be disconcerting that Jesus will assign us no task more important and pleasing than that of being mutton for wolves to devour.

Yet it is important to recognize that Jesus has bestowed a crucial promise on the feeble congregation in its suffering, namely, an all-powerful proclamation: "When they deliver you up, do not be anxious how you are to speak or what you are to say; for what you are to say will be given to you in that hour; for it is not you who speak, but the Spirit of your Father speaking through you" (Matt. 10:19, 20).

In the February, 1967, trial of members of the evangelical congregation in Peressyp, a suburb of Odessa, the accused medical student Borushko said: "The church lives as long as it suffers. If one examines the history of Christianity, one sees that the church is faithful to Christ as long as it is undergoing suffering. On the other hand, when the church turns aside from the commands of Christ, it suffers no more."

No one wants to make suffering a spiritual law for merely this reason, as if we should force ourselves to suffer. But it would be good sense if we took account of suffering. The church has long since been viewed only as an institution that is recognized, respected, and honored by worldly powers. When this situation prevails, however, martyrdom can be perceived only as a misfortune that has come to pass.

But it is martyrdom which calls the congregation of Jesus back to its sources of power. In 1917 the czarist church in Russia was hounded into the desert. If earlier it had only been a well-intentioned desire for service that had prompted the church to marry the state, the relationship nevertheless became more than that, namely whoredom. The church gave its best to the union and enjoyed the protection of the state, but then other values began to infiltrate the church. This dilution has occurred time and again in the history of Christianity. At times it has been cultural Protestantism, at other times a people's, a socialistic, or a nationalistic Christianity.

And then the day comes when these ideologies liberate themselves from the church. They have grown weary of the church's dominance, and have themselves grown strong. Thus, in the Russian Revolution, the state church came rapidly to be seen as a criminal working against the state and no longer received for its service even a prostitute's fee. The age for combining service to Jesus and love of the world was past. The time of martyrdom had begun. This was not a misfortune but the judgment of God. Yet in judgment lay the grace of God's visitation. All of a sudden the congregation of Jesus was no longer acknowledged and honored but was an offense, an irritant; it was battled — and in this it finally received the chance to come to its senses in order to become once more the congregation of Jesus.

We should never react as if suffering were always an unalloyed blessing for God's congregation. Suffering is always and primarily the judgment of God. In many countries of the world there were once flourishing churches. Then persecutions extinguished them, and nothing now remains.

Everything depends upon whether we understand afresh the promises of Jesus to the suffering church. Only He, the Lord, can make His body light and salt in the world.

For this purpose the suffering congregation receives from Jesus the great promises of His presence, so that it can mature in suffering. When it suffers, it learns of its own feebleness and weaknesses. Martyrdom mercilessly exposes the neediness of the church. In the New Testament, in the book of Acts, it is related that the early church never developed a deceptive belief in its own power even during the great revival which gripped thousands of people. The fact that the apostles were repeatedly persecuted and beaten exerted a beneficial influence on the estimate of their own strength, for being crushed by passionate grief makes a person sober.

In the letter to the congregation at Smyrna in John's Revelation this sober observation was made in the face of oppressive persecution: "I know your poverty." Yet at the same time the angel also declared, in total contradiction to appearances, that the congregation, crushed by suffering, possessed an indestructible gift bestowed by Jesus: "but you are rich" (Rev. 2:9).

The Chinese martyr, David Yang, for many years a co-worker at the Kiangswan Bible School in Shanghai, has left us a compelling exposition of this letter to Smyrna. He writes: "It is regrettable that many contemporary Christians aspire to the goods of this world but do not long for the precious things of the kingdom of God. They do believe in their salvation, certainly; yet they are not prepared to be poor for Christ's sake. Comforts and riches are for them the grace of God. . . . Yet the spiritual riches of faith, joy, strength, patience, and many others spring only from poverty."

All of a church's own courage, security, and hope is taken away when it suffers. The suffering church is led to death. For this very reason it must — if it desires to still be alive at all — bind itself completely to Jesus and His promises, and trust in Him. But when that is done, the weak and helpless congregation is so safe and secure in Jesus that even "the gates of hell cannot overcome it" (Matt. 16:18).

Thus, for the church of Jesus poverty and strength, suffering and victory belong together in a definite relationship, however paradoxical that may seem. This, however, will never result in a great victory for the church, but will always be the victory of *Jesus* over a powerless and poverty-stricken congregation. It is a congregation which has been assaulted and beset from every side that receives the revelation of this victory. Paul summarized the close interrelationship of suffering and triumph in this way: we "suffer with him in order that we may also be glorified with him. I consider that the sufferings of this present world are not worth comparing with the glory that is to be revealed to us" (Rom. 8:17, 18).

In periods during which the body of Jesus is respected and recognized, and when it is spared the burden of persecution, the fatal flaw has repeatedly arisen that the church thinks its own charm, its own impact, or its own buoyant form have lent the Gospel its telling force. Christians often express the opinion that they themselves must assist the Gospel in achieving recognition and acceptance in the world. When, therefore, there comes a time to talk of Jesus, we do it bashfully, as if we were defending a subject that was painful to us. And the impression often refuses to go away that we are like someone daring to undertake the totally hopeless effort of pulling a putrid, stinking fish out of our pocket and seeking to sell it solely by our impressive speaking ability and respect for our trustworthiness.

The suffering church does not succumb to this error. And this allows it to experience a true fullness of power. It knows the worth of God's Word and the splendor of Jesus, the Lord who was raised from the dead and is coming again.

Among Christians in the Soviet Union and other Eastern European countries who live with oppression, there is only the faintest interest in most of the discussions of western theology. To many Christians in those areas it is totally inconceivable how one can discuss such things as the divine sonship of Jesus or the binding power of the Word of God. This is what one of them said who had spent sixteen years of his life in a prison camp under harsh torture:

"Such discussion strikes me as a discussion of whether the sun shines in the heavens. We by contrast live in the power of the Word of God alone. My courage, my bodily strength, and my optimism had long since passed away when the sure pledge of Jesus raised me up. Nothing has carried me in these difficult years but this Word alone."

It is not the suffering and afflicted Christians who bear the Word and preserve its validity. Just the opposite, the Word sustains them. Because they have experienced it in difficult times of suffering, this is their testimony:

> "Your Word is the strength of my heart
> and the true defense of the Church's part."

Letters From Prison

(Believers Are Happier)

"Peace to you, my dear mother!

"I have received your letter; heartfelt thanks for it. It gave me great joy. Our thoughts are very much one. This should make our minds easy so that we can face the future with assurance.

"I am especially happy that you are still young in spite of your gray hairs. This tells me that your thoughts are turned to that which is real, to Jesus, and not to sin.

"You carry no bitterness for past years, and even now you can courageously say 'yes!' to the imprisonment of your son.

"My dear mother, how much happier are we believers than the men of this world. We do not despair, 'though our outer nature is wasting away,' for 'our inner nature is being renewed every day'

(2 Cor. 4:16). The people of this world are unhappy because life passes by so rapidly. In old age they must say as Solomon did: 'I have found no satisfaction in my years.' They also tremble before the future.

"I am very happy that you want to lead a holy life in all things. The hymn which believers sing also calls us to this: 'Let the world take our money and whatever else we have, but we will keep a pure conscience. . . .'

"Unfortunately we can now no longer exchange letters with each other concerning our faith. But the time is coming when we will share the joy of faith not only in letters but in great assemblies.

"And our joy will be even more complete when we are in eternity where there will be no more parting (Rev. 22:20). . . ."

(Jesus Stands by His Witnesses)

"I greet you my dear children, and you, my dear wife!

"Accept my hearty greetings in the name of the Lord Jesus!

"May the Lord Jesus bless you, comfort you, and give you the necessary strength and patience for each day of your life.

"I have received your letter; I am very happy that you are all healthy and alive. Also that God is preserving you and still giving you peaceful days. Be thankful for each one. Redeem the time, for it will not always be that way. . . .

"They took my Bible away and said: 'If you want to read about God, we will put you in the hole for six months. You will be sentenced and shipped to Siberia. You will not be dead, but not exactly alive either. We will let you rot. We will have you spied upon. You will be watched to see who comes to you and with whom you speak.'

"They are very likely gathering material against me for a new trial. Conditions are very bad for me. I do not know what more will happen. . . .

"They are trying to force me to promise in writing that I will not speak about Christ and will keep quiet.

"But in everything I sense Jesus as the intercessor. Be brave always. Pray for me. Christ knows what I must still suffer for Him. I want to stay true to His name and my calling. I do not look back on my life, and I will carry out the task laid upon me with joy. Do not be sad. Lay all your sorrow on the Lord Jesus. He keeps our feet from slipping. He will not leave us alone.

Those who believe on Him will not be confounded!
"God be with you until we see each other again."

Pray That We Will Remain Steadfast

The terrors of a time of martyrdom cannot be described adequately. It is too easy to misplace emphasis when only hatred and bitterness have been awakened.

Many Christians keep silent about their time in prison. That which they suffered was more horrible than can be reproduced by words. Individual bits of information testify to the difficulties of imprisonment. A young preacher, not even 30 years old, was shut up with other prisoners in a windowless room in the middle of winter. There were no beds or chairs in the room. The prisoners saved themselves from freezing to death by lying upon each other in turn. The cement floor was so cold that a person could lie on it only for a short time. Since that time the young preacher has been seriously ill.

A Christian lady acknowledges that she had to remain for days in a room where the rain poured through the roof without letup.

But most of those who have been imprisoned are silent about these sufferings. They want to talk about something else. They want to tell how brightly the Gospel of Jesus Christ began to shine in the darkness. They want to tell of their depression which they could overcome by the Word of God. The following excerpts from letters show precisely these things. The senders live in the USSR. Relatives or they themselves were imprisoned because of their unbending obedience to their Lord Jesus Christ and to their conscience. Some of them had already been sentenced, others were still awaiting their trials.

It is unfortunate that of the letters mailed in the USSR only few arrive in the West.

No More Than We Can Bear

". . . I have already been permitted to visit my dear husband three times with the children. He is still healthy and joyful in the Lord. On the 10th of May it will be a year that he has been away from us [in prison]. We can as yet still hold worship services. . . . Now I would like further to report that Sister A. (with her children, whose husband is in prison) received the package with the articles of clothing. We admired it together and were thankful. Proverbs 19:17 . . . M."

". . . Until now we had not known anything about the location of our dear Vanya's place of imprisonment. He has in the meantime been transferred here, but we still do not know what they propose to do with him. Our dear Lord will not lay on us more than we can bear. May He give us strength to trust Him in everything In Psalm 34:16-23 we read comforting words . . . A."

". . . It is often totally incomprehensible how He leads in His wisdom. We have this one great joy, that we may still gather on Sunday and hear His dear Word together. We beseech Him always that He will hold His preserving grace over us so that this situation may continue for a long time . . . K."

". . . The precious words of your letter are profitable for strengthening our faith with thanks and for encouragement. We are poorly equipped with spiritual literature. We had copied many things for ourselves but everything was taken away when my husband was imprisoned. Nevertheless, the Good Shepherd is tireless in His love and takes care to preserve the living bread for the inward man. Your letters are a great help in this . . . M. V."

". . . It is a difficult time, pray for us that we will remain steadfast amidst the storms which raise themselves as high as the Lord allows. For He will also give strength to bear it. Three of our brothers have been put behind lock and key, and rumors have it that our oldest children are to be taken away from us! Yet we want to persist in prayer. He will not allow it if it is not His will. Pray for our persecuted brotherhood. . . . We thank you once again for all that you have done for us . . . J."

Joy in the Bible

"I am writing to say that I have received the package, and it is invaluable beyond all price. I do not know how I could ever thank you for your efforts and for your concern. I thank my personal Savior that He, the Almighty, has fulfilled the desire of my heart. . . . Oh, Book of God, who is not indebted to you? What heart have you not instructed? Did you not kindle the heart of a Moses and of a Joshua and lead them in the way that they should go? Was it not you? Christ read you, John loved you, with you Stephen went joyfully to his death and Peter did not shrink before the cross. Oh, Bible! You have overcome much! You have outlived all laws. . . . The times have changed, millions have passed on but you have remained the same, just as young, unforgettable, and wise. Even if intellectuals do not love you and the proud scorn you, you have been the foundation of life, you book of books, the fountain of salvation and consolation, and you will be so through eternity, book of the utterances of God. With greetings to M. K. (from Siberia)."

No One Understands Me

" 'Rejoice in the Lord always!' (Phil. 4:4).

"Dear brothers in the Lord! Since the opportunity has only just arisen to address a few lines to you, I would like to do that right now. May the Lord give me the right words in this effort. I wish you at first His blessing in soul and body. I would much rather talk with you personally, yet I am content that under the given circumstances I can do it by letter. I am happy to be able to say that, thanks to the Lord, I am healthy and enjoy deep happiness in my beloved Lord due to the prayers of so many saints who remember at the throne of grace my loved ones in their solitude. We can stand firm only when we give ourselves completely to His will and put no trust in ourselves, only when we thank Him for the grace which has come to us and made us worthy to suffer for the sake of our testimony. We want to be prepared as an instrument which He can use in His service. It is so important to me that the peace of God which passes all understanding fills me always and remains like a rock, anchored sure and immovable in my heart. The waves at the surface of the water are what we see, yet deep below is the foundation, Jesus Christ, whom neither storms nor the hardship of this world can touch. The longing to be with Him is often overwhelming. May all things nevertheless redound to His glory. . . .

"I want to close now with this request, that you answer me soon with a few words. That will please me greatly (1 Cor. 1:18). I am so alone, no one understands me. Pray more for me. I know of the large group who remembers my loved ones before the throne of grace in prayer. That is a great comfort to me, for prayers do not go unheard. May the true Lord bless and increase you and give us all the power to fulfill the task which He has given to us. With hearty greetings I remain your brother in the Lord who loves you in his heart." (A letter from a Christian who has five children and who is imprisoned.)

Ten Children Without a Father

"A greeting from far away with Psalm 73:23-27. Dear brothers and sisters, I ask pardon for our long period of not writing. We have waited in order to see how it would turn out with our dear brother. Everything is set now; he has received three years of special vacation [by which is meant labor camp]. Dark clouds threatening rain are now again in the sky. But how glorious that over the clouds the loving eye of our Father watches to see that no more is laid on His child than he can bear. When our brother was led out of court the other brothers and sisters threw flowers. He shouted encouragement to them and they sang a song in the language of that region: 'We fight for the Gospel!' When they had sung two verses of the song he was gone. On his second day in court his tenth child was born. We must pray much for our dear sister; she has obedient and well-bred children."

They Bear Their Burdens Together

"Sergei is currently locked up in a remote prison. He has six children at home, the youngest only a few months old. He was put in prison a few months ago because after he had come to faith in Jesus Christ a year ago, he opened his house to those who had previously held their worship services in the woods. He said these things, among others, in his farewell speech to the Christians gathered in his house: 'How sad I would have been if I had landed in prison a year ago. I would certainly have been there for a crime and with a bad conscience for my drunkenness. But now, as I go for the sake of Jesus' name, my heart is full of joy and thankfulness that He has deemed me worthy to take this path. He has deemed me worthy to leave my family and my home and to suffer for Him and His church.'

"Sergei is now no longer at home, but his wife carries on where he left off. Hundreds of believers go each week to Sergei's house, which lies somewhat off the beaten path. There they sing to the glory of God and praise Him for the blood of the Lamb. God is working in Sergei's home and also in other homes from the Caspian Sea all the way to Murmansk, from the Alps to the boundless tundra of Siberia. Unbelievers come out of curiosity, but God is at work where His pure Word is proclaimed. He is working: 'When one brother is locked up, two come to faith!' the believers say and go on their way.

"The situation is difficult for families who have lost their fathers. But when a congregation understands the words about 'suffering with a member of Jesus body,' it is easier. Not only Sergei's wife and children bear the loss but the whole congregation. Many of those who come to Sergei's house go into the kitchen with a bundle and leave it there. On certain evenings a few girls do the wash and gather wood for the oven, on other evenings the men help. They see to it that Sergei's wife does not feel abandoned in her need.

"Because the congregation is concerned for the suffering ones, it travels a path of great sacrifice. But by this, the harvest field of the Lord is given an extensive demonstration and new ways are found to implement the Lord's command, that command with fatal consequences for a believer's material things: 'Go into all the world and preach the Gospel to every creature.' But this command is very dear to them. If they were quiet and served their Lord only in their small, restricted neighborhoods, the difficulties would be relatively slight. But as soon as the congregation begins to carry out its task to evangelize the world, true difficulties begin.

"The congregation in Sergei's house has been able, in spite of all difficulties, to obey God more than men. It has its two 'missionaries' whose families are supported since neither may return home without being arrested immediately. The missionaries receive no wages and go from village to village into homes where they are accepted. Where they are not accepted they pass on, but where they are received they stay overnight and preach God's Word.

"They praise God that He considers them worthy to suffer for His sake. Of course they bring as well their complaints and tears to God, but also their thanksgiving. That is the secret of their strength and courage. The Bible says that the joy of the Lord is the strength of His children." (From a letter by Christians in the USSR.)

6

CONVERSION TO SUFFFERING

THE 22ND OF MAY, 1719, was a special day in the life of Nikolaus Ludwig Count von Zinzendorf. The young count stood before a picture of the thorn-crowned Jesus by Domenico Feti in the Düsseldorf art gallery. He was on a cavalry ride to Paris, and it is often said that Zinzendorf was converted on that day in front of that picture. The title of the picture spoke to him: "I have done this for you; what have you done for me?"

But what was Zinzendorf really converted to that day?

We know that he had loved Jesus passionately from his early childhood.

Zinzendorf wrote in his diary while still under the impression of that picture and its title: "My blood rushed to my face in embarrassment since I would hardly be able to respond to the question, and I asked my Savior to take me by force into the communion of His suffering even if my intellect was not prepared for it."

This event was a crucial turning point in Zinzendorf's life. Let us understand it clearly: a young man of the highest rank of the nobility, of extraordinary intelligence, a man who could move in all classes of society with conspicuous distinction, desires to be drawn to suffering — by force if necessary. He desires fellowship in Jesus' passion.

The prayer was fulfilled. Zinzendorf was preserved in the communion of passion with Jesus for his whole life. It is well to come to grips with the count's life and wide influence in terms of the harsh suffering which he was forced to undergo. Through personal humiliation, expulsion from his homeland, and under the scorn of theologians and nobility, his testimony achieved a great fullness of power.

Part of following Jesus is, as a matter of fact, being prepared to suffer

Since therefore Christ suffered in the flesh, arm yourselves with the same thought!" (1 Peter 4:1).

Watchman Nee, certainly the most well-known leader of the church of Jesus in China, made the following remarks in an address shortly before his difficult period of suffering in Communist prisons: "Have we yet recognized that being prepared for suffering is part of the armor of a Christian? Being prepared for suffering means that we can repel the devil when he tries to attack us at a vulnerable point. If we lack this part of our armor, we are not fit for the battle of faith."

And in another place he developed this thought further: "There is a limit to our suffering. But there can be no limit to how much we are prepared to suffer, or Satan will sooner or later destroy our ministry."

The Moscow Professor of literature, Levitin-Krassnov, a passionate warrior for a bold confession of faith, who for that very reason has been sentenced several times to long prison terms, wrote in 1968 in a piece published by the underground with the title, "The Cry of the Eagle": "Cowardice — it is the mother of all vice! Cowardice and nothing else. Cowardice is the leprosy which is devouring my homeland. Cowardice is precisely that disease with which the [Russian Orthodox] Church of my homeland is doubly and triply sick."

Cowardice, moreover, is nothing but a flight from suffering.

The preparation for suffering required of a follower of Jesus includes the whole life. "Whoever loses his life for my sake will find it," said Jesus (Matt. 16:25). And in the Revelation of John it was said of believers who had come out of a difficult period of suffering and had overcome all distress: "They loved not their lives even unto death" (Rev. 12:11). Total, undivided surrender is required of a man. Jesus cannot be served half-way. Martyrdom tests people to see if they are ready for His service. And thus even the congregation at Smyrna, in the midst of difficult persecution, was not pitied but called to true obedience: "Be faithful unto death, and I will give you the crown of life!" (Rev. 2:10).

Traugott Hahn, the Baltic martyr, said this shortly before his arrest, in his sermon for the Third Sunday of Advent, 1918:

"My death lies entirely in my Lord's hands. He will order the time and means of my death. I will die — certainly not when chance or blind fate strike me down or when evil men desire it — but at that time when my Lord wills it, not a moment sooner or later, and in the very place where He will require me to die, and in such a manner as He will find it necessary. He will even ordain all the circumstances of my

death as He did once for the death of His Son on Calvary. . . . May
the unflinching mind of the martyr spring to life in us again, not that
we clamor to take the path of martyrdom but that we go to it bravely
when it comes."

Martyrdom is thus the touchstone of our imitation of Christ. In this
regard Watchman Nee once asked a group of Christians: "Is the
preservation of our lives important, or is it the work of the Lord which
must be preserved and advanced? Is it a question of saving men from
darkness or preserving our own lives? What is more important: to
maintain our personal interests or the mighty witness of Jesus Christ
on this earth?"

The so-called crisis in missions of our day shows that there is scant
readiness to suffer among the members of the free, unmolested
churches. But it is not really a crisis of missions. Jesus' mission can
never cease. If we are silent, God will raise children from the stones.
The crisis today is in the missionaries, the witnesses.

If today an adverse wind blows in our face while we are serving the
Gospel by visiting homes, in youth work, or by missions among the
people, we are quick to retreat or prepared even to abandon our ministry. We say in such cases that resistance is characteristic of the
present day. As if that were only true today! We forget that hatred
of the Gospel was much stronger in Jesus' time. When Jesus was on
earth, frenzied cries demanded His death. That was the echo He heard
to the friendly call of the Gospel.

In spite of this Jesus never held back from preaching that Word of
the Gospel, even though it was received as an offense and an irritant.

Atheists are not dangerous. The enemies of the Gospel cannot hinder
the mission of Jesus. The crisis lies with the missionaries, with us
Christians who should serve Jesus with our lives. We lack the zeal.
We lack the submission. But above all we lack the willingness to
endure resistance and rejection.

The crisis lies in the fact that we are afraid. Yet it is often not even
fear of physical suffering! We do not have to confront dangers of that
nature. Often enough the simple fear of enmity and scorn destroys in
us the courage necessary for the public proclamation of the Gospel.

It is, however, a severe blow to the body of Jesus when Christians are
no longer ready to sacrifice their entire lives. The small adversities are
bound to reveal how much we will gladly bear.

Corrie ten Boom expressed it like this a short while ago: "I have
become conscious of the fact that powerless Christians — that is

Christians without faith — disturb God more than powerful atheists."

The New Testament also demands readiness to suffer. "Beloved, do not be surprised at the fiery ordeal which comes upon you to prove you, as though something strange were happening to you. But rejoice in so far as you share Christ's sufferings, that you may also rejoice and be glad when his glory is revealed" (1 Peter 4:12, 13). "Indeed all who desire to live a godly life in Christ Jesus will be persecuted" (2 Tim. 3:12).

During Passion Week the church of Jesus hears year by year the story of the Lord's suffering. It is hard to understand, consequently, how seldom the most natural results appear as expressed by this prayer:

> "Take us now that we with Thee
> May reign and suffer equally."

A Christianity which is not accustomed to suffering will also be a Christianity unaccustomed to the full riches of life with Jesus.

A Church Leader Sought By Wanted Posters

Far in the north of the Soviet Union in the land of the Komi, the city Sosnogorsk lies on the rail line to Vorkuta. On the large bulletin board containing official announcements the picture of Gennadi K. Kryuchkov hangs among the wanted posters of criminals. This electronics technician has been chairman of the independent Council of Churches of Evangelical Christians and Baptists since 1962.

As related by members of this wanted man's home congregation in an open letter to U. N. General Secretary U Thant on 22 August 1971, the following text could be read under his picture: "Gennadi Konstantinovich Kryuchkov, born 1918 in Volgograd, previously convicted. Sought by the government's Criminal Department for Domestic Affairs with the Executive Committee of the Tula region for leading illegal groups of evangelical-baptist believers as well as for the distribution of slanderous writings."

The letter to U Thant related still other particulars of the persecution of this church leader. For instance, the chairman of the Tula police informed Mrs. Kryuchkov that orders to shoot had been issued in case her husband should seek to flee when arrested.

This minister, who is now 44 years old, is the father of nine children. When Kryuchkov was just a four-year-old child, his father was sentenced to three years in a prison camp. Before Kryuchkov's later career as an electronics technician he had served six years in the army. In

1951 he was baptized, was married, and joined the All-Russian Confederation of ECBs.

The persecution of this minister has been going on since 1961. He had developed a plan at that time during a church gathering to fill evangelical churches with new and energetic life. To that end, an Action Group was formed which spontaneously delegated to Kryuchkov, then 34 years old, the responsibility for negotiating in their name with the Moscow All-Union Council of ECBs about the church problems arising from governmental regulations. This activity led to the establishment of the independent Council of Churches. From that time Kryuchkov could no longer live with his family since his house was under constant surveillance by the secret police. The newly-established Council of Churches of ECBs was not recognized by the authorities, but rather, received frequent punishment. All petitions to the government to register gatherings for worship and thereby to sanction them went unanswered.

Spontaneous delegations of these unregistered congregations traveled repeatedly to Moscow. They did not want to be a secret underground church. This is how it happened that 500 representatives, elected from the unregistered evangelical congregations, gathered on 16 May 1966 in Moscow, on the Old Square, in order to explain their request to the Central Committee of the Communist Party. Delegates from more than 130 cities of the Soviet Union demanded to speak with the General Secretary of the party, L. I. Brezhnev; this request was denied. But the delegates refused to be rebuffed. They stayed the whole night through in the Old Square. They wanted, after all their effort, to personally hand Brezhnev their request to free the imprisoned and to recognize the Council of Churches of ECBs. For Kryuchkov this did not mean, however, a capitulation of the church to the state. He was ready, to be sure, to lay open the entire life of the church to state inspection, but as early as 1963 he had formalized clearly the balancing aspect of his position in a letter: "The church must keep itself free from admixture with the world and from mixing worldly power into its internal life."

During the day on May 17, the demonstration on the Old Square was dispersed by mass arrests. Kryuchkov also was arrested, brought to trial on 29, 30 November 1966, and sentenced to three years in a prison camp.

During this trial the church leader pointed out that as Christians they did not desire to protest against their persecutors. The most im portant goal of their activity was to order the church's life in such a way that it could live according to the Word of God. Kryuchkov expanded on this point after he had specifically illustrated the vexations caused by the persecutions among evangelical Christians:

"We believers have endured these persecutions from the outside although they are not justified by the law and are against the constitution. We have not complained about this and will never complain. We accept persecutions which come to us from the outside as something that is laid upon us. . . . It is not our task to instruct the government how it should act toward us. But as servants of the church we bear responsibility for the conditions of the church in its inner life. . . .

"When our spiritual leadership could not support the initiative for calling a conference, we established the organizing committee for the Council of Churches of ECBs and began to carry out business on our own. The organizing committee took pains to ask the government for the permission demanded by law to hold a conference. . . ."

Kryuchkov did not attempt to use this defense as a means to escape from suffering. He was ready to suffer with Christ. But he wanted to make the reason for his suffering publicly visible since the "illegality" of his actions was constantly thrust upon him. Thus in the concluding words of his very strenuous trial, which lasted two days and which finally ended at 1 A.M., Kryuchkov said this:

"I am gathering my last strength together.

"To beat up 400 men in front of the Central Committee building of the Communist Party of the Soviet Union — multiply 400 delegates by the 400 congregations which sent them! — to beat up 400 delegates, that is the same as spitting on the most intimate lives of the thousands of believers who sent them. These brothers who are now in prisons and camps do not suffer because they have violated Soviet laws. No, they suffer because they have preserved their faithfulness to the Lord and to His church. They suffer for Christ who has called them to a new life. . . . I am glad to stand before you as a Christian. I am joyful that the court could discover no crimes in us. And if you now act in accordance with the law, we will be freed instantly. If, however, you act in fulfillment of the prophecy of Jesus which is summarized in the Word, "you will be persecuted," we will be sentenced. We proclaim that one must deny himself and that one must fear neither scorn nor mockery. This is not just a question of bearing scorn. We are cast into prison and we are now forced to behave in such a way that our

words and our works agree with each other. This trial has amazed me.
Yet I am joyful now to become a companion of those who already
have been put in prison."

In the letter to General Secretary U Thant which seventy members
of the Baptist congregation of Uzlovaya sent in the fall of 1971, it was
reported that the secret police had tried to blackmail this minister
during his three-year term in the prison camp. In exchange for coopera-
tion with the KGB he was promised complete freedom and a secure
life for his entire family. Before his release they tried again to charge
him with criminal offenses. There was a particularly dangerous incident
where he was given a New Testament. Shortly after Kryuchkov had
received it, he was searched thoroughly. The New Testament was
found, but Kryuchkov had before this already discovered that the New
Testament also contained a schematic description of a secret atomic
reactor which he, however, had immediately destroyed. It would have
been a simple matter to exile this educated electronics technician for
a long time on the basis of this contrived crime of espionage. It was
in this way that the attempt by the secret police to incriminate him
with false evidence of criminal behavior, even before his release, mis-
carried.

Only a seventeen-day hunger strike could release him from other
charges. Kryuchkov thanks his wife and other Christians that he is still
alive today, for it was their telegrams to the government which finally
brought about his release after he had served his sentence. On 20 May
1969 Kryuchkov returned from Siberia to his home town of Uzlovaya.

After his release he paid a 50-ruble fine for his first sermon. The
authorities were eager to continue the inhuman course of their persecution.

But Kryuchkov went to the authorities. He did not need to fear the
light. He wanted without fail to reach a normalization of relations
between state and church. And he even succeeded in receiving from
the city authorities of Tula permission for a conference of the Council
of Churches of ECBs. This conference took place in December, 1969.

At the conference the members of the Council of Churches, who
after the demonstration on the Old Square in Moscow had almost all
been arrested, were re-elected. Kryuchkov remained the chairman.

Although the conference was carried out with total openness — the
results of the deliberations and an address list of the participants were
sent to the government — the persecution continued. The home of
N. I. Vladykin (14 Krasnodonchev Street, Tula), in which the con

ference had been held, was confiscated by the court on 2 September 1970. As late as the fall of 1971 Vladykin's family had found no new dwelling. The court cited the Bible and prayer meetings for which no official sanction had been produced as its reason for the confiscation, but how could these meetings have been anything but unregistered after so many attempts to gain registration had been in vain?

When the Christians from Uzlovaya wrote to U Thant, Kryuchkov's arrest had been threatened for some time. For this reason he already had been staying at a secret location for several months. The police began to look for him all over the country and photographs were distributed. Kryuchkov's family was forced to let their house be thoroughly and repeatedly searched.

But the primary tone of the letter of the seventy ECBs from Uzlovaya is not one of complaining grief. In an overview of the convulsive events of persecution they write:

"We do not despair and do not even see our situation as hopeless. Suffering is a customary and normal thing for Christ and the church, for Christ Himself said: 'They have persecuted Me and they will also persecute you!' "

The Greater the Difficulties, the Firmer the Faith

A letter from the Soviet Union states:

"Thanks be to the Lord that His work goes forward in spite of the resistance and even persecution which exists in many places. The greater the difficulties, the firmer the faith and more ardent the love for the Lord, for our brothers and sisters, and also for lost men. I am happy that I do not live in a land where everything is at hand in abundance, where men are interested only in hoarding money and have no desire but to accumulate more of it, where money has become their god. There are, unfortunately, enough of such men even among us. Yet there are also men who truly believe, who faithfully follow the Lord, and who are ready to leave all for His sake if it must be that way. When I was in A. in 1968, I met a brother who had been married for 37 years, during which time, however, he had been able to live with his wife for only 13 years. When he was released from prison for the second time, his wife was sentenced to 10 years of prison and exile. But no one could take the joy from his heart. That beamed from his eyes as he gave testimony of his Savior with his head held high. More than anywhere else I found brothers and sisters in that place who were overflowing with the love of the Lord. They were like gold purified in the fire.

"May the Lord also let fruit be seen there. Today I received a letter which said: 'Brother I. relates that a few days ago as he was with some Russian youths in the evening, the Holy Spirit began to convict some of them of their lost condition and many repented in prayers. It was for all of us a great boost to our faith.'"

In Harsh Affliction

"To all believers in the church of the ECBs who live in the USSR.

URGENT NEWS

"'Let not your hearts be troubled; believe in God, believe also in me" (John 14:1).

"'He gives power to the faint, and to him who has no might he increases strength' (Isa. 40:29).

"Beloved of the Lord, brothers and sisters, greetings in peace!

"In spite of our second petition for registration and our effort to give 'to Caesar what is Caesar's,' the greatest persecution of believers of the Council of Churches of ECBs is going on at this moment.

"(1) In many cities the prayer houses are being broken up by the militia, the believers are being kicked out and beaten. The leaders who live according to the Bible and have stepped out courageously are arrested without delay.

"(2) In these last two months, four leading brothers have been arrested and now the fifth has also been added. Among those believers seized in Gorky were Brother Runov and his 22-year-old son. Meeting houses are being confiscated, the doors are sealed, and the congregational leaders are threatened with arrest.

"(3) The Council of Churches is punished with special severity. It was suggested to Brother Kryuchkov that he leave his church work and undertake labor for the state; after that the militia came to him.

"A second accusation has been brought against G. P. Vins in spite of his forced labor of January, 1970.

"Because of the great strength of the persecution, brothers G. K. Kryuchkov, G. P. Vins, C. G. Dubovoi, and P. A. Yakimenkov must leave their homes in order to be able to carry on their work further in the churches. The militia is now harassing their families.

"We are certain that it is the Lord's will, and are thus comforted and accept everything.

"We live in the firm hope that His promise never to leave us will shortly be fulfilled. We trust His words: 'I will come again and will take you to myself, that where I am you may also be.'

"Take the necessary strength from this Word: 'He gives power to the faint, and to him who has no might he increases strength.'

"Pray! Be brave!

"The Council of Relatives of Imprisoned Evangelical Christians and Baptists. 1 October 1970."

The Freedom of Faith Cannot Be Killed

The following poem is by Georgi P. Vins and dates from 29, 30 November 1966, in Moscow, as he was sentenced to three years in a prison camp:

"We stand before you;
we are not guilty
of robbery or murder.
As once before in Pilate's court,
Christ our Savior
is judged here today.
Why are You before the bar today,
Holy Prophet of Nazareth?
Could it be for this, that You are the well-spring of light,
the fountain of love and purity?
Because You give freedom to slaves,
to the children of passions and sin?
Because the sacrifice of Your love
brought salvation to the people?
Once again the children of men
scoff and mock here,
once again slander and lies
rule here! —
But He, He is silent —
and looks with compassion
at the poor sinners.
He knows how weak so many threats are,
He sees the fearful trembling of those people
who have gathered rivulets of tears in their hands,

tears of children, wives, and mothers!
History's evil deeds are forgotten,
and with passion men desire executions.
But no one can execute
the freedom of faith and of conscience —
or isolate Christ
behind barbed wire and bars.
The works of salvation
will live in the hearts of the redeemed.
The silent guards surround His friends
like a ring of steel.
But He is here Himself
and fills them with His Spirit
that they may stand composed before the judge.
We have not called
for rebellion,
we have preached
salvation and deliverance!
We have proclaimed
the beauty of holy desire!
We call the church of God
to take the thorn-filled path,
to wage war now
against cunning and lies
in the name of that Kingdom
which is not of this world.
We stand before you,
or rather, 'have been brought before you' says it better,
for this reason alone: for you to learn
that God the Lord has children still.
All your courts and renewed persecutions
will only confirm belief in God
and proclaim to children and children's children
God's truth anew."

7

THE SERENITY OF FAITH IN THE FACE OF PERSECUTION

On 25-31 March 1969 a trial was held in Odessa for ten evangelical Christians. As early as 1967, five men and two women from Odessa had been sentenced to multiple-year prison terms. The transcript of the later trial, assembled by friends of the accused, was released by the Mission Fellowship *Light in the East* in Korntal. The extraordinarily harsh sentences imposed at the Odessa trial of 1969 set it apart from previous trials. The groups of Soviet Evangelical Christians and Baptists (ECBs) received the news of the "exorbitantly harsh and cruel sentences" with shock. It was pointed out that "such stiff punishments had been meted out only in trials of czarist Russia and those at the time of the personality cult [Stalinism]." Sentences of five years in prison followed by banishment for five years were given at the Odessa trial of 1969 to these men: E. K. Rodoslavov, 19; A. N. Chevchenko, 27; and P. A. Kupriyanov, 41. Sixty-nine year old O. A. Ponomarchuk was sentenced to five years in a prison camp followed by four years in exile, Ostapenko and Dubovoi to four years in a camp and three years in exile. G. Kovtun and N. Krutiko received two years in a prison camp, M. G. Onishchenko, 78 years old, a one-year sentence.

The trial took place in an atmosphere of enmity and hatred inside the "House of Atheism." Christians were prevented by police and state security personnel from entering the court room. Witnesses from the evangelical congregation were abused and violently molested by malicious hoodlums in front of the court house. Girls were struck and clothes were ripped up. The police who were posted in front of the court house did not interfere but rather urged the young people on in harassing believers.

One hundred and eighty young Christians described these incidents in a letter to the government dated 13 May 1969. This is what they wrote concerning the false, incredible charges, none of which could be verified factually:

"The efforts of atheism are in vain. The Church of Christ is invulnerable. When the faith is persecuted for Christ's sake, the church has never weakened, but rather grown in strength. We young people decked with flowers the car in which our brothers rode to the trial. The awful sentence will not destroy our love for our sentenced brothers. The sympathy which many reasonable people have as an inner respect for all that is noble, honorable, good, and credible will also not pass away.

"We are continuously urged to renounce God at our places of work and study. But our experiences in the events we have described convince us all the more of the complete truth and absolute reliability of the Gospel, where it is written: 'They have persecuted me and they will also persecute you. . . . For my name's sake they will hate you.'

As Christians, we young people have no right to meet together. It is impossible for us to go through the streets freely since crowds of hoodlums attack us. Time and again our people are brutally knocked down and ill-treated.

"We can get no education beyond secondary school since we are excluded from college and institutions of higher learning. Besides all this, the press spreads every kind of slander about us. This leads us even more firmly to the conviction that we have no place on the earth. As Christ had no place in the world, it is the same for His sincere followers.

"The legal proceedings against our brothers in the faith will not shake our belief but strengthen us all the more in our conviction to be true to God to the end, even in death. We know that you are not capable of indoctrinating believers. We are prepared, however, to take upon ourselves all the scorn which the world can give.

"If, then, the terrible hand of violence and injustice grips any one of us and we are separated from each other for many years, as we have been separated from our friends, we will even then remain steadfast in confidence to our Lord. We know that He will help us to be as faithful to the end as Stephen and Peter. Indeed, to the end, as our contemporaries have experienced: Khmara of Kulunda, Kucherenko from Nikolayev, Lanbin from Novosibirsk, and Shevchenko. Yes, to the end, as at this very moment our dying brother Minyakova from Barnaul and others are facing death in the camps.

"As long as we live on the earth we will be true to this faith, for which it is well worthwhile to suffer, to struggle, and even to die.

"Penal laws can take away outward things. It is not possible, however, to destroy a person's belief in God by a penal sentence or to remove the sense of moral honor and ethical value. It is not possible for a penal sentence to change a person's moral character or to rob him of everything which belongs to the inalienable aspect of life.

"We are thankful that our brothers have dedicated their lives to building the church. And we, as young people, follow their faith and go their same way. If, however, loyalty and faithfulness is a crime, then all of us are criminals.

"During the trial we ourselves were subjected to outrage for five days: insults, cannonades of coarse jests, and hard reproaches; stones were thrown at us, we were spat upon and brutally attacked.

"After all this was over, we gathered together, praised and thanked the Lord for all that we had come through. At the same time we resolved to remind you of your responsibility for that which has occurred, of your responsibility before the law and before God. Thus, we desire to appeal to your conscience once again afresh with this account. In connection with what we have described above, we ask you:

(1) To acknowledge the innocence of our friends and return from the camps . . . [ten names follow] and all other believers in the USSR who have been sentenced for their faith.

(2) To guarantee believers a normal life and to stop inciting the public against us.

(3) To bring about true freedom of belief and confessions.

(4) To allow believing young people the full benefits of education.

"Signed by 180 young people. 13 May 1969."

Pray for the Persecutors

" 'Do not throw away your confidence, which has a great reward. For you have need of endurance, so that you may do the will of God and receive what is promised' (Heb. 10:35, 36).

" 'Let not your hearts be troubled; believe in God, believe also in me' (John 14:1).

A REQUEST

"To all prisoners, sentenced for the Word of God and their testimony for Jesus;

"To all relatives of the prisoners;

"To all children, fathers, and mothers of those who suffer in prison for the Word of God;

"To all released prisoners who are again threatened by arrest and suffering;

"To all believing brothers and sisters who love the appearing of the Lord.

Peace to you!

"Peace that passes human understanding, peace amid sorrows, joys, and persecutions.

"Praise the Lord for everything, for He was a refuge to the poor, and strength to the lowly in difficult times, a refuge from storms, and shade from the heat.

"After more than sixty brothers and sisters have returned from prison, we turn today to you. We thank God for their release and call upon you to thank God also. How much joy there has been, how many tears of joy and sighs of relief by children who had been robbed of their parents as they greet their dear fathers and mothers after the long separation! Fathers and mothers shed tears of joy when they embrace their children. Prisoners and prison camps leave indelible marks on their faces. Most of them have had their health undermined markedly.

Photo right above: Five hundred members of the independent Baptist Church of Brest gathered on 27 August 1967, in a clearing near Ploski for a worship service. All of their assemblies have been forbidden for years. The occasion of this worship service was the centennial celebration of the congregations of the Evangelical Christians and Baptists in the Soviet Union.

Photo right below: August, 1967: a public baptism in the Bug River, organized by the Baptist congregation of Brest which was dissolved by the state in 1960.

But their hearts glow with love and joy. They burn in the love that God uses to awaken the church.

"In the last few days other brothers and sisters have taken their places in suffering. . . .

"Many churches are in these days bereft of members who have been sent to prison or the camps for their acts of devotion.

"God's harvest field is ready. The people have a hunger for salvation. When we suffer, we do not want to complain but raise our eyes to the things invisible and eternal.

"The harvest field is golden, the harvest is ripe. We hear the call to be diligent. . . . When night begins, all work must cease.

"Our prisoners go to court and to suffering with firm faith. Sergei Terentyevich Golev, a member of the Church Council, was sentenced on 10 September 1969 to three years in prison with strict regulations. This is now his twentieth year in prison which he greeted with the words: 'Even if I must die, I will be faithful to the truth.'

"We should pray for them. We have sent a report once again to the government concerning all recent arrests and the suffering of believers among the ECBs.

"We call on all who are persecuted for the sake of their faith in God and to all who are related to them: 'Trust in God!'

" 'And Jonathan, Saul's son, rose, and went to David at Horesh, and strengthened his hand [trust] in God' (1 Sam. 23:16).

"Wherever your place to praise God, in the forest, in a tiny lowly hut, in a garden, or in a great house, we say to you all: 'Trust in God!' Only firm, deep trust in God will make us steadfast to follow Him.

"The Council of Relatives of the Imprisoned have noticed that through the many persecutions of so many believers of the Christian Church a feeling of rejection can arise toward the persecutors. The Council finds it therefore necessary to remind all believers of these words: 'Love your enemies, and bless those who curse you; do good for those who hate you; pray for those who wrong and persecute you.'

Photo left above: Christians in Brest. In the middle is V. A. Vilchinski (sitting with the two children), to his right is T. K. Feydak, who as leader of the congregation was sentenced to five years in a penal camp on 17 April 1968.

Photo left below: May, 1966: evangelism on the bank of the Don River in Rostov. The leader (in the middle of the picture) and the 29-year-old evangelist, Yosef Bondarenko, who had just finished serving a four-year sentence, were sentenced with other co-workers to multiple-year sentences, some with restricted regulations.

"The Church Council of the Evangelical Christian Church asks the relatives of suffering ones:

(1) To send exact information concerning all those who suffer in persecution for the sake of God's Word.

(2) To forward us news about all children who are separated from their parents because of their religious upbringing. Tell us when the government threatens or attempts to take children away.

(3) To report when brothers and sisters are arrested.

(4) To report on confiscations of religious literature, musical instruments, tape recorders, etc.

(5) To tell us when minor children of believing parents are interrogated by the police or the state's attorney.

(6) To report on the condition of those who are arrested and who are in prisons and camps. Do not lose hope that the great fulfillment is imminent.

"Grace be with you all! Amen! Pray for us! September, 1969."

"Activity Hostile to Society"

In Bessarabia, not far from the Rumanian border, in the district of Bolgrad, lies the village of Novotrayan. Nicolai Ilyich Nikolayev, 41, worked in the collective farm there called, "The Way to Communism." This simple farmer was brought to trial. The case shows with shocking clarity how Christians in the countryside who confess their faith openly are beset. During the trial of 22 May 1969, the following "crimes" were established as having been committed by the accused:

"As one of the leaders of a sect, the accused took an active role in the religious education of children and in so doing transgressed 'the law of separation between church and state, church and school.' At first he taught only his own children. Finally other children also were infected with religious convictions because of his religious preaching in prayer meetings.

"Nikolayev was warned twice by the administrators concerning this lawless activity. He did not heed these warnings and continued instructing the children. In 1968 he set up a music group and instructed the children how to play the guitar and taught them religious songs and poems.

"In the course of a year he finally succeeded in stupefying thirteen children with the sectarian poison. They stopped taking part in the social life of the school and no longer wore scarves and stars. . . .

"To instruct the children in his house the accused used tape recorders on which he had even recorded foreign radio programs.

"The accused claims to be innocent. He does not deny, however, that he held meetings in his house at which his children as well as other children of school or preschool age were allowed to take part at their own wish. . . .

"The guilt of the accused is proved by the tape recording equipment confiscated from him and by the testimony of the child, Konstantinov, who declares that the accused taught her religious poems.

"Bondar, Abdulla, and others declare that the accused carried on activities hostile to society after his reprimand.

"The witnesses Plyakova, Abdulla, Ivanova, and others whom we have heard state that the children came to school peevish, faint, and tired, kept themselves back from other children, and did not take part in the social life of the school. . . .

"Considering the social danger of the accused, considering his person and degree of guilt, in consideration also of the fact that he does not perceive his guilt," the court considered it suitable to sentence the accused to three years and six months in a prison camp followed by time in an improvement colony. The accused is serving his sentence in Bolshoi Tsarin in the Sarpa region. The tape recorder and all accessories were taken away because they were a "means of spreading religion among children."

Greetings to All the Churches of the World

" 'I was in prison and you came to me' (Matt. 25:36).

" 'Have this mind among yourselves [as Jesus Christ also had]' (Phil. 2:5).

"Dear brothers and sisters in the faith of Jesus Christ our Lord!

"We greet you near and far with the words of Christ: 'Peace be with you!' (Luke 24:36).

"Great distances separate us today but the blood of Jesus Christ binds His children in one faith, one hope, and one love.

"The church has from the beginning to this time fought a battle against the powers of darkness and evil, but the church will triumph. Matthew 16:18; Ephesians 6:12.

"The church of Russia is particularly smitten by these enemies, but in 1961 an awakening was sent to it by the Holy Spirit.

"We have gathered together here (fathers, mothers, sons, and daughters of the imprisoned) to thank the Lord for our suffering for Christ. We believe that the Lord is gathering our tears, and He will pour them out on the parched and searching hearts of the Russian people. The Lord is not rejecting us. We ask you, church of the world, not to forget us as long as the Lord tarries.

"We greet the Christians who suffer persecution as we do. 'Be of good cheer, I have overcome the world' (John 16:33).

"Let all of His redeemed children praise the Almighty Lord to the ends of the earth and among all peoples, in every situation of their lives, that every knee may bow before the name of the Lord Jesus.

"With sincere love, the Second Congress of Believers of the Council of Churches of ECBs. 13 December 1970, in Kiev."

The Battle Over the Education of Children

In the Moscow trial of the evangelist Khorev (summer, 1966) the court investigated the various activities of worship in which he had taken part. To do this, the witness Afinagenov of Kiev gave a report which the accused Khorev later corrected substantially. The worship service under consideration took place in the forest near Kiev (Darnitza), since the congregation had not been able to obtain a place for worship for some time.

This is what the accused Khorev, 35 years old, said:

"I would never take advantage of the opportunity to defend myself in order merely to extricate myself. If only this did just concern me! But since the matter with which the church entrusted me is under consideration here, I will speak. . . .

"I cannot be silent about the question of the children. The witness stated that there was an appeal in the text of one of our banners to take action so that children could receive religious instruction at school. I will cite the three texts word for word which were there for the reading:

(1) We proclaim Christ the crucified.

(2) Lord, You know that I love You.

(3) Be an example in word and deed, in love, in spirit, in faith, in purity.

"As you see, there is nothing in these texts which comes close to the charge that was made. I would not like to accuse the witness, but I think that all texts were visible enough to be read correctly.

"The testimony of the witness that a youngster stepped forward at the Kiev meeting with the request that religious instruction should be given in the schools does not accord with the facts. This is what happened: a youth stood up and asked for the floor. He turned to the parents and others present and said that the parents had already sent their children to school for four days in order to gain knowledge. 'We ask you that you pay attention to us in the worship services and pray for all children since our souls are just as immortal as yours.' He asked them to pray that God would help the children to endure all difficulties and to remain true to God. 'I do not speak of my desire alone but for all children,' the young man said. 'Is that right, children?' they were asked. And the children answered in unison, 'Yes, that is right!'

"That which pertains to the question of admitting children into the church has not been an issue for us. In our groups one is brought into the church by water baptism. Repentance, however, often occurs in the meetings. At that very meeting an 18-year-old girl turned to the church and said: 'Pray for me, I want to serve the Lord!' The elder asked whether there were any others who had the desire to give themselves to the Lord. It so happened that there were still a few dozen young people who had this desire. They came to the front and prayer was said for them.

"We will never give up the education of our children. I thank God that there are no laws which forbid believers to train their children. And if indeed there were such, we are ready to sacrifice our freedom and our lives for the sake of the children."

The court sentenced preacher Khorev to two and one-half years at forced labor.

When he was led to the prison car, his friends threw flowers toward him and sent him off with these words: "Stay true to the Lord! Keep preaching! Warm the frozen hearts!"

Parents May Not Instruct Their Children in the Faith

K. Teregulov, President of the People's Court in Sumgait, together with the people's attorneys, V. P. Podzevalova and S. D. Murzalov, sentenced seven Russians and one Ukranian to prison terms of from one to three years on 31 March 1969. In this city on the shore of the Caspian Sea, 25 miles northwest of Baku, the verdict, spoken in the name of the Azerbaijan Republic, was based on this argument:

"The group of sectarians of ECBs which operates illegally arose about 1958 and separated itself from the registered Baptist congregation in Baku for religious reasons. The Baptist group in Sumgait numbers some seventy to eighty people, so-called members of the church, and also includes a portion of the believing Baptists of the Shemakha district as well; the group belongs to the illegal organization of the Council of Churches of ECBs.

"The said group of sectarians has for ten years gathered regularly, in violation of the law, at the individual dwellings of their fellow believers for prayer meetings. At the religious rites carried out in these meetings a great number of citizens have gathered, including young people and minors. The meetings were carried out in persistent disregard of public order and communal regulations. . . .

"Although the Baptist sect had been repeatedly warned by the members of the city's governing council and the police, the group did not cease its activity, but to the contrary stepped up their work. The place of the illegal gatherings changed from meeting to meeting. . . .

"The residents of Sumgait as well as the indictment now prepared testify to the unlawful activity of this group. Thus, for example, on 1 March 1964, in the residence of the Baptist, Michail Grigoryevich Tarusov (Sumgait 1, Mikrorayon, House 25/36, Apartment 1), an illegal gathering was held with some thirty people present. It involved the participation of underaged children.

"On 7 April 1958 (according to the indictment) an illegal meeting was held in the residence of the Baptist, G. I. Popov (Sumgait, Quarter 4, House 6, Apartment 3, settlement Stroiteli), at which seventy believers participated, including forty-six young people under 20 years of age, among whom were included children of 7-15 years. In this meeting Nikolai Timofeievich Gurov preached from the Bible. Kolodin Shubin, who is presently under accusation, was among those present.

"It was established in the trial that the meetings in private homes lasted up to two hours with great general participation. These services were accompanied by loud singing.

"The other residents were roused to anger by these since their peace was disturbed and since these large meetings violated sanitary regulations.

"The indictment for trial further shows that on 12 June 1967, an illegal assembly of Baptists was held in the residence of Nikolai Dimitrivich Taranenko (Sumgait, 65 South Vurgung Street, Apartment 58) where sixty people, mostly youth, were led astray. M. P. Kabanov led the meeting. He read aloud from the Bible and preached.

"After the Sumgait prosecuting attorney had begun criminal proceedings and after several of the accused were warned to discontinue the unlawful meetings, an illegal meeting was held in Sumgait on 7 November 1968, on the holiday memorializing the great Socialist October Revolution at Mikrorayon 4, House 17, Apartment 29, in the residence of Timofei Vasilyevich Losnikov, to which sixty-five people were allured. M. Kabanov led the meeting and also preached. Afterward the children read the Bible by turn.

"During the trial the witness L. V. Bagdatyev declared: '. . . and what is most important, children and youth went to choir practice. It irritated me to see that. My wife is a teacher. She recognized her students among the children. We feel that we are abused since spiritual people force themselves violently into the lives of our children, poison their child-like souls, and in fact rape their spirits. Look here, at that time I wrote a furious report urging that measures be taken concerning the Baptists.'

"The witness stated further: '. . . The accused Khvorov was invited to a meeting of parents of School No. 12 with cooperating representatives of the city where 156 people were present. In connection with the fact that he compelled his daughter, Lyubov Khvorov (who was then 12 years old), to forsake social activity, he told that meeting of parents that he was educating his daughter in the religious spirit, that he would educate her in it, and that no one could stop him from doing it. . . . On the strength of this, the parents appealed to the proper organizations in the city to set aside Khvorov's rights as a parent and to expel him from the city. . . .'

"The accused who are named and other members of the Baptist sect drew their children into the Baptist sect and induced them to forsake social activity in school by forcibly stifling their desire for independent social activity.

"The Baptists standing before the court and those not standing before the court succeeded in exerting psychological pressure on the children at an early age since it was, as a rule, their own children whom they gradually trained day by day in a spirit of servile subjection to the will of their parents. Beyond this, the age of the children plays a role here, as well as the great skill of the Baptist sectarian preachers standing before the court.

"The accused and other Baptists induced their minor children not only to take part in prayer meetings, to learn religious texts, to practice religious rites, and to sing religious songs, but often also to participate in religious instruction and to copy religious literature and placards with proclamatory slogans: 'Trust in God!' and the like. . . ."

8

THEY HAVE SOMETHING TO SAY

NOT ALL SUFFERING IN the body of Jesus is done for Christ's sake, even though we are never in a position to make final judgments of anyone else's actions. In such a matter we most often know too little of the martyrs, for it is the nature of oppression to falsify the truth and isolate those who suffer from their fellow believers. A final decision as to whether a particular act of suffering conforms to Christ or not is often impossible for that very reason. And we do know and should never forget that suffering also arises because of our own sin that God is punishing.

However we are not discussing this problem now, but rather the suffering of the church for Christ's sake.

To take an interest in the affairs of the martyrs is to confirm time after time that they are suffering on account of their testimony. The church in suffering has a Word which it proclaims. And because it cannot release itself from this Word, it is oppressed and trampled.

This is an absolutely essential point. Those who persecute the church know a great deal about how the sincere Word works. For that reason they must not allow it to be heard.

A church which merely discusses religious questions and topics will hardly be affected at all. Why should it be? But the sure Word of proclamation is often enough a cause of deep enmity.

For the Word is the only thing that the church retains in martyrdom. Everything else, all outward beauty and influence, can be stripped from it. It is thus precisely in suffering that its witness is most clearly developed. The enemy's assaults on it are consequently of even greater strength.

The church has, therefore, a Word for which it is worth dying. When it no longer has this Word, it is dead. It is only its witness to the Word of God as the sole and ultimate reality which makes the church unconquerable. And this Word which a believing church possesses is the Word of Jesus, the Son of God and Lord of the world.

To maintain such a position today is shocking, even though we suffer under a flood of religious talk. And now it is the simple Word, testified to by believers, and this alone, which provokes persecution and suffering.

This fact was stated openly in the final summation of charges against three evangelical believers on 23 March 1966, in Lugansk.

The concluding speech of the state prosecutor in the trial of V. A. Golub, N. I. Butkov, and A. N. Balatski, which was ratified by the court magistrate in the city of Lugansk, was as follows:

"Golub, Balatski, and Butkov preach in prayer meetings held two or three times a week. Not only were adult members of the congregation continuously influenced by the preaching, but also children of school age. They were led to believe in God and in a paradisiacal life beyond the grave. They teach that the earthly life is incidental and transitory and that it must be lived according to the teaching of the Bible: 'everything is permitted, but not everything is useful.' True life begins only on the other side of the grave. With the intention of interesting children in attending church, the group's leader [Butkov] taught the children to play musical instruments. They also learn to sing spiritual songs to the accompaniment of these instruments." (Extracted from the letter to the General Secretary of the U.N., U Thant, sent by the Council of Relatives of Imprisoned ECBs on 15 August 1967.)

The question rises instinctively: what should be characteristic of a religion if not faith in God and life on the other side of the grave? An academically trained jurist — even in the Soviet Union — certainly must have known that he was enumerating banalities in saying this. That, in any case, is the impression these statements make on us. But the prosecutor and the judges who sentenced each of the believers to four years in a prison camp for their preaching grasped more than we suspect. They sensed the power which Christian preaching has. The message of these accused believers, which seems so simple to us, must have had a deep effect on them.

It was not the teaching in and of itself that was objectionable. Even in the Soviet Union groups of believers who teach these things are still helped by the state. No, it was not the teaching in and of itself which caused such a stir. The Communist Party was forced to attack in Lugansk because of the *testimony* which believers bore so impressively to that simple and well-known teaching.

With the devaluation of Christian preaching in the West we are unable to grasp how the testimony of simple members of a congregation could have such effective power. But it happened here in Lugansk. And for this reason the three accused believers were dignified by the charge that they, with their preaching in a small Christian gathering, had dealt a telling blow to the communistic doctrine of salvation. For according to this concept of salvation there is only one reality, namely the visibly material. The word of preaching, however, had pierced this one reality. Believers testified to the living God and the immortality of everlasting life, and all at once this was no longer a "myth" but the reality of faith. The word of a simple witness created this effect. The Word alone!

The church finds its understanding of the "Word" with the Lord Jesus Christ Himself. The Revelation of John calls Him the "true witness," or in Greek, the *martus*. Jesus proclaimed the Word which had been given to Him. He could not alter that Word to suit His own tastes. The Word was His, a charge communicated to Him. "My teaching is not mine, but his who sent me," Jesus said (John 7:16). From this knowledge alone rises the unwavering steadfastness of the *martus*, of the true witness of the Gospel. He neither invents or sustains the Word to which he testifies. The witness only passes on what God has revealed to him. Consequently he can never compromise himself to say only that which men like to hear. It is unthinkable for him to silence or weaken his Word merely because the powers resist it. Thus, the authority of an empowering God rests with the Word of the *martus*, the witness. And the witness is prepared to seal this Word even with death if that is required.

It is an idea completely foreign to the suffering church that it twist the Word of proclamation according to the desires of the hearers or somehow adapt the Word to them.

There is only one criterion for the object of witness: it must be true! It must be worth more as the Word of testimony than the life of the one who testifies to it.

When a church proclaims the Gospel like this, the powers of the world will be disturbed. This applies not only to governmental powers, but the church also will expound the truth in the teeth of the fashionable dictates of culture, society, the spirit of the age, and all ideologies. It is only a Word. No more. Yet it is a Word which does not accommodate itself, and so it judges the powers because it testifies to Jesus' Lordship, His irrefutable power.

Christians often are entirely unconscious of how greatly the prevailing movements of the time fear such a firm testimony.

This was evident, for example, when Helmut James Count von Moltke was sentenced in the People's Court of Germany's Third Reich. He himself had predicted the course of his trial: "The decisive sentence of the verdict will be: 'Herr Count, we National Socialists and Christianity have one thing in common and only one thing — we demand the whole man!' The question is if the judge will really know what he is saying." And von Moltke said further: "I do not stand before the court as a Protestant, as a great landlord, as a nobleman, as a Prussian, or as a German, but as a Christian and as nothing else."

A man brings unrest even when his thoughts are heard as a simple Word, but this is a Word which has taken complete control of the one who speaks it. Wherever this is lacking, Christian preaching is empty.

This became clear in the course of the proceedings against Count von Moltke when the president of the People's Court, Freisler, exulted: "The time of cowardice is up. Where do you get your orders? From the next life or from Adolf Hitler? To whom do you offer your trust and belief?"

Freisler's discovery here seems as banal as the prosecutor's speech in Lugansk. Is it really not self-evident that a Christian lets himself be commanded by God?

Therein lies the need of Christian proclamation at all times. Words are cheap, but in spite of the inflation of pious rhetoric, the true witness of faith has not lost its explosive power. Martyrs have found that out, and their lives are a testimony of it to all Christians. It is a Word with which there is no negotiation, no compromise. Testifying and suffering are all, for the convinced Word of testimony can no longer be humored by the world's common standards of tolerance. It leads to judgment and suffering because the powers of the world feel themselves attacked, and rightly so.

But by whom?

By the simple Word of a man who is sure of his testimony. This Word is truth and therein lies its power.

That which Christians must confess as truth will always be an offense to the world. That which we confess and believe is totally opposed to the thinking of the world. The world can build only on the visible. We can build only on the invisible.

Even when he strictly follows all of God's commands, a Christian will still strongly provoke his environment. Hatred is bound to appear. "Because you are not of the world . . . therefore the world hates you," said Jesus concisely (John 15:19).

It is therefore a mistake when someone expresses the opinion that the confessor of the Gospel can be at peace with the world, that his service can be offered in such a way as to reap thankfulness and respect. The service laid upon us by Jesus is in fact different from all that which the world regards as a beautiful or great accomplishment.

It is in these insights that the suffering church can be a decisive help for the contemporary need of the church to proclaim the Gospel. From it we can again learn what the church's real constitution is and what it means for a witness to make a proclamation. Christian preaching is more than teaching and instruction, more than meditation. It is confession of that which is ultimately true.

It is not necessary to make the witness of faith biting by way of preparation in order to gain a wide effect for it. It is provocative and offensive in its origin and can, as a consequence, exercise an immeasurable effect on its own. For that which we confess in faith can only be that which has entered our own life and thought as an unknown reality. This recognition will always predominate over our thinking. It is not we ourselves who have grasped the truth of the faith, but it is Jesus who as the living Lord has taken hold of us and our thinking. For this reason Christian preaching which desires to be effective is, in the last analysis, a testimony.

Current tactics used in the Soviet Union to persecute religious groups show that essential distinctions are made in the battle against religion. Church groups enjoy, for the most part, considerable freedom. Yes, they can even be supported. And why not? Yet the more resolutely the ECBs pursue open missionary activity, the stronger the persecution grows.

A great nation of the status of an unmolested world power could not express more clearly the explosive power which the biblical Word possesses today. In their missionary efforts the ECBs preach nothing in public except the Word of the Bible. If it is possible to check biblical missionary preaching at all, it can apparently be done only with brutal violence. Events of our day in the Soviet Union show this to be true.

It would be good for all Christians in the world to recognize that, for they then would know the only way for their witness to have value.

Part of the suffering which martyrs must endure is that their zeal and submission are misunderstood. It is a great burden for the suffering church when people contend that imprisoned Christians are merely ineffective, bungling people who have provoked their own suffering.

But the truth always bring the persecutors to light. Blockheads are not the objects of hatred, of sentences to prison camps. Acts 5 relates the story of the martyrdom of a group of apostles around Peter: the apostles were publicly flogged in order to intimidate them. While this was going on, they were forcefully commanded: "You may no longer preach in the name of Jesus!" (Acts 5:40).

A small point must be noted here. It was not forbidden to speak *of* Jesus. The world is tolerant. But it was forbidden to speak *in the name of* Jesus. That is the final, authoritative command. In the name of Jesus one can forgive sins, drive out demons, heal the sick; in the name of Jesus a great plentitude of power is passed to the church. And men hate this all-powerful witness. The hatred is not always clearly visible, yet it most often is the cause of the animosity. So much hatred directed against the testimony of the believing church has as its cutting edge the reproach: "They speak so confidently! They are so authoritarian!"

The world is turned on its head. A mauled congregation is confident. And yet this is true, for the Word of Jesus is certain and sure and full of authority where it is spoken in His name.

Concern for the Free Churches

" 'If God is for us, who is against us?' (Rom. 8:31).

"Dear brothers and sisters, young heirs with us and followers of Christ from the entire church, confirmed in difficulties and persecutions, but still true to their Lord;

"Peace be with you!

"We greet you all heartily in the name of Him who once gave up His life for us and who called us in our youth to follow Him, in the name of 'the most beautiful among the sons of men' — Jesus!

"We want to praise Him along with you, thank Him heartily, and honor Him for all His provisions and blessings which we four prisoners . . . [four names] have experienced and continue to experience the whole time we are apart from you.

"Thanks be to the Lord for this temporary separation and honor to Him for the storm which we have yet to pass through.

"Dear friends. We know that you who are not in prison pass through

Sergei T. Golev, age 76, a total of twenty-one years in the camps.

Vassili D. Zhovmiruk, 78, a total of fourteen years in the camps.

Georgi T. Ossipov, 74, si[...] with TB.

Nadezhda F. Nikitina, 24, sentenced to three years in a prison camp.

Yevgeni K. Rodoslavov, 22, sentenced to a total of ten years (to 1978).

Vladimir P. Sinchenko, 2[...] sentenced to three years [...] a prison camp.

The family of Ivan A. Afonin who died in a work camp in the Tula region on 22 November 1969.

Aida Skripnikova in the summer of 1971 after he[...] three-year term in a priso[...] camp.

idia Vins, president of the ouncil of Relatives of Imrisoned Evangelical Chrisans and Baptists, senenced in 1971 to three ears in a prison camp.

Gennadi K. Kryuchkov, chairman of the Council of Churches of Evangelical Christian Baptists, sought by wanted posters in 1971.

Georgi P. Vins, general secretary of the independent Evangelical Christians and Baptists.

"Church, do not forget them!" With this cry under this photo-filled document the Council of Relatives of Imprisoned Evangelical Christians and Baptists draws attention to Mrs. Lidia Vassilyevna Kryuchkov who with her nine children lives in Tula; her husband has been forced to leave his family.

great affliction and are enduring oppression. . . . We can say one thing and only one thing: God is for us!

"And are there conceivably powers in the world which can force us to betray the Lord and divide the people of Christ?

"No, such powers do not exist. Because everything which concerns God's church concerns the apple of our heavenly Father's eye. Therefore, dear friends, with this in mind, let us go forward! Let us join together into one family in our trust in Christ! The way is not much longer, not much longer at all. The day when we will meet our Best Friend and His mansions of wondrous beauty is near.

"The present, temporary sufferings mean nothing compared to that splendor which will be opened for us.

"We feel very confident. We recognize constantly that you who are free are in much greater difficulty than we here in custody. We never forget to remember you in our prayers. We believe that we will soon meet you and at that time serve the Lord in the congregation with ever greater surrender and energy. Our present testing is only for our healing. It is a great joy for us to hear that you have manfully borne the storms that assailed you.

"We are at present united with you in spiritual communion. May the Lord bless this communion. We desire perfect peace, love, and unity to reign among us.

"The Lord permits these afflictions so that His children might see themselves as a family, friendly and sincere with each other. He would have our hearts praise and exalt Him constantly and sense the need for His blessing.

" 'Blessed are the men whose strength is in thee, and whose hearts walk after thee. As they go through the barren valley, they make it a place of springs, and the early rain covers it with blessings' (Ps. 84:5, 6)

"Dear friends! Let no one lose heart or courage. Think of this — the world without God looks at us: we must hold up Christ as an example and point to Him. Our faces, our eyes must shine with joy. We must have perfect inner peace and let it shine forth.

> To live for Jesus, to die for Him;
> Can anything better be desired?

"Greet all young people on our behalf, all prisoners, and also the entire church with all its members.

"Let us consider that this difficult time which the church is passing through will not be in vain.

" 'Let this be recorded for a generation to come, so that a people yet unborn may praise the LORD: that He looked down from His holy height, from heaven the LORD looked at the earth, to hear the groans of the prisoners, to set free those who were doomed to die' (Ps. 102:18-20).

"The Lord bless you! Know that we are joined to you in spirit. We ask you to sing this song:

'Oh, no, no one in the entire world
can take freedom from those who are faithful.
The body may fear to molder away,
and prison gives it a fright!
But the God of love Himself gives freedom
to thoughts which darkness has subdued.
And the world has not yet been able to smash
the freeing-chains of love.'

"Your friends in Christ [the names of four young prisoners]; 1971."

Parents Organize Worship Services for Children

On 29, 30 November 1966, Georgi P. Vins, the General Secretary of the independent Baptist church, whom we have already had occasion to mention frequently, and Gennadi K. Kryuchkov, the chairman of this brotherhood of faith, stood on trial in Moscow. Both were sentenced to three years in a prison camp. The indictment tried to maintain that the two church leaders had seduced the members of the church communion into disregarding Soviet laws concerning religion. But both accused leaders were able to prove easily during the trial that it was the congregations who first of all had wanted to be active in unhampered missionary work. It had only been much later that the request came for them to assume the spiritual leadership of the Initiative Group. The vigor of this church group was actually based not in the fact that direction came from above (as was customary in other churches), but that the many activities of the church members first arose by themselves and were only then handed over to the spiritual leadership for coordination. It is important to establish this in order to have a clear picture of the beliefs of the majority of these ECBs and their courage in bearing testimony.

Gennadi K. Kryuchkov expressed himself in the trial as follows in regards to those actions which the court found objectionable:

"The Council of Churches of ECBs has developed an arrangement for those aspects of ECB activity which come in contact with social and legal norms of civic life, a plan for the Confederation of ECBs. [At this the noise grew in the chamber.] I can understand the atheists and their indignation. I am, however, a believing man. I believe in a kingdom where there are no jails and prison camps. We are under accusation for illegal activities. That, however, has been shown to be absurd. Since we were organized, we have been writing to the government constantly. We have stood before the doors of various organizations with our explanations and petitions. But they drove us away and said: 'We do not want to know anything about you; you are acting illegally.' At that time, as we were exercised about our affairs, we could not get in touch with you, Comrade Prosecutor. But now you are here to hold court for us. And one would like to ask you, Comrade Prosecutor, where did you make your mistake? Earlier when you exonerated our brothers, or now when you pass judgment for the same thing?

"We are charged with the fact that we organized children's schools — i.e., Sunday schools. This contention has also found no confirmation. The Council of Churches has not organized any Sunday schools or never even commisisoned them. The parents do this themselves.

"We have always said that the church may not forbid the presence of children at worship services, but the Council of Churches has organized no Sunday schools. If, however, there was such a hero — I say it forthrightly, a hero — who acted from his own zeal and who on his own initiative wanted to organize the instruction of children in the spirit of the Gospel, could I protest that? I could not, however, recommend anything to anyone for which that brother or sister could have been responsible in court.

"We are charged with having organized the delegation in May, 1966, on the Old Square in front of the Central Committee building in Moscow, but there is no proof of this in the charges. All the statements by witnesses are not from eye witnesses but from third- or fourthhand sources; and there are no witnesses and participants in the delegation present here. We ask you, therefore, to summon these witnesses so that they can report on why they came to Moscow and so that they can make the necessary statements. You charge us with having organized the delegation. If some 500 participants gathered on the individual initiative of the believers, I can assure you that the Council of Churches could have called as many as 3,000 together and carried through the conference in the course of a few days, unless someone was able to prevent us. We did not take that approach but desired everything to be ordered according to law."

What Are We Passing on to Our Children?

It takes a healthy dose of naivete to accept Soviet propaganda to the effect that ECBs are sentenced because they have incriminated themselves before Soviet laws through the forms of their meetings. The massive oppression of evangelical congregations cannot be justified by an ostensible breaking of laws concerning religion. The actual facts tell an unequivocal tale. As a goal for valid existence communistic ideology can tolerate only an exclusive focus on this life. And thus when Christians think and act in accord with the biblical concept of the future proclaimed by Jesus, conflict arises with the purely this-worldly materialistic ideology of Communism. This was made clear, for example, in 1964 when Georgi Vins, together with six other leaders of the church, wrote a letter to all parents who shared their common faith. This appeal was attacked vigorously in the press as anti-Soviet: the rearing of children in biblical faith was an activity inimicable to society. Evangelical parents take the responsibility which they have before God for their children all the more seriously in light of the massive atheistic influences exerted upon their children.

The parts of Georgi Vins' letter which were like a red handkerchief to the Communists were the following:

"Dear brothers and dear sisters! . . . Are your children going the same way as you do? Do they know the Lord? Do they love other people? Do they wait on the teaching and the commands of the Lord as He Himself commanded (Eph. 6:4)? The Word of the Lord commands believing parents to instruct their children about Him. . . .

"The greatest thing that you can gain and pass on to your children is the unpurchasable possession of faith. . . . Some day it will be possible to see in your children how you yourself have treasured the gift of faith and what the Lord means to you.

"Dear parents! If your children stand outside at the last day, will they not testify against you with tears? Is your salvation certain to you?

If all in your family are believers, is the congregation in your home visible and is Christ their sole glory?

"Dear brothers and dear sisters! If you have any brother or sister who does not come to the worship services and who perhaps has renounced God, care for that one and strive to save his life."

Faith Found in a Prison Camp

"Honored government!

"I, Vassili Ivanovich Kazlov, was born into the family of a poor farmer in 1924. I am by nationality a Russian.

"My father died in 1933. We five fatherless children were left to ourselves.

"The street drew me and I became a thief. When I was just 15 years old, I went to prison on a four-year sentence, a severe penalty for a child

"Imprisonment at such an age did not serve to rehabilitate me but only strengthened me in my criminal ways.

"After my release I went to the front in 1943, and after one year was severely wounded in the chest. When I was released from the military hospital, I returned to the army after a short leave. In 1945 I was demobilized and returned to my life of crime. In 1946 I received another five-year sentence, this time for storing weapons.

WITHOUT GOD, WITHOUT MORALS

"Thus I lived without God and without morals and did not stop my criminal activity. In 1947 my sentence was extended to ten years for thievery in prison.

"I was often close to despair and looked for a way out of this situation. I had lost all interest in life. I did all I could not to have to live any longer. And yet I wanted to live, only not as before.

"I began to look for the source of my life's tragedy. Today I can say where the root of my fall lay: I was born in 1924 and at school the idea was instilled in me that there is no God! And when one has no faith in God, one also has no morality. As a consequence, the ruin of the soul follows as well as the path to moral and physical disintegration.

THE SHINING EXAMPLE OF CHRISTIANS

"But among the other prisoners I had the opportunity to get to know some people with a high morality and a high goal in life. These were Christians, believers. They were stripped of their freedom and put with criminals for their living belief in God!

"I saw that I was serving a sentence I deserved: for theft, robbery and banditry!

"But these people who were arrested for their convictions were sentenced to higher sentences than I was, from 20 to 25 years.

"While criminals like myself fell into general despair and cursed themselves, the camp, the camp leaders, and everything in the world and tried to open their arteries, to cut open their stomachs, or hang themselves, etc., the Christians did not despair.

"Life in camp and the terrible conditions there did not disconcert them. A spiritual beauty shone from them. Their pure, upright lives their deep faith and devotion to God, their diffidence and outstanding bravery became a shining example of real life for many thousand prisoners. In their faces Christ was mirrored! To lead such a pure life with its high goal became my wish!

From Criminal to Christian

"Just such a shining and inextinguishable example seemed one of the arrested ones — the Christian Kh., whom I met in 1953 in an East Siberian camp. That was not his first imprisonment for faith in God.

"He is also in jail now. He is 56 years old and of these years he has spent more than half behind the walls of prison and prison camps as a Christian. . . .

"Notice well that many hundred believing ECBs, our people's finest sons and daughters, walk the way of long-term suffering!

"But their chains and suffering have brought many to an awareness of Christ. The transforming power of Christ, the power of the Gospel, has won over not only my criminal heart, but hundreds of others who like me were contaminated by godlessness and depravity.

"Russian jails and prison camps become for many people the place of spiritual rebirth and of encounter with Christ.

"In 1953 I broke completely with the world of crime and with my criminal past. I became a Christian. . . !

Captured Again — for Jesus' Sake

"In 1954 I returned from exile and married. But from that same moment persecutions began for me as a believing Christian.

"In 1961 — I already had five underage children by then — I was sentenced to forced labor for my Christian life.

"I had not yet paid this penalty when I was, in the same year, exiled to eastern Siberia for five years because of my witness for Christ.

"Thus began the second stage of my life under arrest, this time not by any means for banditry and robbery but for Christ's sake!

"I was brought under escort to the Krasnoyarsk region, but I did not have the feeling of despair as earlier. I had already tasted the love of Christ and knew His promise that it was my privilege, 'not only to believe in him but also to suffer for his sake!' (Phil. 1:29). That comforted me.

"I was in exile for three years far from my family. My wife and my six fatherless children likewise bore the burden of suffering for Christ's sake.

"In 1964 I was freed and could return home, but I was not permitted to remain there long.

"The militia and other agencies did not leave the believers in peace — not only in our city but throughout the land — but continued their persecutions. . . .

Petitions Gain No Hearing

"In August, 1965, more than 100 leaders of believers in Moscow turned to the President of the Presidium of the Supreme Soviet, A. I. Mikoyan, with a request for admission and a hearing. When we received this permission, I was one of the five men received by Mikoyan.

"To the Chief of State we handed in writing thirty particularly characteristic incidents of unlawfulness and arbitrariness against believers. Besides this, sixteen conclusive photographic documents — such as the destruction of prayer houses, the thrashing of believers, etc. — were also submitted. Mikoyan promised to re-establish freedom of conscience in the land.

"In reality, however, the situation of believers did not improve but only became more difficult.

"I myself was ordered to court again in April, 1966, and sentenced to a year's forced labor for religious activity.

"I stood again as a Christian in court! This was the fourth time that I had been sentenced because of my belief in God.

"I was sentenced to three years in a prison camp with strict regulations.

"My family again remained behind without their father, but we have long since forgiven you for all that.

The Blessed Answer of the Christian

"From the first days of imprisonment believers have prayed for you! God has heard this prayer, the gloomy walls of the Lefortovsk prison — the greatest political prison of our land — have also heard.

"We prayed for you as we have been taught by our teacher, Christ, who said: '. . . bless them that curse you; do good to them that hate you; pray for them that despitefully use you and persecute you' (Matt. 5:44).

"I believe that these prayers which rise day and night will not be in vain. . . .

"All illegal activity of the authorities, all persecutions which I and my family have had to endure are directed to the end that I renounce

Christ and return to my earlier life of sin, which I still today do not recall without horror and revulsion.

"I must often hear my masters say: 'It would have been better if you had remained a bandit instead of becoming a Christian.' I still recall the first legal proceedings for me as a Christian in 1961. The public prosecutor wanted to make my past a rebuke to me. . . .

"Yes, even the chairman of the Council of Religious Affairs, V. A. Koroyedov, has taken the effort to air my sinful past anew in the newspaper *Izvestia*. But Kozlov — the bandit and thief — has long since died and been buried and now by the goodness of God lives Kozlov the Christian. As one who has experienced to the full the total abomination of a criminal, sinful life and who has recognized the liberating power of Christ, I urge you earnestly: do not inflict evil and suffering on innocent people — the Christians. They are your most honorable and best citizens! They desire good for you, and only good.

"And the persecutions will not be crowned with success, for it is written: 'No weapon that is fashioned against you shall prosper, and you shall confute every tongue that rises against you in judgment' (Isa. 54:17).

"Do not draw the wrath of God upon yourselves!

"I ask you urgently once more to grant me a conference with you.

"Very respectfully. (Signed) V. I. Kozlov. 23 October 1970."

Many Publish Christian Writings

Gennadi K. Kryuchkov, chairman of the Council of Churches of ECBs, spoke these words on 29 November 1966, before a Moscow court.

"We have already proposed several times that the writings not signed by the Initiative Group, the Organization Committee, or the Council of Churches be removed from our legal records. The magazine *Vestnik Spassenia* (*Messenger of Salvation*) is not an official organ of the church. Neither is it edited by the Council of Churches, published by it, nor distributed by it. . . . For five years the Council of Churches has been in a situation where we are subject to arrest at any moment whatsoever. We are not underground people. I have a pass which contains my name. We have appeared personally with our statements before governmental authorities. The magazine *Messenger of Salvation* is published by believers who are of one heart and mind with the Council of Churches and they are the ones who also distribute it. [Laughter in the chamber.] I must say to you that the Council of Churches does not at all know all the places where the writings are printed. Duplication is easily done. I already knew how to do it when I was a very young child. One takes gelatine, glycerine, and glue; that is all dissolved and poured onto glass; later one makes a print. This method is very simple. Every young girl, every young boy who wants to serve God in any way at all can do this. Dozens of believers publish writings by this method of whom the Council of Churches often has absolutely no knowledge at all. I can say that with certainty."

From the Standpoint of Atheistic Propaganda

Even atheistic propaganda has revealed how senseless it is to simply revile the religious feelings of Christians. It has thus tried to attack the causes which lead unbelievers to become Christians. A Moscow Party Commission investigated the reasons why the ECBs are so widely dispersed among the people. The Chief Ideologue of the Soviets, Ilyichev, named four "evils":

"(1) They are without exception good skilled workers. For this reason they are respected.

"(2) They have solved the alcohol problem for themselves. They are increasingly entrusted with tasks demanding special reliability. In such key positions as truck drivers, crane operators, and others they display a thorough efficiency.

"(3) They do not, to be sure, subscribe to any peace resolutions in world politics, but they stand up for peace concretely where they live. They live peacefully with their families and also help other families to live in peace when these threaten to disintegrate.

"(4) They do not let anyone die comfortless."

At no time in their history of now over 100 years has it been possible for the ECBs of the Soviet Union to carry out public missionary work among the people. And yet these Christians, living apparently ingrown lives, have been light and salt to their surroundings. This lively faith leaves deep marks behind as evidence of new life. Examples of this are found in atheistic propaganda, which concedes by inference how the Christians are valued even by unbelievers.

The first example comes from a 1965 newspaper and was reprinted as follows in an article by K. Ikramov in the Soviet magazine *Journalist*, March, 1968. It is clear from this article how helpless people are who stand in the face of death with only communistic materialism to buttress them. Evangelical Christians consider it a most important task

to stand by dying friends in their final hours. Of this the article of
atheistic scorn writes:

"... a man took sick. A serious illness chained him to his bed for a
long time. Paralysis held human life tightly in its claws . . . convales-
cence came slowly. *They* came faster. Like black carrion birds smelling
easy prey, they circled the house. *They* — pious faces, lips pressed
sweetly together, black shawls wrapped tightly about themselves, like
shadows they creep around the bed. The gospel and psalms appear.
The soul-saving talk flows at him. The 'soul-grabbers' go into action.
The dead antennas of the sectarian sea-monsters stick tightly to the
body of the falling sacrifice. . . ."

The only question to ask the author is why, then, do enlightened
Soviet citizens open their doors when the Christians, seemingly so
contemptible, ring and express a desire to visit the dying one?

The other example comes to grips with the ethics of evangelical
Christians. As is well known, Communism awaits the New Man as the
fruit of altered societal relationships. After 50 years of Communism
the morality of converted Christians in the Soviet Union has remained
proverbial, as this citation from an atheistic propaganda magazine
indicates:

"On a Sunday evening a Volga-style automobile was traveling on a
highway to Moscow. It began to rain. The Volga overtook a bus jam-
packed with travelers. At the next bus stop three people stood in the
rain, a lady with a child, and a man.

" 'They will not be able to find any room in the bus,' the driver
thought, and he braked to a stop.

" 'Are you headed for Moscow? I can take you along.'

"The passengers got out at the Metro Station, and the father held
out some money for the driver.

" 'Thanks,' said the driver, 'I don't take money.'

" 'Is that right?' the father asked, openly surprised. 'You have done
me a good turn. I must therefore do something for you.'

" 'Do something good for someone else,' the driver said.

" 'Baptist!' the father sneered scornfully, put his money in his pocket,
and declared to his wife: 'A Baptist!'

"Why did he think that? Who gave him the idea that only Baptists
acted this way? Obviously the man was convinced that what the driver
said revealed a morality which we so gladly call hypocritical. I do not
contend that it is just our journalistic efforts against religious morality,
against the 'little Christs,' which gave him such notions and elicited

such a reaction, but I believe that they have played an important roll.

"Besides, the driver of the Volga was not a Christian but an author of well-known atheistic works. . . ."

Harassment and Suffering From a Different Perspective

Many Christians in the East are reluctant to report their sufferings, if they talk about them at all. It is not that they are afraid. It is much rather an example of spiritual self-discipline. They know how easily stress on such things is converted to hatred and bitterness, and for this reason they do not enumerate the horrors. They know how to distinguish between important and unimportant matters. And the most important thing to them — even in the midst of oppression — is testimony to Jesus Christ. We quote from a report about a prisoner who, as a preacher, spent many years in a Siberian prison camp:

"When Nikolai was taken prisoner he had his New Testament with him. He had it all the years he was in prison. He even brought it home again with him. As soon as he was arrested, his belongings were searched. The Testament was found and taken away. A policeman threw it in the dustbin. Nikolai protested vigorously, and demanded it back. 'Without this book I will not survive the journey!' he cried. 'You will be able to take me off the train as a corpse!' The police thought that Nikolai had threatened a hunger strike. The officer was called. There was endless discussion, and finally he was allowed to take his Testament along, something which only a very few others have been allowed.

"In the train there were many prisoners together with Nikolai. The guards came to count the prisoners each day, and often they beat them with clubs. Twice Nikolai stood up to the guards boldly, and that won him respect from the other prisoners. They began to watch him when he read his New Testament. And finally they asked him to read it aloud to them.

"Of his six years of labor in the prison camp, a mine, Nikolai had only this to say in restrospect: 'One who belongs to God's kingdom sees the harassment and suffering from a different perspective than do other men.'

"The news spread rapidly in the prison camp that Nikolai was a preacher. The barracks' residents often gathered together secretly in groups. Nikolai was not only able to read aloud to them from his Testament and explain the Word, but many prisoners also came to him with their needs and concerns.

"Among the prisoners was a biology professor, an atheist, who wanted to win Nikolai over to his conviction. His world view was: 'Education and culture are the pillars which hold us up when all else fails.'

"Shortly thereafter they were unable to see each other any longer, having been separated and transferred to different camps. But one day they met again during their work. The professor was totally dispirited. He was forced to shovel coal although he had been sick in the meanwhile. In despair he said: 'It's all up now; even education and culture no longer help.' Nikolai wanted to give him new hope through the Gospel, but he had the impression that in the face of open despair the professor could understand nothing at all.

"Hopelessness was the greatest danger to the prisoners. Many pined away from it and died.

"When someone once betrayed to the guards that Nikolai read to others from the New Testament, he was shut up in the notorious lock-up. But Nikolai began a hunger strike. He became very ill, and was put in the military hospital. In the next room was quartered a young man, a former officer, who was in deep despair. He did not want to eat anything at all and would just exchange his rations for tobacco. Nikolai gave him his tobacco ration under the condition that he would finally eat. This concern had its effect on the former officer. He ate and began to slowly regain his strength.

"Out of the blue he asked Nikolai one day: 'Are you a Christian?'

" 'Yes,' answered Nikolai.

" 'Do you believe in God?'

" 'Yes.'

" 'Do you believe that Jesus stilled the storm in the boat that time?'

" 'Yes.'

"Slowly Nikolai brought this very ill person to put his trust in Jesus. He gave the prisoner this sentence: 'With Christians there is no hopelessness!'

"When Nikolai was able to be released from the military hospital, his friend gave him a small piece of paper on which it said: 'It is still true, there is no hopelessness!'

"Another fellow-prisoner belonged to a different group. He refused to work on Sunday because he did not want to violate the Sabbath commandment. For this he was locked up and beaten, but the next week he did the same thing. Nikolai tried to show him that forced labor was not a profanation of the Sabbath. Then he made this proposal: the prisoner should celebrate Sunday in his heart while working and in so doing say to himself, 'voskressenye' which in Russian means both 'resurrection' and 'Sunday.' Finally the prisoner was ready for this, and Nikolai went to work with him. The other mumbled constantly to himself, 'voskressenye, voskressenye,' and became genuinely happy in doing this.

"When Nikolai was released after many years, he still had first to earn the money for his trip home. The trains were so full he couldn't buy a seat ticket. He finally found a seat in a compartment with a professor, a teacher, a married couple, a major, and a girl student. After the Russian fashion they soon became friends in the compartment. They had a thirteen-day trip ahead of them before the train was due in Moscow, so first of all every one in the compartment introduced himself and gave his occupation. When Nikolai reported that he was a convict, it must be stated that the others were startled. Nikolai therefore withdrew into his sleeping area while the others took out their provisions in order to prepare the evening meal. Nikolai did not have much with him, so he read a little in his Testament in his sleeping compartment. The student finally came and invited him to eat. She had taken an interest in his reading, but Nikolai did not want to take part in the eating.

"Through the student the others also found out that Nikolai was a Christian. Then the major also came to the sleeping compartment and asked Nikolai in a friendly way to share in the meal. Otherwise, the people would be offended. From then on he belonged to the group and received everything he needed. His fellow travelers were interested in him and asked about the contents of the New Testament. The trip became a thirteen-day period of evangelism.

"Every day at a set time Nikolai read the New Testament aloud to his fellow-prisoners in the compartment and explained it. Finally even travelers from other compartments came to these meetings. After a couple of days there were exchanges as some got off and some came on board, among whom were a policeman and a 10-year-old boy who had run away from home and now had to be brought back by the officer. When on the next day it was time for the Bible reading, Nikolai was afraid the policeman would make trouble. The others, however, spoke with him, and with a dark look he commanded: 'Begin!' The whole time they traveled together the policeman listened attentively. . . ."

WITNESSES TO THE FAITH BROKEN

NOT ALL MARTYRS ARE Christians, for many people suffer for the sake of their convictions. It is certainly proper to recognize that there are true heroes outside of Christianity, heroic martyrs who endure suffering in the fight for right and justice and who are persecuted for this fight.

But martyrs for Jesus' sake are different. They are not really heroes. The nature of their suffering is different from that which a hero undergoes, for they do not bear the burden laid upon them heroically. Martyrs for Jesus' sake are people affected by their suffering. Heroes, on the other hand, are somehow not affected by it but are kindled with an almost fanatical will to endure.

We know from the reports of innumerable suffering Christians that to the end of their lives they are beset by the dread of renouncing the faith or growing weak in it. The strength of Christian martyrdom, in fact, is not in the remarkable endurance of individual personalities.

The martyr for Christ's sake can be understood only in the light of faith. Everything he says, indeed his whole life, is aimed only at testifying that in all weakness Jesus upholds him in a marvelous way.

When Corrie ten Boom was a child, she told her father that she was afraid that she would lack the necessary strength to die as a martyr if this was ever required of her. Her father responded: "When you go on a trip you receive money for your traveling expenses from me. But do you receive it two weeks before the departure date?" The child answered: "No, you give it to me on the day that I leave." The father then explained to the child: "The Savior is just like that. He does not give us the grace now for those things to be suffered in the future. But if the moment ever comes that He honors you with a martyr's death, he will even give you the strength for that." When Corrie ten Boom

later experienced the hell of the Ravensbruck concentration camp, sh
found that an unconquerable witness had been given to her.

We always stand in danger of basking in the martyr's personal bri
liance, but when such a brilliance suddenly fades, we will benef
inevitably.

It was a great shock for Christians who had taken the suffering (
Russian believers to heart when the news became known that a tru
witness to the faith had grown weary. Her name was widely known i
the West. She had shown herself — in spite of her youth — to b
unbending in service for Jesus. She had held children's worship servic
here and there in private homes; she had been sentenced to five yea
in a prison camp; and she seemed firm as a rock in her faith. Her im
prisonment was very severe, and although she was ill, food parcels fror
her parents were kept from her. To this day we do not know the tactic
which were used in the prison camp to break the witness of this Chri
tian girl.

Opposition is great. The ones who suffer are "winnowed like wheat
(Luke 22:31). It was the reports of this girl's weakness which fir
showed many believers how important it is to intercede constantly fc
the suffering church.

We have a false picture of martyrdom if we fail to realize the distre
caused when witnesses crack. And these are not merely isolated cas
or just painful breakdowns. This is a decisive matter which measur
how well Christians understand themselves today. God is pleased t
describe witnesses in all their frailty. Our mortal bodies see to it tha
we do not fill our mouths too full; our earthly personalities, our chec
ered spirits, keep us humble before God.

Paul called himself an "earthen vessel" (2 Cor. 4:7), but even th
breakable pot that he described still had to be smashed to pieces.

Paul said: "While we live we are always being given up to death
(2 Cor. 4:11). We should look askance at those Christian biographi
which always picture death as the triumph of heroic people, for i
death only the grace of Jesus still avails for us.

We have testimony from the suffering churches that they do not l
down even their fellow Christians who have grown weary in the fait
They know that it is expressly in the face of martyrdom that Jesu
promise rings true: "No one shall snatch [my sheep] out of my hand
(John 10:28).

In this weakness, therefore, martyrs in the faith stake all on th
power of the ever-present Jesus. Martyrs are courageous because the

thoughts are focused on Jesus. Trusting in His power, they can conquer all oppression.

When Luther was at the Coburg Castle in 1530 and so concerned about the small group of men bearing an evangelical witness at the Diet of Augsburg, he wrote in this same vein in his exposition of Psalm 118: "They can buffet, they cannot make us fall; they can torture, they cannot eradicate us; they can pommel, they cannot compel us; they can hinder, they cannot restrain us; they can bare their teeth, they cannot devour us; they can murder, burn, hang, and drown, they cannot wipe us out; they can drive out, rob, and seize, they cannot silence us. For our calling is sure: the Lord helps me. Who could ever do anything against someone whom the Lord is helping: God's Word remains forever. They would have to say that God Himself and His name no longer existed — let them be so foolish and insane."

The Book of Revelation was sent to congregations in martyrdom. It never grows weary of emphasizing that only that one who has been cleansed by the blood of Jesus is able to gain the victory. Christian martyrs are not without personal failings or personal sin, for they have "conquered . . . by the blood of the Lamb" (Rev. 12:11). And those who survive the great battle do not march into eternity as carefree victors. Their clothes, Revelation relates, have become filthy in the heat of the battle. They are not themselves the perfect ones, but those who have been made holy. The only reason they are able to survive is that they have made their robes "white in the blood of the Lamb" (Rev. 7:14).

The ancient church used the Word of the Bible to declare atoning power to suffering martyrs. To do this they stood constantly and exclusively on the atoning power of the death of Jesus.

No Christian possesses unshakable steadfastness. It is a gift of grace. Chambon wrote at the end of his book *French Protestantism*: "An essay could be written with the title, 'Views on Christian Heroism,' although indeed it would be necessary to call it more correctly: 'Thoughts on Special Evidences of God's Power in His Children'."

We do not understand martyrdom when we stress the ways in which men hold fast to Christ. The exalting theme of martyrdom is how Jesus Christ holds fast to sinful men.

The Way of Maria Braun

The Kirghiz Soviet Republic lies on the border of the Chinese province of Sinkiang. The snow-covered mountains belong to the Ala-

Tau chain. At the foot of the northern slopes the river Chu forms a wide valley in which the capital city of Frunze lies. A khan had been the ruler here in earlier days, but today both land and people are part of the great Soviet state. The war had even driven a group of Germans into this Asiatic region.

On 11 March 1966, in the Kirghiz SSR, Maria Braun and her friend, Yelena Tkhertskaya, were each sentenced to five years in a labor camp under normal regulations because they had conducted illegal Sunday schools.

Maria Braun comes from a German family. She was born in the village of Arkhangelsk on 14 October 1946, and attended primary school for ten years. She did not belong to any Party organizations, lived in the village of Novopavlovka, and worked as a tailor's cutter in a knitting establishment in Frunze.

The following is taken from the judgment pronounced by the court:

"Maria Braun and her friend belong to an unregistered congregation of ECBs. Since 1964 they have organized and led an illegal religious school for children in Novopavlovka. Through her initiative and above all by her active participation more than 80 children not yet of school age were taught in this school. Since the second half of 1964 Maria Braun has trained a group of 27 children. The local authorities warned both of the accused repeatedly about the illegal activity, i.e., the instruction of children in a religious school. In spite of this, both of the accused continued to lead the religious school and to establish a course of instruction, thereby poisoning the children's essential being by keeping them from society. In their teaching they used an ideology foreign to the Soviet system, and they encouraged the children not to join or visit Soviet youth groups. A student in the fifth class of the primary school, Viktor Kran, who attended the religious instruction held by the accused, sent the following request to the Council of Young Pioneers of Novopavlovka on 14 October 1965: 'I ask you to exempt me from the Pioneers since I cannot wear the red kerchief because of my beliefs.' Both of the accused plead innocent and refuse to make further statements to the court."

Maria Braun was in a labor camp for three years. From a letter to U Thant (summer, 1967) we extract the following note: "Maria Braun, who is imprisoned in the camp at the city Kungura, Perm Province, has been denied the right to receive food parcels from home for an entire year. The director of the camp contends that this is an educative measure." In 1968 Maria Braun went into the prison hospital

Nikolai K. Khmara from Kulunda, slain by mistreatment in the Barnaul prison on 9 January 1964.

On the way home from the worship service which with many people entails a trip of over sixty miles.

One of the heavily attended youth meetings in the Ukraine of the independent Evangelical Christians and Baptists who are persecuted by the government.

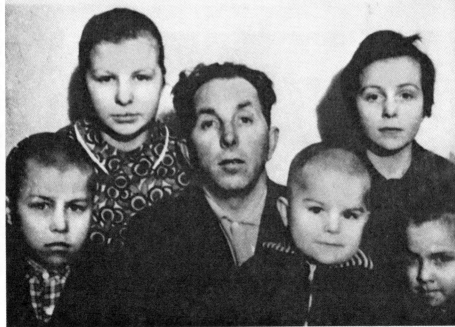

for four months. She recovered and was again able to perform light labor at the beginning of 1969. Our last news was that Maria Braun had once again taken sick and was still not allowed to receive food parcels.

She let it be known personally that she sensed the great number of prayers being offered for her. She greeted all children of God with Philippians 4:4: "Rejoice in the Lord always; again I will say, Rejoice."

The life story of this courageous witness was published in Christian magazines. Her picture was printed, and Christians began to be interested in her.

Then came the shock. By letter her family was told that Maria had defected from the faith. It took a long time for people in missionary circles to understand what that meant. Many Christians felt instantly that they had been negligent in intercessory prayer. A biblical sense of decorum had also been lacking. It had been such a comfort to be thrilled by Maria's story.

Because of all these things, it is especially important to read both of the following letters which tell us different things about Maria Braun. She herself wrote about her own life in the newspaper *Soviet Kirghiz* on 23 March 1971.

The second letter comes from Christians who were very close to Maria Braun. This letter recognizes with almost unfathomable depth that it is Jesus Christ and He alone who redeems. This Lord has not yet ceased to deal with Maria Braun, and it would be good for all Christians of the world to be less enthralled by martyrdom and more anxious to live by the Word of this Lord, whose grace is much greater than our sin and unbelief.

"I Think About My Past With Shudders"

This girl who had been a confessing Christian became a Communist and reported how she had found the way from Jesus Christ to "faith in herself."

". . . . For activity contrary to the law and for training underage

---

Photo left above: This house, belonging to Eduard Hauf, was destroyed on 17 March 1966, in Barnaul because Bible hours were held here.

Photo left below: Ivan Sloboda with his five children, Shura (Alexandra), Galya (Galina), Kolya, Lyussia, and Pavlik, who were taken away from him by the authorities and placed in a children's home. The mother has been in prison for several years on account of her faith.

children in an illegal religious organization I was sentenced to five years imprisonment by a trial of the People's Court in the Sokuluksk district of the Kirghiz SSR with the stipulation that I serve my sentence in a rehabilitation work colony of the central government.

"Because of the fatiguing worship services and the extravagant fasts, my health was so shaken that I was taken to the district hospital in Perm. I was very astonished that the doctors as well as the nurses treated a sick person so humanely, even one who was a criminal. There in the hospital I was charmed by the progress of the men in the white smocks. These were the people who constrained me to look at my environment with different eyes and to see that these men served the people in selfless surrender. Who forced the surgeon to seek out a patient on his day off, encourage him with a joke or a kind word, and instill in him faith in his own strength so that he could at last master his illness?

The therapist, Nina Alexandrovna, guided me like a small child, sought ways (and found them) to get me back on my feet again. After four months I was able to return to my work. A great desire grew in me to be useful to mankind through medicine. I had a great desire to learn more and entered the eleventh class. In places of exile I finished trade-technical school with a special skill in shoe manufacturing. My awakening began here — it was here that a light went on for me.

"Different people and circumstances were working on my consciousness. There were first my school friend, Tamara Mitrakova, and all the teachers, and next the All-Union Subotnik [voluntary labor during free hours for the good of the state or the public]. I will be thankful to Tamara for my whole life. She sat next to me in school and tried for a whole year to convince me that there was no God. In her I came to know a resolute and dedicated person who had fallen in love with her country, her home village, and nature. For a long time we were friends as far as education was concerned but opponents when it came to beliefs. Later as we walked the same way she became my best adviser and friend. I would not wish to forget my beloved teachers — Katarina Ivanovna Kotova, Lina Alexeievna Shilova, Valentin Nikolaevich Volkov, Svetlana Ivanovna Krylov, and others. I remember how Svetlana Ivanovna read aloud to us from the newspaper in class about events on the island D. We were all roused to indignation by the provokers' bandit raid. I do not know how the Baptist young people, who are urged not to take up arms, would have reacted to this case, but our class was ready to do our all for the holy Russian soil, for the homeland.

'How would you act?' I asked myself. 'Could you sit in the bushes while the others were sacrificing their lives?' At that moment I found myself convinced for the first time with my whole being that I did not agree with the rule of the sectarians, that I should refuse military service in order to follow archaic biblical laws.

"The All-Union Subotnik led to my conclusive break with the Baptists. When my 'sister in Christ,' Valentina K., who was also sentenced for 'soliciting children for the Baptist congregation,' found out that I wanted to take part in this activity, she was enraged and said to me: 'What, do you want to work for the atheists?' (She pretended to be a pious person, but in reality led the young people of her group in Perm astray.)

"We had a serious altercation, but the next day we went to work together. I convinced Valentina that the Baptists acted deceitfully. On the one hand they demanded that people do 'good,' yet on the other hand they were not prepared to take arms to defend their homeland. And in just this way they refused to work for the well-being of their homeland. Where is in this the charity with which we pride ourselves so? We are only willing to do 'good' when it brings us advantage or salvation while the atheists do good unselfishly.

"In April, 1969, I became an unbeliever and soon afterward was freed, before the end of my sentence. The Soviet Agency for the Administration of Justice gave me credit for my conscientious work. Last summer I successfully finished my course at a pedagogical institute. I hope to be useful to my land as a teacher.

"I have satisfied myself time after time that I am surrounded by good people who understand my difficulties. I have obtained a place in student quarters and a small business which allows me to pursue my studies successfully. I am in the social science department and hope to be able to work as a journalist. I intend to join the Communist youth organization.

"My thanks go to all people who have had a share in my fate. If you knew, my dear comrades, how happy I am now. I think about my past with shudders. I appeal to parents and teachers: protect your children from the influence of church people and sectarians, otherwise the 'servants of the Lord' will try to make them spiritual slaves, and it will not be an easy task to break the religious chains later on.

"That is actually all that I have to say . . . M. Braun, a student of the Kemerovo Pedagogical Institute."

At the End of Their Own Strength

"Greetings, dear sisters in the Lord, dear brothers! Many thanks for your letter which we received yesterday, 17 February. We know that you have not forgotten us. I will try to answer a few of your questions: Is our dear Maria at home? She was transferred from the camp to Siberia and a place called Frieansiedlung. It is much more difficult now for them than earlier, but the greatest pain is that her faith has been shipwrecked. So long as she held it firmly and agonized, she grew stronger and stronger in the faith, and they saw that they had misplayed their hand. But then Satan approached in the form of an angel with love and began to praise, and so Satan won. Her mother has been with her as a guest for two and a half weeks. Dear Maria no longer prays . . . . and yet we confidently believe that she will find her way out, for the old God still lives, has never yet made a mistake, and is stronger than all enemies. And the Lord has promised that when two or three people ask Him something in firm faith, nothing doubting, they will receive it.

"There are thousands here, I believe, and your dear brothers and sisters who will also help us to pray in spirit and in truth. Imagine that you are Job and you will understand my situation. One messenger has not even left before another one is here. But I do not want to murmur or complain. The Lord does not impose more than each can bear. He causes wounds, but He also heals them and helps us to bear the cross. When it becomes too difficult, He lays His pierced hands under us so that our shoulders and backs are not weighted down so much, and he helps us bear it when we go on our knees. A horse, when it is over-loaded, throws itself on its knees and draws the load still farther, and we must also do the same. Help us pray!

"Two of our sons have also been put in jail, for drinking, and the oldest wants to separate from his wife now. With what should I comfort myself? I hope in You! I also belong to this Redeemer. You do not send me suffering to torment me. No, only to tell my soul something. How should I comfort myself? It is all so empty . . . my hands so tired, my feet so heavy. And yet I hear You admonish me softly and say: Look upward and forward, you must not lose heart! To vanquish sorrow and pain — quiet — until we are gloriously comforted — to become a comforter . . .

"Farewell, until meeting again. Your brothers and sisters."

HIDDEN MARTYRDOM

WHEN WE SPEAK OF martyrdom, we usually mean an act of Christian confession displayed in a public drama as a brave demonstration of courageous faith. Yet this is a misconception with which we ought not burden those who must suffer for Christ's sake.

Some of those who report on martyrdom want to picture it as a human accomplishment. By contrast true martyrdom is frequently hidden or concealed, and this indeed is often its gravest difficulty. The Christians who are harried by external pressures do not have an easy time in deciding how they should behave. It has always been difficult to recognize clearly the way which one should take in persecution. The path to public suffering can even be a flight if it is a path taken on one's own initiative. What is the difference between confession and provocation? A church beset by martyrdom often divides over this fundamental question.

When is martyrdom unavoidable? When is the wisdom of serpents demanded?

In this crucial question, so fraught with difficulties, every Christian can only decide for himself.

We must understand that the uncertain period before actual martyrdom is a difficult time of inner distress. Should a hard or soft line be taken? When once this decision has been made and a clear confrontation between irreconcilable spiritual powers has been joined, the way of oppression is a much easier way to go. The tangled web of lies beclouding the choice makes this decision monstrously difficult.

Actually, it is not martyrdom itself which threatens our service to God; it is often only a deficient view of the current situation that pushes us to lazy compromises. But that is fully capable of crippling our ministry and our testimony.

When Luther left the hall after the proceedings of the Diet of Worms in 1521 and saw his friends, he cried: "I have made it!"

Over Luther's head now hung the imperial ban. It would really have made much more sense if he had cried: "It's all over with me now." But he was happy, although the time of martyrdom was just beginning.

Luther had been truly liberated in that moment. After months and years of uncertainty, a decision finally had been reached. The inner struggle had lasted for a long time; uncertainty and the need to search for the right way had burdened him severely. Luther must have been relieved when the lay of the land was cleared, even if it disclosed that all the power of the emperor was arrayed against him.

The distress of Christians in the Soviet Union is not over the battle against atheism in itself but over the tactics, uncertain for many, with which this struggle is to be carried out. It is not just foreign observers who are falsely oriented. Official religious policy intends to offer a fully paradoxical picture. Certain cults are promoted in order to testify to the generosity of religious freedom. For propaganda purposes the state uses the spiritual leaders of the church. Of necessity such activity has consequently had a damaging effect on the confidence of believers. In the end one can even see unnerving signs that such "services of convenience" have destroyed the respect of spiritual leaders for themselves.

The phrase "martyrdom of lies" which circulates within the churches tolerated by the state makes it clear that those Eastern churches tolerated by the state suffer from this relationship.

A martyrdom of lies is senseless in itself. Lying can only be sin. It can only be martyrdom of the truth, but we can sense what a great deal of suffering goes on under the fog of all-out seduction. Even church groups not touched by oppression suffer from the confusion and are divided over it more than we realize. And the most difficult thing is that they cannot talk about it with anyone.

There are no Christians in the East who, without scrupling, can say they approve of Soviet religious policies. When one of them nevertheless denies that Christians are afflicted, we can intimate from that the affliction which he himself is under. And that is also suffering!

The harshness with which both groups of ECBs carry on their disagreement spreads the suffering, in spite of earnest attempts at reconciliation. The impression will not go away that it could even be the aim of Soviet religious policy to aggravate this division by massive, mutual incriminations.

Both sides know well that in the end atheism's enmity can mean only martyrdom. Stalin's persecutions resolved that difficulty and removed the last doubt. But the disturbing question in 1961 was, nevertheless, whether the injunctions officially prescribed for the church leadership were unimportant laws or the signal to begin the last battle against all religion. It was in the area of tactics that clarity was lost on this issue. And when such a situation exists, it is systematically beclouded.

This kind of suffering, therefore, cannot even be recognized by others and certainly not combated. For the oppressed body of Jesus, this search for clarity is an effort involving great distress, as has become evident in many ways. Since we ourselves are not under persecution, we should guard from passing judgment on other Christians just because we do not understand their current situation. These casual judgments often are the kinds of talk which end up being the most dangerous in the Eastern countries. So many things in this world remain veiled that never can be explained. It should be enough for us that many who now live in the officially recognized churches have spent a substantial part of their lives in the comfortless prison camps of Stalin's time. No one outside the Soviet Union should take it upon himself to censure these people because of their "loyalty" to the state. Yet, at the same time, one should listen critically to many statements about religious freedom in the Soviet Union made by representatives of the officially recognized churches.

It is even difficult for us to know whether combat or patient love is demanded in our churches and in our associations with other Christian groups. The battle can be borne only when one knows that it is ordained by God.

Separated From the Society of Believers

"My dear ones, greetings to you and all friends!

"It is only yesterday that we parted. And today there is already such a great distance between us. I arrived in X. at 12 noon. I went immediately to the city militia. I told them that I was under surveillance and would have an emigration permit for city X. A lady official telephoned to someone about me, and I was led into a small room where two officials of the criminal department were waiting. Later two more also came. I found out only after they had gone away again that they were officials of the secret state police. They had already known for many days that I was to come, and so they interrogated me as to why

I had not come immediately. I explained that after the years in prison I had to rest up. Also I had sought to be put under police surveillance in my home territory. They beat it into my head immediately and with firmness that I could stay in X. only and nowhere else. . . .

"Finally they asked me if I had any believing acquaintances in the city. They were able, they said, to put specified groups of acquaintances and visits to individual houses off limits to me. They also wanted to know if I would go to a registered or an unregistered congregation. I answered only that there was no unregistered congregation in this city. Why, I asked, were they so afraid? In any case, I was not to be allowed to leave the house after 9 P.M. And what I would do before that was my concern. Then the officials of the secret police became agitated: 'We do not want an unregistered congregation to spring up here because of you!' They asked me: 'Have the three years in prison had any affect on you?' I could only answer that the things desired by the ones who arrested me at that time had not occurred. Actually this interrogation was longer than I can now describe. One of them asked me: 'Why have you been put under police surveillance? You have probably agitated a lot for your belief!' To this I answered that I was always very happy to be able to tell of my faith, especially when my listeners were paying attention. . . .

"It is a peculiar situation. I am not in prison. And yet I am treated like a prisoner. . . .

"(One day later.) Today is Saturday. During the day I again looked for a room, but all was in vain. I will have to search further. I also wanted to find a prayer house but at the city information bureau they did not know the address of any. They could not tell me about any church at all. I am now all alone. Nevertheless, I am pleased. I am listening to the radio. It is good that I brought it along. Hopefully it will be better for me next week.

"Give a hearty greeting to all! I have an ardent desire to be with you soon — even if it were only for two days. In great love, your. . . .'"

Under Pressure

"To the Prime Minister of the USSR, Comrade A. N. Kosygin.

"Copies: Chairman of the Krasnodar UKGB, Council of Relatives of Imprisoned Evangelical Christians and Baptists (ECBs).

"From: Citizen Peter Danilovich Peters. Krasnodar, 50 Sychevaya **Street.**

EXPLANATION

"Honored Alexei Nikolaevich!

"On 5 November 1969, an unknown comrade extended me an invitation and brought me to the house of the military officers, where a second comrade joined us.

"When we had entered the room allotted to us, they told me they were agents of the KGB [secret state police]. The first called himself Comrade (I think he said, Comrade Starostin), the other Comrade Sokolov.

"In order not to tire you with long descriptions of our discussion, I will explain myself briefly.

"The above named comrades tried to persuade me to work with them for the agencies of the KGB. In order to acquire my assent in writing they began to describe as criminal activity my service in the congregations of the Council of Churches for which in reality I could have been criminally responsible.

"If I consented, I was promised my freedom; if I declined — prison.

"This is an outrage. In our country there is no law which strips freedom from those who are not willing to be secret collaborators of the KGB. So far as I know, the administration of justice in our land does not allow the agencies of the KGB to build a place of refuge to which criminals who deserve a just penalty can remove themselves and escape justice if they declare themselves ready to act as collaborators.

"When the comrades noticed my weariness, due to strenuous work before the holidays, they postponed my final decision to 6 November. Since I had unmistakably declined their offer at the first meeting, I considered a second discussion of the matter superfluous and did not show up at the second meeting.

"During the holidays these comrades appeared at my residence while I was away and told the landlord: 'If he had been here, we would have arrested him.'

"I am, thus, unjustly threatened with arrest and forced to leave my place of work and my residence for that reason.

"I do not think that even you yourself would countenance the opinion that agents of the KGB have the right to make such a proposal to me if I really am subject to a criminal penalty.

"The conditions forced on me constitute convincing proof of my innocence and of the fact that the KGB itself bears the full responsibility for my present way of life.

"I ask that the causes of my present circumstances be investigated and that justice be done for me.

"Peters. I request an answer at Krasnodar, 50 Sychevaya Street."

Mortal Danger for the Suffering Church

The independent Baptists often speak against the officially tolerated All-Union Council of ECBs in Moscow with a ferocity inconceivable to us. It is a question, for them, of the life or death of the congregations. The atmosphere is also fouled by the difficult lives of suffering which burden congregations and families. The battle for truth and for a true following of Jesus can be waged only when a congregation of Christians has complete certainty. And yet the All-Union Council in Moscow expressed an opinion, October, 1971, in its *Fraternal Herald* concerning this very matter, an opinion which must be studied by the Council of Churches if it does not want to lose the fullness of its spiritual power. The danger of passing from martyrdom to fanaticism appears to be present here. We quote from the newspaper of the officially tolerated church leadership in Moscow:

"The Council of Churches has zealously spread its appeal of 6 December 1970 to all brothers and sisters. From reports reaching us it is said that this appeal by the Council of Churches was received with skepticism even among the separated congregations. The children of God have grown weary of this sad rupture and do not need the kind of appeals foreign to the spirit of Christ, but the kind which call all those who are redeemed by the blood of Calvary to reconciliation and to common labor.

"Nevertheless, it is necessary to pay serious attention to the appeal by the Council of Churches — in particular to the false teaching which it contains. The false teaching is this: the Council of Churches has begun to teach that there are saving and non-saving churches. In this the Council of Churches dares to contend that only those churches belonging to it are saving churches. The churches which belong to the All-Union Confederation of ECBs are by comparison non-saving churches and even ones which corrupt those who belong to them.

"This false teaching, unprecedented in the history of our brotherhood, could only arise among people who have forgotten the great and dear truth that the church does not save us (it makes no difference which church) but Jesus Christ who died for us on Calvary. 'And there is salvation in no one else, for there is no other name under heaven given among men by which we must be saved' (Acts 4:12).

"We consider it our holy duty to warn our dear brotherhood, every single congregation, every sister, and every brother, away from this false teaching into which to our regret the Council of Churches has fallen and which arises clearly from its appeal of 6 December 1970.

"The salvation of each of us is only by one Savior, Jesus Christ, who has rescued us from eternal destruction by His holy precious blood.

"May the Lord keep all of us from proclaiming any other way of salvation. Jesus Christ Himself says to us plain and clear: 'I am the way, and the truth, and the life; no one comes to the Father, but by me' (John 14:6)."

A Christian Lady Is to Be Prevented From Speaking

Dubravy is just a small village in the forests of White Russia. It lies apart from the great industrial city of Vitebsk in the Verkhnedvinsk district. This village had an object of pride. There were no churches there, no Orthodox Christians, no religion. Everyone was class-consciously atheistic. But suddenly a change occurred. It started in the family of Ivan Feodorovich and Nadezhda Stepanovna Sloboda. The father composed a detailed report in March, 1970:

"In 1962 one of our relatives came as a guest and had with her a New Testament. She proposed to us that we read it, but we were afraid and declined. But the Lord moved the spirit of Nadezhda, and she got up once in the middle of the night when all were asleep, took the Word of God from the pocket of our relative's clothing, and read it. She did this a few times. Then we read with her secretly; later we did it openly. Other relatives joined us in reading this wonderful book. I myself and our relatives had a radio, and we now began to listen to spiritual broadcasts. The Lord sent us the spirit of repentance and we, twelve in number, turned to the Lord and were born anew. Our life was changed.

"This was noticed immediately and it brought persecutions upon our heads. Stones flew through the windows of our homes. In order for us not to be able to receive radio broadcasts we were cut off from the electrical current; they banged open our doors and barged into the room where we were reading God's Word. I was excluded from the collective farm and we were deprived of a parcel of land which had been allotted to us. But our faith was strengthened. There was not the slightest doubt that the Gospel was true since we had also read the words: 'They have persecuted me and will also persecute you.'

That was fulfilled in our case on the spot. The world grew more and more enraged, but we were strengthened in the Lord.

"My brother, Vikenti, was sent to us — he is now a prisoner — in order to undermine our convictions, but he heard the Word and was converted. Persecutions descended upon him also, but he was strengthened by them. His wife set herself resolutely against him, shut him out, and wanted neither to read nor hear the Gospel — but when she was alone at home listening to the radio, she repented and was converted. In this way the fire of the Holy Spirit had already gripped four homes.

"The governmental authorities now began to take action. They decided to take our two oldest daughters, Galya and Shura, away from us. They did take them away and through a court order deprived them of their parents' home and of loving, motherly affection. The children on two occasions fled from the children's home (Dyetdom) which was 55 miles from us, but the unmerciful hands of the persecutors, with the power of governmental authority and the authority of the sword, recaptured them and took them back there. The children cried out in terror: 'People, people!' and put the whole village into a fright. But the people only spread out their arms helplessly. Thus it was that the first act of violence was carried out on my children.

"At that time we still did not belong to the church and were not yet baptized. The Lord trained us immediately through suffering. He led us to the thorny path, and on that path we met believers and were baptized.

'The persecutions did not cease. At the end of 1968 my wife, Nadezhda Stepanovna, was arrested, and also my brother, Vikenti, and my wife's brother, Piotr Kurash. They were hauled before the court for their testimony to Jesus Christ and sentenced to four and three year terms. As the state prosecutor led Nadezhda out of the house, she sang: "When the testings come upon you, when you grow weary in the battle and cannot cope with it, do not fall, but struggle on and do not deplore your fate — for faith, hope, and love are there!" And the little three-year-old baby, Pavlik, ran after her and wept, 'Mother, mother!'

"The court passed a resolution to take away our radio, 'for reception of religious broadcasts from foreign countries,' which was carried out by the sheriff. But the Lord did not leave us even when our houses were watched secretly and we lost the right to visit each other.

"A year and a half passed. On 16 January 1970, a new judicial

ocess was staged, and they took the other three children away from
to the children's home: Kolya, 10; Lyussia, 7; and Pavlik, 5. Who
able to tell our sorrow? He who gave His life for us — He carries our
row and strengthens us. Will the children's hearts ever be able to
get these difficult days? The sufferings of little Pavlik are undescrib-
e.

"Our house is empty now. Evenings they creep under the windows
d search for my soul.' Pray for us. I believe that the prayers of
od's children rise to the throne of His mercy. In all may His will be
ne. Ivan Feodorovich Sloboda."

Father Asks for His Children

"To the Chairman of the Council of Ministers of the USSR, Com-
e A. N. Kosygin.

"To the Chairman of the Supreme Soviet of the USSR, Comrade
B. Podgorny.

'To the Attorney General of the USSR, Comrade Rudenko.

'To the Attorney General of the BSSR.

To the President of the Supreme Court, Comrade Gorkin.

'From a believer of the evangelical-baptist confession, Ivan Feodoro-
h Sloboda, resident of the village Dubravy, district Verkhnedvinsk,
ritory Vitebsk, BSSR.

'An open letter.

'I turn to you, the rulers of the land, and ask you to take an interest
my affairs. Five years ago I was like all other residents of my village
o did not know God. When I became a believing person, disdain
l persecution struck me at once. Stones flew through the windows
our house, people forced their way into the room and in so doing
e the doors off their hinges, cut the electrical current, and later —
lowing a court order — took away the children, Galya and Shura,
m me. You have already been told all this in another letter.

'The children have gone through a great deal. Who could describe
ir suffering? They fled home twice from the children's home (Dyet-
m), but search parties were organized to recapture them, and they
k them back.

'All this oppression was led by Chairman Bykov of the collective
m, Secretary Soltan of the Party Organization of the collective,
xander Kurash, and other village activists.

'When they saw that our complaints against them did not lead to
ventive measures, they took action against my wife, Nadezhda Stepa-

novna, mother of five children, who was sentenced to four years
prison on 16 October 1968. They took her to court for proclaimii
Jesus Christ here in this dark, backward place which had never receive
the light of Christ. My brother, Vikenti Sloboda, and her brothe
Piotr Kurash, were also sentenced with her.

"I was left behind with the three children: Kolya, 10; Lyussia,
and Pavlik, 5. I exerted every effort to replace their mother for the
Their home was loving and warm. Mother Ustinya and my brothe
wife, Galina, helped me to look after them. But the militant atheis
the absolute rulers of the village, would not yet be satisfied. Th
watched us sharply and forbade all my relatives to visit one anoth
But even that was not enough for them. On January 16 of this ye;
with the help of other officials, they assembled a false indictment
the basis of which the court has taken away our remaining childre
My 10-year-old son, Kolya, was present at the legal proceedings.
was taken into another room where he was interrogated by the jud
and the state prosecutor. When they returned from the interrogatic
the judge said: 'It was enough for us that he said, "There is a God!
After this the youngster was not allowed to stay in the court room a
longer. I was not allowed any witnesses to present my case. T
witnesses were officials who signed the indictment under the ruse tl
they were simple village residents. They were: Viktor Drosd — ac
ally, however, the director of the school; Paul Styepanovich Andrucl
nok, village resident of Velikoye — actually, however, chairman of t
Chapayev village council; Arseni Filippovich Bykov, village resident
Dubravy — actually, however, chairman of the Zhdanov collective far

---

Photos right, top row: I. S. Savelyev (1907), Baku, 12-1-70 — four years, w
Maria P.; V. A. Orlov (1939) Novosibirsk, 12-2-70—two years, mother: Vera
K. V. Polyakov (1925), Tula, 2-12-71 — two years, wife: Ludmilla; N. T. Pr
sanov (1929), Tambov region, 12-8-70 — one and one half years, wife: Lyubov

Photos right, middle row (the ladies): M. V. Rempel, Chu district, 8-21-70; L
Klassen (1938), Omsk region, 2-71; L. M. Vins (1906), Kiev, 12-1-70 — th
years, daughter-in-law: Nadezhda; E. J. Klassen (1936), Omsk region, 2-
L. S. Losinskaya (1950), Tula, 2-3-71 — one and one half years, mother: A
R.; N. I. Kravchuk (1931), Pavlodar, 12-9-70, father: Ivan St.

Photos right, bottom row: T. F. Shovgan (1922), Odessa, 2-17-71 — wife: '
yana P.; I. I. Dyck (1911), Chu district, 6-24-70 — two years, wife: Susanna
F. D. Penner (1928), Omsk region, 2-71; E. P. Bormann (1932), Chu distr
9-9-70 — one and a half years, wife: Johanna G.; A. A. Viebe (1933), P
lodar, 12-19-70, wife: Nina G.; I. M. Mirozhnichenko (1925), Novosibirsk, 1-
71 — two years.

ВЫЕ УЗНИКИ ЗА ДЕЛО ЕВАНГЕЛИЯ

„ВАМ ДАНО РАДИ ХРИСТА
НЕ ТОЛЬКО ВЕРОВАТЬ В НЕГО,
НО И СТРАДАТЬ ЗА НЕГО"

...ЬЁВ Л.С. 1907г. 1/ХП-70г. осужден к 4 г.лагерей, Баку-19 1-2 Подпрониая 79. Жена-Мария Павловна.
...В.А. 1938г. 2/ХП-70г. осужден к 2 г.лагерей,Новосибирск-2 Павловая 95б. Мать-Вера Антоновна.
...ОВ Н.В. 1925г. 12/П-71г. осужден к 2 г.лагерей, Тула Промышленный проезд 10 кв.1. Жена-Кылица.
...АКОВ Н.Т. 1929г. 8/ХП-70г. осужден к 1Р.Зм.лагерей,Тамбовская обл.
...мкий ?-он с.Фрунзе п/о Агласово. Жена-Любовь В.
...А.Г. 1930г. 21/П-70г. осужден к ЗГ. стр.режима, Киргизская ССР ст. Ивановка ул. Московская тон 16. Жена Иринна Геккарловна.

...М.В. КЛАССЕН Л.И. ВИНС А.И. КЛАССЕН Е.И. ЛОЗИНСКИЙ Л.С. КРАВЧУК И.И.
...г. осужде- 1938г.-арестована 1906г. 1/ХП-70г. 1938г. арестована 1950г. 3/П-71г. 1931г.-арестован
...лагерей, в феврале 1971г. осуждена к ЗР.ла- в феврале 1971г. осужден к 1 г. ла- 19/ХП-70г.
...ам ССР Омская обл. Моска- герей УССР,г.Киев Омская обл. Моска- герей.Тула ул.Бол- Город Павлодар
...-Лешка ленский р-он 114,ул.Совенко ленский р-он дина 147-б кв.1. ул. Совхозная 74.
...120. село Миролюбовка. 11-б.Невестка- село Миролюбовка. Мать-Анна Романов. Отец-Иван Степано-
... Винс Надежда И. вич.

... T.X. ...ИК И.И. ...ПЕНКОВ А.С. ...АН ... ...ЗНК А.А. ...ИРОКОНСКИЙ А.А.
...стиан 1811г. 24/ХП-70г. 1938г.-арестован 1932г. 6/Х-70г. 1911г. арестован 1971г. 1932г. 14/Т-70г.
...Олесса-60 осужден к ЗР.ла- в феврале 1971г. осужден к ?.г. ...Ташкент-4, ул. ...осужден к ?г.лаге-
...л.Волошня герей,Киргиз. ССР, Омская область ...Киргиз р-он, ...Тановская 23. рей,...содержится
...Гена- Чуйский р-он,с. Москаленский р-он ...Чираевская ул. ...Отец-Иван Г. по...оерихонка
...етровка. ...Ивановка,пер.Фридма- село Миролюбовка. ...дом ?30. Том 71-8 кв.11.
... Тула ул. Хво-
... рудная Ховорка.

БЮЛЛЕТЕНЬ №1 1971г.
СОВЕТ РОДСТВЕННИКОВ УЗНИКОВ ЕХБ В СССР

Evangelical Christians, Baptists, and Mennonites who were arrested in 1970.
With these pictures (from left to right and top to bottom) are given in
sequence on page 146; name (year of birth), residence, date of arrest —
length of sentence, and name of relatives.

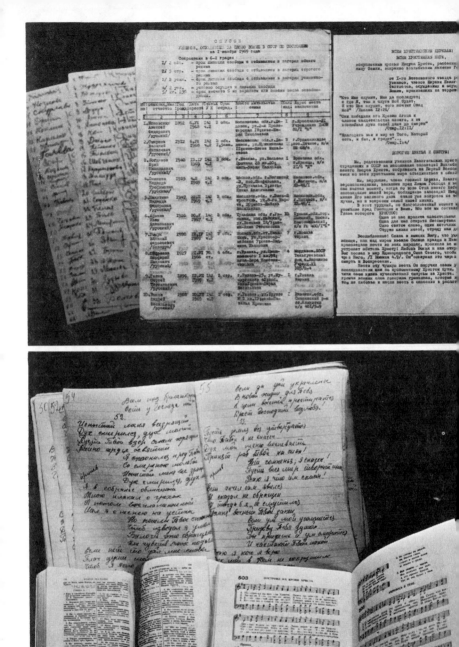

iktor Ignatyevich Soltan, resident of the Zhdanov collective — actu-
y, however, the secretary of the Party Organization; Eduard Dubro,
sident of the village Dubravy, is on his part the director of the club.

"They stated that my children were trained in the religious spirit.
y children are well-nourished and cleanly dressed. The children were
ken away on February 13 of this year under the following circum-
ances. My son Kolya was told in school: 'Go home!' But he did not
ant to get on his overclothes. So the director, Drosd, dismissed all the
ildren. When Kolya got dressed and left the school building, the
rector grabbed his arms and stuck him in a police car which had been
ding behind the school. He was not even allowed to say good-by to
s father. Meanwhile, an ambulance from the Ozvei hospital came to
e house. These people got out of the car and entered the house:
e sheriff of the court at Verkhnedvinsk, the school director Drosd, a
cal policeman from Ozvei (Polevechko), two voluntary auxiliary
olice (Alexander Kurash and Vassili Kuntenko) from Dubravy, the
erkhnedvinsk district superintendent (Sinyavski), and a nurse from
e Ozvei hospital. The sentence was read aloud to the poor children
d they were ordered to get dressed. They began to cry desperately.
hey were seized forcibly and put in the car. I was ordered to go
ong. They took us in this way to Verkhnedvinsk where I was let off.
ut they — my weeping, my unhappy, my lonely little children — were
iven further. According to the accounts of the older children, they
ere taken first to the city of Novopolotsk in the Vitebsk region to the
ildren's home for preschool children. They took Pavlik by the hand
ere and led him up the stairs. He looked back steadily at his brother
d little sister and cried desperately and bitterly. It was night. The
vo others, Kolya and Lyussia, were driven by strange people to the
ty Ostrovno, to children's home No. 28. They arrived there at mid-
ight. The children wept. The next day their father found the chil-
ren in the city of Ostrovno; both cried bitterly over the fact that

---

hoto left above: Original pages of the letter, "To all Christians of the World,"
' 1969, with signatures and an original page of the list of imprisoned ones of
November 1969.

hoto left below: The lack of spiritual literature is unimaginable. In the picture
a hand-copied hymnbook from the Soviet Union. Next to it is a New Testament
d a hymnbook, both produced in a printing establishment of the persecuted
hristians working at an unknown location in the Soviet Union. The books are
ry thick since only the kind of paper which can be bought in stores for letters
n be used for paper.

Pavlik was missing. The oldest child showed his father where they ha been driven, and the father found his little one.

"Where can I get the words to express the grief of my children and the torment of my sorrow! They were taken away and like sma flowers they are plump and fresh among the other children. Wl should I tell of my sorrow? The Most High alone knows my path. I gives me the strength to endure the unbearable burden of my childrer sorrow. Who has any human feeling? Can it be that your hearts c not wince? The party organizer, Soltan, together with Bykov ar Kuvalek, came from house to house with police dogs on a leash.

"I am left at home alone; in the empty house one hears the voic of neither my children nor my wife. This thought comforts me, the Christ said: 'They have persecuted me and will also persecute you Oh, you persecutors of the living God, come to your senses, hold bac repent of your course, for the tears of orphans are a heavy burden. Th Lord gathers these tears in the cup of His long-suffering and patienc You have taken away my wife, you have taken away my five childre1 but the Lord has not left us. Whether I live or die I will belong t the Lord.

"Give my children back and let my wife return home — but let tl will of the Lord happen in everything!

" 'Unless a grain of wheat falls into the earth and dies, it remair alone; but if it dies, it bears much fruit' (John 12:24).

"4 March 1970. Sloboda."

COMMUNION WITH THOSE WHO SUFFER

THE OPPRESSED CHURCH OF Jesus does not need our pity. It is often very close to God. An extraordinarily secure faith often is given to it because Jesus' promises are to the weak.

But the church of Jesus throughout the whole world ought to be sharing the martyrs' victorious strength in the faith. The suffering church does not desire to come to terms with the world and its questions — it desires to overcome the world. "It waits for new heavens and a new earth in which righteousness dwells" (2 Peter 3:13).

No Christian, therefore, should write off the martyrs and their difficult suffering. If this is done, the fruit of their suffering will also be lost, their brave hope, and their freedom from the domineering events of the day. "Remember those who are in prison, as though in prison with them!" (Heb. 13:3). Our unity with the suffering church must be close. All that happens to it is an example for us. In reality, it is our own following of Jesus which should be tested by its example.

Are we joined to the suffering church as members of the one body of Christ in such a way that we feel it when a fellow-Christian cracks who has suffered much? God speaks to His entire congregation. There can be only one body.

The more one is involved today with the suffering church, the less one is able to hear the words of the strong, powerful, modern church. This is our temptation: we desire victory, visible effects, success, and fruit for the congregation. Of course we want all this not for ourselves but for God, but we are not prepared to become poor in order to attain this goal, to die for it. Yet that is still the fundamental principle of the kingdom of God: The grain of wheat must die before it can bear fruit (John 12:24).

Persecution should make the church sober; God is stripping away our false power; He is taking all our false glory; we stand there we and helpless.

That is the fruit of the suffering church.

For when the congregation of martyrs is poverty-stricken, it expe ences victory, and it is no disgrace to bring to light the weakness of t martyrs. Where individual personality has become very small, faith c take hold of the great promises of Jesus.

But the martyr-church is under attack. Whoever is associated wi it will be frightened about the things he hears. They are not words faith, for the loneliness and forsakenness of the congregation ca become so great that hatred and bitterness will reign. It is consequent of great importance that Christians everywhere in the world suppc the martyrs with their love, their prayers, their hope. They should n be alone! Their loneliness should not be allowed to grow without lim

The night of suffering with Jesus is darker than most people realiz During the night of His Passion Jesus told His disciples that the dev himself wanted to test them then. The only power able to withstar such an onslaught was His intercession: "I have prayed for you th your faith may not fail" (Luke 22:32).

The most difficult attack upon the suffering church is still its isol tion. These people are isolated from those who could strengthen the in the faith. And many try to persuade the suffering congregation th it has long since been scorned and betrayed by its brothers in the fait That is also a great source of suffering.

The suffering of Christians in the East is consequently a dire concern of ours. Paul once said to the Colossians: "I complete wh is lacking in Christ's afflictions for the sake of his body, that is, tl church" (Col. 1:24).

Paul meant that every generation of the church of Jesus in the wor needs its share of suffering to retain its grasp of reality. This sufferin however, is distributed in many different ways. It could be that tl suffering would lie on only a few and affect only them. In that ca there would be just a few who bore all the suffering, who "completec it for the others. But how can the suffering of a few serve for tl maturing of the whole body of Christ?

A Russian proverb says: "By pressing the olives you get oil, and c gives off light!" And Präses Humburg, the leader of the Confessir Church in the Rhineland, said during Germany's Third Reich: "Whe the minister goes to the mill, the congregation gets the oil."

Thus, suffering has a broad influence even on those who do not themselves suffer but who are bound with the suffering ones in the brotherhood of faith.

One product of the suffering undergone by the church in the East should be that the church in the world returns again as the body of Jesus to the fullness of its power and the essentials of its ministry.

A suffering church has a clear vision. It knows the most important thing and separates the less important matters from it. When in the middle ages the citizens of the imperial city Ulm were forced to decide concerning the Reformation, this was a critical decision which the citizenry could not pass over lightly. The little city desired to set itself against emperor and empire and to put its life, its wealth, and its freedom on the line. The two questions put to the citizens of Ulm at the voting bore a classic form: "Would you rather have the emperor's grace and God's displeasure? Or God's grace and the emperor's displeasure?"

The citizens of Ulm voted by an overwhelming majority for the grace of God. In so doing they knew full well that the emperor's displeasure would now fall upon them with full force. But the grace of God was their assurance.

Great sacrifices are required in martyrdom. Here a family is destroyed, there essential preparation for a career is relinquished. The physical body can be so weakened by the hardships of a long term in prison that it can never again be restored.

But in reality martyrdom that is authentic never brings God a sacrifice. Martyrs are like people who collect pearls and who for the sake of the one great pearl will give up everything else. And the pearl for the suffering church is the grace of God and the royal majesty of Jesus Christ. When Christianity as a whole participates in this — through the bond of empathy — it will itself be rich in its inner life.

The knowledge of the path of suffering taken by the church of Jesus must occupy an important place in the lives of believers.

In 1932 the YMCA's governmental observer in Germany, Erich Stange, wrote something which at that time could not yet be understood to its depth: "To do youth work today means to prepare youth for suffering."

Why are such sentiments heard so seldom today when those who are reformulating concepts of youth work set their goals for evangelical youth? Have we really become superficial in this area? Or do we believe that we can help young people in other ways?

A year after Stange wrote this remark, the only choice for evangelical youth in the battle against the grasp of the Nazi state was hypocritical submission or suffering.

The hard words of Blumhardt deserve much thought: "At present we teach children the song: 'Since I am Jesus' little sheep . . . He leads me to good pastures.' I say: No, since you are Jesus' little sheep, you therefore have wool. And you must let yourself be sheared. Sheep are not kept for the meadow's sake but for the wool! We should oppose all those mottoes and songs which merely flatter the hearts of our children from earliest youth so that they no longer think that they have to give up their skin for the loving God."

In martyrdom witnesses to Jesus often enough are completely crushed. Nothing pious is left over, there are no more holy masks. Dietrich Bonhoeffer expressed this with great clarity before his execution:

"Who am I? They often say of me
that I leave my cell
composed and calm and firm,
like a squire coming out of his castle . . .
Am I really the way that others think I am?
Or am I only what I know about myself? —
ill at ease, longing, sick, like a bird in a cage,
struggling for life's breath, as if someone were choking my throat,
hungering for colors, for flowers, for the voices of birds,
thirsting for good words, for human companionship,
quaking in wrath at caprice and the pettiest wrongs
. . . tired and too empty to pray, to think, to create,
faint and ready to take leave of it all?
Who am I? Lonely questioning mocks me.
Whoever I am, You know me, I am yours, O God!"

It is the hand of Jesus which sustains those who are oppressed. With this certainty Archbishop Benjamin could cry in 1919 in front of the firing squad: "Farewell, you dead ones, I go to the living!" This is the martyr's testimony in the death of his individual life.

If suffering in the body of Jesus distresses us, what should we think about our own sloth, as when we retreat from lost ground when the world turns its hate on the congregation of Jesus? We must be wide awake. Does God have to bring even harsher preparation for His church in the West, basking in its security? Must He prepare the oven of distress? For the church to be awake means nothing other than to grow firmly in the bond of faith with Jesus Christ, the crucified and risen one. But so many Christians who face no opposition have become negligent in this task.

God is never concerned that His church merely squeak through. He wants His congregation to proclaim His Gospel. And this cannot be done except with the firmness of a witness who does not value his own life.

If only Jesus' kingdom be built!

Everything else may fall away, yes, must fall away. Jesus remains alone. Nothing else.

"Pray for Me": A Circular to all Churches of ECBs.

"Worthy churches! Dear brothers and sisters in Christ!

"I, Lyubov Vassilevna Rumachik, mother of six children, turn to you with the request that you would undergird me with your prayers before the Lord. For on 11 December 1970, I was summoned to the Administrative Commission by an order of the City Council. . . .

"The representative of the president of the City Council, Comrade Ivan Ilyich Solchov, read aloud in the presence of the five-member Commission from an indictment which had been gathered together in March, 1970. That which was read was invented and fabricated. In it I was accused of urging openly in a meeting of believers that they not submit to the government.

"On the strength of this, they decided to take my children away from me and stick a criminal charge on me because my children and I attended the worship service together. I am to be judged as an 'idler and a parasite'. . . .

"With fists banging on the table and in wild rage they hollered at me and told me once more that for my attendance at the worship service of believers my children would be taken from me. The Commission will also convict me and ship me out so that I can serve a sentence in common with my husband.

"My husband, Piotr Vassilevich Rumachik, has been sentenced for the third time as a servant of the church and as a member of the Council of Churches of ECBs. He is now in a prison camp.

"On 20 December 1970, the police again came to the believers' meeting. Two members of the Administrative Commission were also there. In the presence of the believers they screamed at me and threatened again to take my children away. They also threatened to lock me up.

"Dear brothers and sisters. Support from God through your prayers and your petitions to the authorities is very precious for me as a wife of an imprisoned one and mother of six school-aged children. Perhaps the menace and terror against my family can be lessened by that. . . .

"My children also turn to you with child-like requests, dear fathers and mothers, not to be silent in the face of this terror and to do what you can so that the dreaded event does not come to pass.

"As a fellow-member of the church, standing in great suffering, we will, dear friends, bear affliction and sorrow as it is given to true Christians. And when one member suffers, the whole body also suffers with him. . . .

"In the hope of brotherly sharing in my distress with love, motherly disquiet, and concern . . . Your sister in the Lord, Lyubov Vassilevna Rumachik, Moscow district (Oblasti), Dedovsk city, 13a Bolchinaya Street, Apartment 51. 9 January 1971."

A Letter From the Soviet Union to All Christians of the World

" 'If any one serves me, he must follow me; and where I am, there shall my servant be also . . . the Father will honor him' (John 12:26).

" 'And they have conquered him by the blood of the Lamb and by the word of their testimony, for they loved not their lives even unto death' (Rev. 12:11).

" 'Grace to you and peace from him who is and who was and who is to come' (Rev. 1:4).

"To all Christian churches; to all Christians of the world, who, saved by the blood of Jesus Christ, are scattered over the entire globe and who sincerely love the appearing of the Lord —

"From the First General Conference of the Relatives of the Imprisoned, members of the church of Evangelical Christians and Baptists in the USSR who have already been sentenced or who are yet to be sentenced for the sake of the Word of God.

"Beloved brothers and sisters!

"We, the relatives of Imprisoned ECBs who suffer in the USSR for following the commands of our beloved Lord Jesus Christ, are gathered for our First General Conference, and we turn to all Christians of the world with the request that we unite in common prayer before the Lord.

"We believers, members of the persecuted church of the evangelical Baptist confession, declare before the face of the Lord and before you all that according to the will of our heavenly Father, the time has come when a more extensive confession of our faith, full adherence to the commands of Christ, and the fulfilling of His great work has become for us not only a question of our well-being but also a question of our self-preservation.

"In this difficult, but blessed moment, we testify to our trust in God and in you. For we all form one body whose head is Christ!

One blood has flowed for all our salvation,
one immortal love stands open to us all;
one holy word, one fountain of living water, refreshes us all!

Joyful Tidings for Russia

"Beloved! Praise God in the highest! Two thousand years have passed since the sun of truth arose over the world, and the Gospel of salvation has been preached to almost all peoples and has penetrated to many hearts where Christ has found lodging. The love of God has been revealed in this, that He sent His only begotten Son into the world that we might have life in Him (1 John 4:9). This He accomplished through His suffering, His death, and His resurrection.

"Then He commissioned His disciples to proclaim this wonderful news. They and their followers took the way which Jesus had prescribed for them, and many of them gave up their lives for Christ with a martyr's death. The blood of the martyrs spoke more loudly to sinners than words were ever able, and these were kindled by the same love and were emboldened to carry on the tidings of the crucified Jesus.

"We thank God that His messengers preached the pure teaching of His Word to our people 100 years ago.

"The evangelization of our country has its own history. It is expressed in our national Christian hymn:

'The sea of life rages fearfully,
Strong waves distress the boat.
In terrors of death, in despair of suffering,
God, O my God, I call upon you.
Have mercy upon me, deliver, pardon me.
I have had to battle fearfully from the first days of life.
I do not possess the strength to struggle any more.
Have mercy, O God, I call upon you . . .

"The evangelical Baptist church arose under such conditions in Russia, but at every moment it has been 'like the dawn, fair as the moon, bright as the sun, terrible as an army with banners' (Song of Sol. 6:10).

Martyrdom Bears Fruit

"The church's servants in those days were driven by the Holy Spirit. Selfless, with upright hearts surrendered to the Lord, they fulfilled their service to the Lord, And the church, in chains, in exile and persecution, in prison and privations of many kinds, proved in daily life to be true unto death.

"Although the Christians were persecuted outwardly, God, who saw their inner purity, could not withhold His blessings from them.

"In order not to make groundless accusations, it is enough for us to rely on an official historical document by that statesman of our country, Bonch-Bruyevich: 'The Russian czars did not spare the schismatics and sectarians. They tortured, tormented, and trampled them, had them executed or imprisoned them in prisons and forts. They were martyred and their blood was not spared. And this has been their lot even to our day when the laws and customs have become more mild. Although sectarians and schismatics are no longer executed before the eyes of the people, they are now judged, arrested, and evacuated, put in prisons, dungeons, and houses of detention, and tormented in disciplinary battalions. Not infrequently they are beaten to death' (Journal, *Rassvet* [1904]). 'In 1875 the law code of the Russian state contained 755 different ordinances for the persecution of sectarians and Old Catholics.' (From the *Publications of the Academy of Science of the USSR* [1961], p. 545.)

"The first Russian brothers evangelized by following the bloody footsteps of first-century Christians. They testified of their fidelity to the Lord by the good fight of faith, by their suffering and their martyrdom. To them belonged brothers Pavlov, Ryaboshapka, Ratushnyi, and many other witnesses to Christ. The church grew. By the end of the twentieth year of this century there were between 500,000 and 600,000 believers. The earth, saturated with the blood of the martyrs, bore fruit, and the spirit of repentance moved in rich measure among the people.

Calm and New Storms

"Time passed. After a short period of freedom sent by the Lord, persecutions and suffering began anew. The basis for this was the unlawful decree appearing in April, 1929. According to the January, 1918, constitution of the country and the ordinance on church and state, it was forbidden to promulgate any decrees whatsoever which contradicted it. Disregarding this, the government at that time — it was the period of the personality cult, namely in 1929 — issued a decree whereby believers, in total contradiction to the constitution, were forced to stop following the commands of Christ or be stripped of their freedom. In the 1930s the chairman of the Confederation of Russian Baptists, Nikolai Vassilevich Odintsov, died an excruciating death in the cold taiga far in the North. In exile and in camps, in cold snow and thick forests, these brothers died unknown deaths: A. S. Ananyin, G. I. Shipkov, P. J. Vins, P. V. Ivanov-Klyshnikov, A. P. Kostyukov, P. J. Datsko, V. Sinitsyn, F. Sapozhnikov, A. Velavin, Pachivalov, N. W. Assiyev, and many other servants of the church. Thousands of witnesses to Jesus Christ were thrown into prisons where they succumbed in mass numbers. A mere few returned. Only in eternity will the secret of their unknown graves be revealed.

"That is the path of those who in Russia proclaim peace and redemption through Christ. The apostle Paul wrote to Timothy: "Be always ready to suffer for the Gospel!" The 1940s and 1950s passed with similar suffering.

A SPLIT IN THE COMMUNION

"We must call special attention to the fact that in the life of our brotherhood in recent years the moment came to take freely the narrow, thorny path of persecution and suffering in loyalty to the Gospel — or to choose the broad way of personal well-being but also compromise with the world. To our great distress, the leadership of our brotherhood (The All-Union Council of Evangelical Christians and Baptists = AUCECB) chose the second way. Resigned to thorough compromise, they sacrificed the truth of the Gospel and abandoned the principles in the command of our Savior: 'Go into all the world and preach the gospel to the whole creation' (Mark 16:15). They forbade youth to attend church and did not permit children to take part in the worship services. In spiritual questions they did not fulfill, and still do not fulfill to this day, the commands of Christ, but rather align themselves with outward regulations while, in so doing, they destroy the inward life of the church. These measures led to a situation in which the condition of the Laodicean church prevails.

"Many believers who saw this obvious destruction of the work of God were tormented in their souls and sought a way out. In 1961 God in His love awoke the church. Many awoke from spiritual sleep and entered the path of true service for the Lord. This kindled a new storm of general persecution, by the leadership of the AUCECB as well as by the government. The sincere children of God were driven out of the congregations of the official church. They were forced to hold their worship services in private homes, in forests, and under the open sky, while the older church which had adopted the broad road of compromise gathered peacefully in their churches. A persecution broke out upon those who had chosen the narrow way of Christ.

"The persecuted church turned at this juncture to the government with a formal request for permission to hold a fraternal conference, something which had not occurred for 76 years. An organization committee was established (now the Council of Churches of ECBs) which was to plead the request for permisison to hold a conference before the government and to take in hand the preparations for the conference. In place of permission for holding the conference, all of the members of the Council of Churches were arrested and put in prison. Arrests, the dispersal of meetings, beatings of believers, and house searches were poured out in a broad wave over the land.

"In 1963 the direction of the conference was taken over by the AUCECB which had joined with the worldly powers to justify the destruction of God's work and to undertake the conference under governmental regulations.

EXAMPLES OF MARTYRDOM

"We cannot give an exact number of believers who in the years 1929-1961 died by the tens of thousands in imprisonment and exile But the cup of the tears and the sufferings of martyrs for the Gospel of the tears of children, the tears of wives, mothers, and fathers is filled to the brim. The Lord holds them in His hand. Since 1961 more than 500 brethren, chiefly servants of the church, i.e., elders and ministers have been arrested and put in prison. Among them are also some of our young sisters who, pure of heart, are cast into prisons and camps — into an abyss of the sin and unchastity of fallen women. 'Thou hast gathered my tears and noted them in thy book' (Ps. 56:8).

"In many cities and villages — as for example Odessa, Chelyabinsk Frunze, Brest, Gomel, Kiev, and others — our meeting houses have been seized and homes in which meetings were held have been confiscated. With the goal of liquidating the congregations, prayer houses have been destroyed in a few cities — as for example Vladivostok Barnaul, etc.

"Meetings for worship are dispersed violently by the authorities, in many places by soundly thrashing the believers, as was the case for example in Krivoi-Rog, Saporoshye, Chelyabinsk, Sverdlovsk, Vladivostok, and other cities and villages. In Kiev hounds have twice been released during police raids.

"Many police raids among the believers have resulted in arrests for two weeks during which the bread winner of a family not only loses his wages but also has to take the responsibility for his maintenance in jail. This money is garnished from wages or pensions. Their families are forced to lead a hunger-filled existence without resources.

FINES

"The penalties are determined by law. They have reached hundreds of thousands of rubles in these years. Among these are included fines for families with many children and for pensioners, which have reached a colossal total, unmercifully, so that many are not able to pay them to the end of their lives. And these are levied for merely participating in prayer meetings or because one has put his apartment at the disposal of the group for this purpose. As an example, let us consider the congregation in the city of Nizhniy Tagil, district Sverdlovsk. It has 23 believing members and has been beset by fines totalling 4,956 rubles, of which 3,242 rubles already have been collected. To pay these fines the people's property is taken and sold at auctions for a pittance; and pensions are dug into. Of the 23 believers, 13 are pensioners. The four elderly ladies living in the house of an old prisoner, A. J. Sholl, relatives of this believer, and all pensioners between 60 and 80 years of age, have been fined 1,100 rubles.

LITERATURE IS CONFISCATED

"Even in our extraordinary poverty of, and need for, spiritual books — Bibles, gospels, hymnals, and other spiritual literature — uninterrupted confiscations are carried out by constant searches in the homes of believers, in the meeting houses, etc. The use of force often accompanies these efforts. Thus, the wife of brother Sergei Prokofyevich Kravets (village Lovachevo, district Volodarko, Kiev region) had her hands wrenched and her face beaten bloody by the leader of the search party when the hymnbook, *Guzli*, was confiscated. This hymnbook was precious to her as a gift from her dead father. She had guarded it for forty years. It was taken away.

"Confiscated Bibles are not returned. Recently the Bibles have been sentenced to be burned as for example at the Riazan court during the trial of brother S. T. Golev.

Children Are Taken Away

"Our children find themselves in a difficult situation. They are subjected to interrogation by the state's attorneys and the police with questions concerning their Christian training, and are forced violently to testify at the trials of their parents. The confession of their Christian faith in the Lord and their firmness before cruel judges is enough to move one to tears. The Son of God who suffered for our redemption prophesied of even these days when He said: 'Truly, I say to you that he who does not receive the kingdom of God like a child will not enter into it.' There are children who are taken away from their parents by the People's Courts because of their Christian upbringing and are, accordingly, separated from their fathers and mothers. We cannot pass over the fate of the children Shura and Galya in silence. These were taken from their parents, Ivan and Nadezhda Sloboda, out of the village Dubravy (district Verkhnedvinsk, region Vitebsk) because of their Christian upbringing and put into a children's home. Their mother also has been sentenced to a four-year term for the Christian education of her children and the proclamation of the Gospel in her home village. The father remains behind with the three small children [but see p. 149]. The children Shura and Galya have turned to all believers with the request that they pray for them and share thereby their difficult portion which is certainly more than a child's lot. We do not want to forget them!

"In accordance with a resolution of the court they have taken away this family's radio and those of other families for 'tuning in to religious broadcasts.' A commentary on this is superfluous. It should be clear to everyone why Christians are sentenced in the USSR.

Hardships in the Camps

"The lot of prisoners in the camps and prisons is difficult. For praying in front of their sleeping quarters and for witnessing to Jesus they are deprived of nourishment and are not permitted to see their relatives. Letters from their relatives mentioning religious matters are not permitted, and their own letters are not mailed. They do not have the right to possess or to read a Bible. They are subjected to all possible reprisals and interrogations with the suggestion that they could obtain a conditional freedom at the price of renouncing their faith. At this present moment we have sick relatives among the prisoners whose situation is so bad that they are on the brink of death.

"The following believers have died agonizingly during interrogations in the camps and prisons: Khmara from the city of Kulunda, Lanbin from Novosibirsk, Kucherenko from Nikolayev, and others. They have gone the way of suffering and have been true to God until death. Of them one can say with the words of the song:

'Many saints have already crossed over to those shores;
The most blessed time nears when we will also be there.'

"That is a short review of the path which we have walked to now. 'Remember all the way which the LORD your God has led you . . .' (Deut. 8:2).

WHERE DO WE STAND?

"But by His grace we have not disappeared. We are placed in very difficult circumstances today. As in the days of Joshua we are again asked the question: should we be true to God or should we deny Him? When our loved ones return from serving their sentences, they are spied upon from their first days home. They are challenged to give up their religious activity and threatened with imprisonment if they do not. The servants of the church, who by election and the laying on of hands are called to a spiritual ministry, are forced to accept work with the government and to give up their ministry in the congregations. If they do not comply, they are threatened with arrest and imprisonment as indolents. On the other hand, they are also refused employment. All the members of the Council of Churches of ECBs who are not in prison have been menaced in this way. This is a direct violation of the laws regarding the separation of church and state on the part of the authorities. The servants of the congregation are faced with the critical question whether they will remain true to God and go again to jail or abandon God. This is the reality.

NO RESISTANCE

"We declare to you all that there is not the slightest resistance to, or disobedience of, the state in the revival movement in our land. Our petitions of the last eight years, presented by the thousands in writing and through representative delegates (as for instance, 17 May 1966, when 400 believers were beaten in front of the Central Committee building of the Communist Party of the Soviet Union and thrown into prison), acknowledge expressly over and over the high calling of state authority. In response we receive a persecution that is even stronger and more terrible.

"In the last months of this year [1969] yet another twenty-one believers, mainly servants of the church, have been arrested and sentenced. Their number grows daily. New investigations are hastily thrown together in many cities and villages. On the 10th of September of this year in Riazan, elder Sergei Terentyevich Golev, a 74-year-old servant of the church only recently released from prison, who had already spent nineteen years in prison for his faith, was sentenced once again to three years in a prison camp with strict regulations. This sick man, who could hardly stand on his feet, was led into the court held up by the arms. To maintain him in prison is immeasurably difficult. In the city of Odessa young believers were sentenced to five years in a prison camp and five more years in exile. One of them, Yevgeni Rodoslav, is 19 years old.

"At this moment we have again 170 prisoners and 700 orphaned wives and children.

The Way of Following Jesus Truly

"The believing ECBs are systematically slandered in the press and on radio in such a way that through cunning falsehoods they are linked with the most disgraceful criminals and immoral people. Thus in the newspaper *Izvestia* an article appeared under the title, 'The Agitators,' in which the author tried to shift the blame for the present situation, which is of his own making, to believers. The author is the chairman of the Council for Religious Affairs in the Council of Ministers of the USSR. The article contains not even a kernel of truth concerning the true sufferings of believers in the USSR. The vexed tone employed in this major newspaper was picked up by the rest of the press in order to incite the public against believers. 'Blessed are you when men revile you and persecute you and utter all kinds of evil against you . . . on my account' (Matt. 5:11). We comfort ourselves with this. We believe in the Word of God and the speedy return of Christ to the earth to take His purchased congregation to Himself. We, therefore, rejoice in the midst of sorrow and inevitable tears with unspeakable joy, but we cannot make our service for the Lord dependent upon outward circumstances, for 'we must obey God rather than men' (Acts 5:29).

"We receive all of the ever-greater persecution and suffering from the hands of our dear heavenly Father. They cannot separate us from the love of God which is in Christ Jesus, for: 'Who shall separate us from the love of Christ? Shall tribulation, or distress, or persecution, or famine, or nakedness, or peril, or sword? As it is written: "For the sake we are being killed all the day long; we are regarded as sheep to be slaughtered." No, in all these things we are more than conquerors through him who loved us' (Rom. 8:35-37). As once before in circus arenas God ordained the blood-spattered martyrs for Christ to be a spectacle for the world, angels, and men, so has God ordained us (1 Cor. 4:9). We are sentenced as in the days of Esther; all of us, one after another, are given over to prisons, the terrible camps, and exile.

"We have checked the investigatory material carefully, the interrogations of witnesses in court, and the sentences — we declare before the whole world that our relatives suffer for their belief in God! Here are some proofs: it is constantly proposed, both to those not in prison as well as those in the camps and prisons, that believers will be left alone if they abandon God; Bibles are taken away from prisoners; Christian literature is confiscated everywhere; and there are other demonstrations of this.

It Is Time to Awake

"Dear children of God, Christians all over the world who love the Lord! In our persecutions we recognize the soon coming of the Lord and the fulfillment of the Word of God. The time has come for us to awaken, to ready our lamps, and to let them be filled by the rich outpouring of the Holy Spirit as we petition the Father for this outpouring in common prayer.

"The question stands before us all in fiery letters today: are we ready to meet the Bridegroom of our soul? Is He dearer to us than the things of the earth? Does He hold the first place in our hearts? His footsteps can be heard, He is drawing near!

"Beloved children of God! Our purpose in writing to you is to express the sincere request that you might share zealously in asking almighty God to look down upon the threats of our persecutors and bestow upon His servants the strength to proclaim His Word courageously (Acts 4:29).

"We believe firmly in Almighty God and in our prayer together (Matt. 18:19, 20). Our desire every day, with which we turn to all who sincerely love the appearing of the Lord and who are true to Him, is that they join with us in prayer:

(1) for all who suffer for the sake of Jesus' name,
(2) for all persecuted churches,
(3) for a spiritual awakening in our land,
(4) for all of us to be prepared to meet the Lord.

"And thus we desire to gather with prayer and fasting around our crucified and risen Lord.

" 'The grace and peace of our Lord Jesus Christ be with you all!'

" 'Even so, come, Lord Jesus!' (Rev. 22:20).

"Your brothers and sisters in Christ Jesus, the relatives of prisoners, members of the church of Evangelical Christians and Baptists, who are sentenced for the sake of the Word of God.

"November, 1969. Signed on behalf of the conference: [62 signatures]."

From Letters

". . . We are as yet still not molested when we gather inconspicuously to hear the Word preached. How thankful we are for that in consideration of all that is happening around us. We have also been sent the joy of seeing how lively our young people are in spite of all the hostility. Last Sunday over sixty young souls were gathered in my house. They sang, glorified, and praised the Lord from child-like hearts to the accompaniment of music. There are even more young people with us than this, for this group of sixty did not even include them all. We see that with all of the evil intentions of the enemy the ways of our great God are wonderful, yes, 'My counsel shall stand, and I will accomplish all my purpose' (Isa. 46:10). Yet we must remain dependent upon Him in all things which are to be said in our prayers. Pray for us. The evil of the adversary is great. . . ."

". . . It has already been three months since I have again been allowed to be free with my family. The three-year school of my heavenly Father [imprisonment] has ended. Yet I must still learn much from Him who said: 'Learn from me; for I am gentle and lowly in heart, and you will find rest for your souls' (Matt. 11:29). The grace of God will carry us even in the days to come if it should be His will to allow us to pass through still further trials (2 Tim. 3:12). The earnest prayers of many people rise to Him. He has wonderfully helped and wonderfully sustained and preserved us in every need. To him be praise and thanks for this! The desire of our heart is that He be glorified wherever He may lead us further. Once again many hearty thanks to all beloved brothers and sisters who by prayer and active love have shared in our oppression. The Lord will recompense them. May He richly bless all of you. . . ."

". . . I send a hearty greeting to you, dear brothers and sisters, deeply moved and with my heart full of thanks for the labor of love which you have again displayed so helpfully to my dear family for the four years of my imprisonment. Once again I have been instructed by a new gift sent to them, and for this I thank you from my whole heart and praise and glorify my dear Lord and wonderful Preserver. When in times of quiet I am reminded of all the goodness and faithfulness which He has shown us, I again must ask the question: 'Lord, are we worthy of all your goodness and faithful concern? Yet by taking thankfully all His good gifts from His hand, we honor Him. We must truthfully say that we have lacked nothing during these years that I have been absent from my family, and as a matter of fact, the daily needs of my family were often met more richly during that time than when I myself was still at home providing for them. By sharing with active love in our circumstances and conditions you have caused many prayers to be said to His glory from hearts filled with thanks. . . ."

". . . May His perfect will alone be before our eyes at all times; it can only be to our good and our effectiveness when we are in accord with this will (Mark 10:29, 30). The enemy's intentions are not unknown to us, but he must see what God does for His children by moving hearts in the far distance to help us. Although we have not yet seen each other face to face, we are yet joined in love as the bond of perfection. And the basis for it all is the sacrificial death of His beloved Son on the cross of Calvary, where His precious blood of atonement flowed and purchased us for God. 'Now there are to be sure many members, but the body is one' (1 Cor. 12:20). . . ."

BIOGRAPHICAL NOTES

Alexander I, Russian Czar (1801-1825).

Alexander II, Russian Czar (1855-1881).

Johann Christoph Blumhardt (1805-1880), a German Pietist minister who directed an extensive international missions work from his home center of Bad Boll, Germany.

Dietrich Bonhoeffer (1906-1945), a German Lutheran pastor active in the Hitler resistance movement in World War II for essentially Christian reasons; he was executed for this activity by agents of the Third Reich.

Chekists, members of the Soviet secret police in the early years of the USSR (ca. 1920) who exercised life or death power over most of society.

Convention for Human Rights, a document including a "Universal Declaration of Human Rights" drawn up by the United Nations Commisison on Human Rights and ratified 10 December 1948, which guarantees certain basic rights to all people.

Ludwig Andreas Feuerbach (1804-1872), a German author of such works as The Essence of Christianity, who believed that Christianity was a projection of man's own finest and highest instincts into God.

August Hermann Francke (1663-1727), is known with P. J. Spener as the motivating spirit behind German Pietism.

Johannes Gossner (1773-1858), a Roman Catholic convert to Lutheranism who was active in the German awakening of the 1810s and active as a pastor in Petersburg from 1820 to 1824.

Aloysius Henhöfer (1789-1862), a Roman Catholic convert to Lutheranism who was active in the resurgent German missions effort, who combatted German rationalism, and who suffered abuse and scorn in this effort.

Jan Hus (1369-1415), the Czech reformer executed at the Council of Constance for criticism of the morality of Roman Catholic clergy and the correctness of Roman Catholic doctrine.

Lenin (Vladimir Ilyich Ulyanov) (1870-1924), the first great leader of Russian Communism who was the leader of the Bolshevik party and the first chairman of the Soviet of People's Commissars.

Marx, Karl Heinrich (1818-1883), author in 1848 of the *Communist Manifesto*, who saw religion in general, and Christianity in particular, as a narcotic used by the middle and upper classes to keep the working class in its state of oppression.

Helmut James Count von Moltke (1907-1945), an important German landowner and official who came to participate in the anti-Hitler movement at least in great part for specifically Christian reasons and who was executed by the Third Reich.

Nicholas I, Russian Czar (1825-1855).

Nicholas II, Russian Czar (1894-1917).

Peter the Great, Russian Czar from 1682 to 1725. From 1682 to 1689 he shared the throne with Ivan V.

Pietism, a movement dating from 1675 in Germany when Philip Spener published his *Pia Desideria* which stressed the devotional, practical side of Christian life and practice as opposed to arid theological and philosophical speculation.

F. D. E. Schleiermacher (1768-1834), a German theologian who based Christianity on the feelings, particularly that of one's absolute dependence upon God.

Nikolas Ludwig Count von Zinzendorf (1700-1760), the founder of the Herrnhuter Brotherhood and influential member of the Moravians who opposed barren rationalism and Protestant orthodoxy in favor of a heart-religion tied to Jesus as creator, redeemer, and sustainer of the world.

GAZETEER

1. Aral-See = Aral Sea
2. Asowsches See = Sea of Azov
3. Astrachan = Astrakhan
4. Biisk = Biysk
5. Blagoweschtschensk = Blagoveshchensk
6. Brjansk = Briansk
7. Buchara = Bukhara
8. Charkov = Kharkov
9. Dnjepr R. = Dnieper R.
10. Dubrawo = Dubravo
11. Duschanbe = Dushanbe
12. Estland = Estonia
13. Frunse = Frunze
14. Gelbes-Meer = Yellow Sea
15. Gorki = Gorky
16. Innere Mongolei = Inner Mongolia
17. Jaroslawl = Yaroslavl
18. Jenissei R. = Yenisei R.
19. Joschkar = Yoshkar
20. Kara-See = Kara Sea
21. Kasachstan = Kazakhastan
22. Kaspi-See = Caspian Sea
23. Kaukasus = Caucasus
24. Kemerowa = Kemerovo
25. Kiew = Kiev
26. Kirgisistan = Kirghiz SSR
27. Kirow-Ola = Kirov-Ola
28. Kisel = Kizel

29. Komi ASSR = Komi ASSR
30. Lettland = Latvia
31. Lgow = L'gov
32. Litauen = Lithuania
33. Mongolei = Mongolia
34. Moskau = Moscow
35. Nordsibirische Tiefebene = North Siberian Plain
36. Norwegen = Norway
37. Nowosibirsk = Novosibirsk
38. Ochotsk-Meer = Sea of Okhotsk
39. Ordshonikidse = Ordzhonikidze
40. Orscha = Orsha
41. Pjatigorsk = Piatigorsk
42. Polen = Poland
43. Rjasan = Riazan
44. Rostow = Rostov
45. Schachty = Shakhty
46. Schwarzes-Meer = Black Sea
47. Schweden = Sweden
48. Sibirisches Bergland = Siberian Upland
49. Swerdlowsk = Sverdlovsk
50. Taschkent = Tashkent
51. Tscheljabinsk = Chelyabinsk
52. Türkei = Turkey
53. U.d.S.S.R. = USSR
54. Ukraine = Ukranian SSR
55. Ural Gebirge = Ural Mountains
56. Usbekistan = Uzbekistan
57. Weiss-Russland = White Russia
58. Weisses-Meer = White Sea
59. West-Sibirisches Tiefland = West Siberian Plain
60. Wladiwostok = Vladivostok
61. Wolga R. = Volga R.
62. Wolgograd (Stalingrad) = Volgograd (Stalingrad)
63. Workuta = Vorkuta
64. Zelinograd = Tselinograd

* Marks the known places of imprisonment for Christians 1968-1971.

CHRONOLOGY

11 January 1813	Founding of the St. Petersburg Bible Society which was dissolved after twelve years. Since then it has not been reestablished.
1820-1824	Johannes Gossner is pastor in Petersburg.
1825	Czar Alexander I is replaced by the totalitarian Nicholas I.
1855	Liberalization at the beginning of Alexander II's reign.
1856-1858	The awakening in the German colonies in Odessa. In the wake of this Ukranian congregations of "hourlies" arise.
20 August 1867	The first Baptist baptism, in the Caucasians near Tiflis (the beginning of the Baptist movement).
1874	The awakening preaching of Lord Radstock in Petersburg.
1884	The conference of South Russian "hourlies" and the Petersburg evangelicals broken up by persecution.
1888	An increased battle against the "hourlies."
16 April 1905	Toleration proclamation, the "hourlies" achieve partial freedom of belief.
1905-1907	The First Russian Revolution.
1917	The October Revolution.

3 January 1918	Lenin's decree on separation of church and state.
1917-1928	Limited freedom for non-Orthodox denominations.
8 April 1929	The law concerning religious meetings. The start of the persecution of evangelical congregations.
1934-1938	The high point of the Stalinist terrors.
1942	Relaxation of Christian persecution.
27 October 1944	Union of Evangelical Christians and Baptists into the confederation called the All-Union Council.
1945	Inclusion of the Pentecostals in the All-Union Council.
1959-1964	Church persecution under Khrushchev. Many congregations are dissolved.
May, 1961	The initiative for the calling of an evangelical Congress. The start of organizational schism.
25 February 1962	The Initiative Group forms an organizing committee. The beginning of the arrests.
1963	Inclusion of the Mennonites in the All-Union Council.
1964	Foundation of "Council of the Relatives of the Imprisoned."
1964	The fall of Khrushchev; breathing space in the battle against the churches.
September, 1965	Transformation of the organizing committee of independent Baptists to the "Council of Churches of Evangelical Christians and Baptists."
1965-1966	Misisonary activity of the independent Baptists.
16, 17 May 1966	Demonstration of the 500 in Moscow.
1966	Beginning of the second phase of persecution of the independent Baptists.

APPENDIX

New Lists of imprisoned evangelical Christians and Baptists: An extrac
from "A List of Prisoners who have been sentenced for the sake o
God's Word in the USSR."

Seven lists of imprisoned ECBs had reached the West by the middl
of 1972. In all about 600 prisoners are counted. The list of 15 Octobe
1970 included 49 new names.

Explanation of the tables which follow:

Column 1   indicates the number under which the imprisoned persor
was entered in the original list by consecutive numbering

Column 2   gives the family name, the first name, and the first initia
of the paternal name. The transcription of the Cyrillic
letters is given so that the reader approximates the Russiar
pronunciation; "o" is always pronounced as in "open" anc
"kh" as in German "ich."

Column 3   lists the year of birth.

Column 4   names the date of arrest.

Column 5   gives the sentence in years: a = sentence in a camp with
normal regulations; b = strict regulations; c = furthei
heightened regulations; d = conditional sentence; I =
detention pending investigation; E = exile.

       In almost every case the sentences were assigned for
"violation of the laws for the separation of church and
state and school from church."

Column 6   names the residence of the relatives of the imprisoned. In
the original lists columns 6 and 8 usually gave the complete address; here we give only the residence or place in
which the trial was held: district (D), region (R), or
Republic. Transcription conforms to the Diercke Atlas.

Under the place names are the names of wives (W),
mothers (M), or husbands (H).

Column 7   gives the number of dependents incapable of working who
are supported by the imprisoned one.

Column 8   names the place of imprisonment (see the explanation
under column 6).

Forty-nine Additions of 15 October 1970

90	Bavin Ivan I.	1930	10-17-69	4/a	Piatigorsk W. Nina A.	7	Okhansk R. Perm
138	Belyayev Yevgeni Y.	1916	3-13-70	2/a	Gomel W. unbeliever	2	Mogilev
132	Beloussov Vladimir M.	1923	12-31-69	3/b	Gomel W. Irina I.	4	Ivatsevichi R. Brest
23	Bytin Vladimir V.	1951	12- -69	1/a	Netyinka R. Briansk W. Lyubov K.	1	Klintsy R. Briansk
133	Khivuk Artem A.	1904	-69	5/a	Rogosno R. Brest W. Yekaterina I.	2	Volkovysk
92	Khorev Michail	1931	12-18-29	3/b	Kishinev W.Vera	4	Kishinev (prison)
115	Demina Vera M.	1939	8-22-69	3/a	Smiyev R. Kharkov		
30	Durmanova Rosa N.	1944	7-16-70	1½/a	Gorky H. unbeliever	2	Gorky
18	Elfimov Alexander A.	1938	9-23-70	I	Rostov/Don W. Lidia A.	3	Rostov (prison)
142	Gavrilovich Sofia V.	1931		I	Lamuty R. Vitebsk	2	
40	Golyashov Alexander Y.	1911	8-19-70	I	Omsk W. Yuliya (without work)	1	Omsk (prison)
141	Karpovich Ivan S.	1925	6-17-70	5/a	Berezino R. Minsk W. Yelizaveta		
41	Kasyanova Klavd'a	1929	5-14-69	2/a	Omsk M. Avgusta V. (without work)	—	Chelyabinsk

89	Kostenko Grigori N.	1935	10-31-69	3/a	Piatigorsk W. Alexandra A.	1	D. Verkhnekams R. Kirov
69	Kostyuchenko Grigori	1934	3-30-70	3/b	Mogilevsk Krasnodar W. Lyubov F.	7	Krasnodar
21	Kruchinin Nikolai N.	1943	12-10-69	3/a	Dedovsk R. Moscow W. Lyudmilla V.	2	Yurgamysh R. Kurgansk
32	Kulikova Tatyana I.	1947	7-27-70	¾	Novosselki R. Gorky M. Alexandra	3	Gorky
129	Lasuta Nikolai N.	1919	3-18-69	5/a	Borodichy R. Grodno W. Nina I.	3	Volkovysk
24	Mitin Ivan S.	1933	12- -69	3/a	Briansk W. Maria A.	1	Klintsy R. Briansk
81	Moissenyenko Styepan M.	1925	1-14-70	3/a	Pavlodar M. Maria St.	3	Pavlodar
68	Nikolenko Vassili P.	1921	4-13-70	4/a	Kurganinsk Krasnodar W. Nadezhda G.	9	R. Sverdlovsk
87	Ossipov Alexander G.	1924	4-13-70	2/a 1/b	Piatigorsk	—	Arkhangelsk
88	Ossipov Georgi T. (ill with TB)	1898	10-17-69	4/b	Piatigorsk W. Pelagea K.	1	Rakpass Komi ASSR
135	Petrenko Ivan I.	1932	3-18-70	2/a	Gomel W. Valentina A.	6	Bobruisk R. Mogilev
144	Puyonon Feodor	1937	11-29-67	3/a	Omsk	—	Omsk
39	Poyunov Ivan A.	1924	7-16-70	5/a	Omsk W. Maria (without work)	10	Omsk
143	Rishi Martin K.			I	Berezino?		
17	Rogostin Alexander St.	1912	7-23-70	1½	Rostov/Don W. Maria S.	—	Shakhty R. Rostov
117	Rotar Grigori F.	1929	7- 8-70	3/a	Khorinsk R. Voroshilovgrad W. Xenia V.	8	

30	Rudenko Ivan N.	1921	1-14-70	2/a	Pavlodar W. Anna F.	5 Pavlodar
20	Rumachik Piotr	1931	1-16-70	3/b	Dedovsk R. Moscow W. Lyubov V.	7 Tavda R. Sverdlovsk
27	Runov Ivan O.	1899	7-20-70	3/a	Bor R. Gorky W. Yelizaveta	1 Gorky
28	Runov Pavel I. (son of #27)	1948	7-15-70	1½/a	Bor R. Gorky M. Yelizaveta F.	— Gorky
16	Sayez Ivan F.	1919	4-16-70	4/c 4/E	Belyev R. Khmelnitsky	3
34	Shinkarenko Ivan K.	1923	3-14-70	3/a	Gomel W. Yelizaveta I.	6 Orsha
29	Shishkina Tatyana Y.	1948	7-15-70	1½/a	Gorky M. Rakhil I.	1 Gorky
16	Shostenko Anatoli I.	1933	8-26-70	2/a	Rostov/Don W. Nadezhda	6 Rostov (prison)
15	Shostenko Grigori F.	1912	7- 7-70	I/a	Rostov/Don W. Anastasia (ill)	1 Rostov (prison)
10	Shugalo Nikolai V.	1928	12-18-69	5/a	Borodichy R. Grodno W. Lyubov V.	4 Minsk
14	Zhovmiruk Vassili D.	1894	7- 7-70	2/a	Rostov/Don W. Daria S.	1 Rostov (prison)
35	Sotov Anatoli A.	1947	9-16-67	5/a	Orel W. Nina D.	— Sheltye Vody R. Dnepropetrovsk
11	Soldatova Rakhil	1938	7-23-70	½	Gorky M. Anastasia	1 Gorky
11	Sviridyuk Alina M.	1940	10-21-69	2/a	Ordzhonikidze M. Anna V.	— Yavass Moldavian ASSR
—	Trostinkov Kuzma N.	1910	4-24-68	3/a	Uti R. Gomel	3 Minsk
9	Cheryopka Vassili T.	1902	11-18-69	5/a	Prudok D. Ossinovichy W. Nadezhda A.	1 Minsk

140	Chudakov Roman M.	1919		3/a	Ossinovichy W. Yekaterina A.	3	Orsha
25	Chuchkov Karp St.	1898	12- -69	2/a	Netyinka Briansk W. Yevdokia	1	Klintsy R. Briansk
118	Vins Georgi P.	1928		I	Kiev W. Nadezhda I.	5	
137	Vladyntsev Semen K.	1909	3-19-70	2/a	Gomel (single)	—	Minsk

Fifty-six Additions of 15 September 1971

On 1 January 1971, 163 Christians, who at that time were in prison prison camps, or exile, were known to us by name. In the course the year forty-seven Christians had been added to the list, and thir eight were released after serving their sentences. The lists include on the names that have become known. The actual number of prisone may be a good deal higher. The following new prison terms we known by 15 September 1971.

A14	Artyushchenko Boris T.	1920	8- -70	3/b	Kursk		
A1	Bartoshchuk Michail D.	1925	8-20-70	5/b	Brest W. Maria V.	2	
566	Bondaruk Piotr V.	1949	7- 5-71	3/a	Dubrovka R. Brest W. Yekaterina		
A4	Borman Edgar R.	1932	9- 9-70	1½/a	Ivanovka R. Chuisk W. Johanna G.	10	
B6	Boronyuk Ivan A.	1924	2- 3-71	5/a 5/e	Khmelnitski Ukranian SSR W. Yeva P.	8	
555	Khmelyeva Matwei P.	1937	5- 4-71	5/a	Kropotkin Krasnodar W. Anastasia	1	Ust-Labinsk Krasnodar
553	Khmelyeva Vera V.	1937	5- 4-71	2/d	Kaliningrad		
554	Danilichenko Nikolai G.	1928	4-27-71	5/a	Kropotkin Krasnodar W. Nadezhda Y.	9	Pervomaiskiy

5 Dyck Isaak I.	1911	9-24-70	2/a	Ivanovka R. Chiusk W. Susanna N.	6	
9 Fedyatshin Yakov M.		1-28-71	3/b	Penza	3	
5 Fegalskikh Jakov P.	1926	5-30-71		R. Omsk W. Marinovskaya Sofia S.		
2 Gelis Vladimir A.	1928	2-27-71	2½/a	Kaliningrad W. Tatyana	3	R. Kaliningrad
2 Golub Natalia T.				Kiev		
1 Gorievich Stepan V.	1938	2-27-71	2½/a	Kaliningrad W. Polina	3	Kaliningrad
9 Goryanin Alexandr N.	1914	5-25-71	3/b	Maikop Krasnodar W. Yelizaveta	12	
0 Gorobets Bronislav P.	1931	3-26-71	3/a	Brody R. Lvov W. Galina M.	3	
6 Hamm Abram H.	1930	10-21-70	3/b	Ivanovka R. Chiusk W. Maria G.	10	
3 Yastrebov Vladimir S.	1924	5- 3-71	3/a	Dergachi Kharkov W. Nina P.	9	
4 Kasdorf Helena A.	1924	5-30-71		R. Omsk		
1 Kirilko Nikolai M.	1902	4-24-69	3/a	Trilesy R. Kirov		R. Kherson
2 Klassen David D.	1927	9-27-70	3/b	Karaganda	8	
4 Klassen Ella Y.	1936	2- -71		Mirolyubovka R. Omsk	1	
2 Klassen Lisa I.	1938	2- 3-71		Mirolyubovka R. Omsk	2	
7 Kopenkov Feodor Y.	1909	5- 3-71	3/b	Uti R. Gomel W. Galina A.	7	

562	Kosoresov Alexei T.	1933	4-14-71	5/b	Omsk W. Alexandra T.	9	
B7	Kravchuk Alexei S.	1930		3/c	Krivoi Rog	9	Nikolayev
A18	Kravchuk Nadezhda I.	1931	12-19-70		Pavlodar Father, Ivan S.		
561	Kukssenko Yuri F.	1930	7-21-71		Fergana Uzbek SSR W. Anna F.	10	
571	Linnik Daniil I.	1934		3/b	Zhitomir W. Olga D.	7	
A12	Losinskaya Lyubov	1950	2- 3-71	1½/a	Tula M. Anna P.		
A11	Mirozhni-chenko, Ivan N.	1925	1-18-71	2/a	Novosibirsk	3	
573	Moznitski Nikolai A.	1927	8-24-71	2½/d	Vinnitsa Ukranian SSR W. Leonida A.	7	
569	Mukhin Alexandr S.	1931	8-19-71		Fergana W. Valentina M.	6	
567	Olennikov Feodor Y.	1903	6-29-71		St. Liubertsy R. Moscow W. Nadezhda		
A10	Orlov Valeri A.	1939	12- 2-70	2/a	Novosibirsk M. Vera A.	3	
A20	Penner Franz D.	1928	2- 4-71		Mirolyubovka R. Omsk	11	Omsk
563	Poyunov Feodor A.	1937	4-14-71		Omsk W. Melania D.	6	
A13	Polyakov Konstantin V.	1925	2-12-71	2/a	Tula W. Lyudmila		
A15	Prossanov Nikolai T.	1929	12- 8-70	1½/a	Ryzli R. Tambov W. Lyubov	8	
B68	Rasumouski Yevgeni P.	1933	8-19-71		Fergana Uzbek SSR W. Taissia	6	
A3	Rempel Maria V.		8-21-70	1½/a	Ivanovka R. Chuisk		

Rissovuk Andrei P.	1928	4-20-71	4/a	Malorita VSSR W. Nadezhda	6	
Shepel Aleksei				Shostka R. Sumsk		
Shoshenko Vassili				Sumy Ukranian SSR		
Sossin Viktor				Sumy Ukranian SSR		
Shovgan Terenti F.	1922	2-17-71		Odessa W. Tatyana	7	
Savelyev Stepan I.	1907	12- 1-70	4/a	Baku W. Maria P.		
Savchenko Michail S.	1927		3/c	Krivoi Rog Ukranian SSR	6	R. Voroshilovgrad
Savchenko Nikolai R.	1925	4-14-71	3/b	Omsk W. Lyudmila	7	
Terekhov Yuri M.	1931	4-14-71		Omsk W. Lyubov A.	8	
Tretinkov Kusima N.	1910	4-24-68	3/a	Uti R. Gomel	3	Minsk
Viebe Abram A.	1933	12-10-70		Pavlodar W. Nina G.	7	
Viebe Aron A.	1910	3-11-71	5/b	Pavlodar W. Margarita A.	2	
Vins Lidia M.	1907	12- 1-70	3/a	Kiev Sister, Nadezhda I.		Kharkov
Vinogradsk Daniil M.	1930		3/b	Zhitomir W. Raissa I.	6	
Vladykin Nikolai I.	1925	2-20-71	¾	Tula	2	

The Fifth Letter to U Thant

To the General Secretary of the United Nations, Mr. U Thant.

From the Second All-Union Congress of Relatives of Evangelical Christians and Baptists who for the sake of God's Word are imprisoned in the USSR. The Congress was held on 12, 13 December 1970.

The most honorable U Thant!

The second Congress of the Council of Churches of ECBs in the USSR is very concerned about the disregard for fundamental rights:

(1)   free confession of faith in God;

(2)   the ability to have prayer meetings;

(3)   the distribution of Christian literature to believers, i.e., Bibles and gospels;

(4)   private training of children according to one's own conviction and the laws of the land.

Our believers have not been able to enjoy these rights from 1962 to the present. They are persecuted and punished; 524 have been put in prison; 348 were released after serving their sentences; eight died in prisons.

As of 12 December 1970, 168 are still in prison. The 524 servants of the ECBs were all arrested for certain of the following reasons:

(a)   preaching God's Word,

(b)   open confession of belief in God,

(c)   distributing Christian literature,

(d)   visits and meetings,

(e)   raising children according to their own conscience,

(f)   putting homes at the disposal of prayer meetings,

(g)   refusing to give information in court against church and leaders, and

(h)   refusing any compromise with atheism and the All-Union Council of Evangelical Christians and Baptists which has turned aside from the teaching of Christ.

Many houses have been searched and all Christian literature taken away. Many are now without spiritual food. This is the true lot of the believing ECBs in the USSR.

We turn your attention to the terrible events involving the Sloboda family of the village Dubravy, BSSR.

On 20 April 1965, two children were taken away from the family — Galya and Shura — and taken to a children's home.

On 12 December 1968, the mother of the children was sentenced to four years in a work camp.

Three radios were also confiscated because they listened to foreign religious broadcasts.

On 16 January 1970, the three remaining little children of the Sloboda family were taken away.

We cannot describe the distress of this family.

On 1 December 1970, a 64-year-old lady — L. M. Vins — was also

rrested. Her son, G. P. Vins, had already been sentenced for the
econd time in 1970. His father, P. J. Vins, was arrested in 1939 and
hen died in prison, but 20 years later his wife received the news that
.e had been posthumously exonerated.

We would like to ask you to exert every possible effort to improve
he situation, including:

(1)   the release of the prisoners,
(2)   the return of children to parents,
(3)   an end of the persecution of the Council of Churches of Evan-
elical Christians and Baptists, and
(4)   the return of spiritual literature to believers.

We ask you to publish this letter for public judgment.

This is the fifth letter which we have addressed to you; the earlier
mes were dated 21 January 1967; 5 June 1967; 15 August 1967; and
1 August 1968.

With sincere respect to you,

The Second All-Union Congress of the Relatives of Imprisoned
Evangelical Christians and Baptists. 12 December 1970.

The Thirty-ninth Petition to the Government

To the government of the Soviet Union.

From the Second Congress of the Council of Churches of Evan-
elical Christians and Baptists.

ADMONITION

When in 1969 the First Congress was held, you received reports on
the situation of believers in our land. Yet the persecutions did not
stop, so that one can draw the conclusion that you approve of them.

We recall for you that from 1961 to the present day, 524 people have
been in prisons, of whom 44 were ladies, and of whom 8 died in the
camps.

During the persecution by the militia and the office of the state's
attorney, 2,840 Christian books, musical instruments, letters with Christian content, tape recorders, and wall plaques have been taken away
during house searches.

There have been 791 people held in jail for two weeks because they
had attended meetings.

Meetings were broken up 986 times by force and at such times the
people present were often struck.

There have been 1,380 people interrogated and exposed to threats.

Three hundred and ninety children were also interrogated by th state's attorney and in the schools.

Fines were assessed amounting to 94,300 rubles.

Hundreds of believers were refused access to higher education be cause they have relatives who believe in God.

All this is probably only 50 per cent of what actually happened.

As early as 1960 believers were called all kinds of names in the press radio, and magazines.

All this has happened with your consent, and you have not answered any of our thirty-eight petitions. Today there are still 168 of our believ ers who sit in prisons. You have now directed the persecution against the leaders of the Council of Churches of ECBs so that certain broth ers must flee to fulfill their tasks.

This Congress asks for free permission for:

(1)   Confession of faith. Equal rights for the believers and thei children in matters of employment and education.

(2)   Cessation of persecution.

(3)   Rehabilitation and release of our relatives.

(4)   Return of the children.

(5)   Return of confiscated houses.

(6)   Return of fines and confiscated literature.

The tears of fathers and mothers, of orphans, and the blood of inno cent Christians should remind you of this great injustice — the perse cution of Christians — and make your heart gentle. 13 December 1970

Russia Must Be Able to Hear the Gospel

To Prime Minister Kosygin of the USSR.

To Chairman Podgorny of the Supreme Soviet of the USSR.

To General Secretary Brezhnev of the Communist Party of the USSR.

To Attorney General Rudenko of the USSR.

To Chairman Gorkin of the Supreme Court of the USSR.

To the Chairman of the Committee for State Security.

To Minister Shchelkov of the Ministry for Internal Affairs of the USSR.

To the Editors of Newspapers: *Pravada* (Truth), *Izvestia* (News), *Sovietskaya Rossia* (Soviet Russia), *Komsomolskaya Pravda* (Truth of Communist Youth).

To the Editors of Magazines: *Sovietskoye Gossudarstvo i Pravo*

The Soviet State and the Law), *Nauka i Religia* (Science and Region), *Rabotnitsa* (The Lady Worker).

To the Confederation of Society, Snaniye (Knowledge).

To the Chair of History and Theory, Moscow University.

To the Company, Mysli (Thought), Moscow, Leninsi Prospekt 15.

To the Council of Churches of Evangelical Christians and Baptists.

To all Believers of the Evangelical-Baptist Confession in the USSR.

From the Council of Relatives of Imprisoned Members of the Church of Evangelical Christians and Baptists who have been senenced in the USSR for the sake of the Word of God.

Nahum 1:3: "The Lord is slow to anger and of great might, before which no one is innocent; he is the Lord whose way is in whirlwind nd storm, and the clouds are the dust of his feet."

Psalm 103:6: "The LORD works vindication and justice for all who re oppressed."

EXTRAORDINARY PUBLICATION

The daily sighs and tears of the wronged and the suffering do not top. The earthly world is filled with them. This is the twentieth etter concerning the persecution of believers which we have written ince 1964. Around 500 believers of the ECBs have served or are still erving prison terms. Our last communication to you concerning the uffering of our relatives dates from half a year ago. We have time fter time waited patiently for your hearts to soften toward the believers. But the reply is constant new persecutions and a new throng of orphaned children, deserted wives, mothers, and fathers.

1) *Harassment in the Camps*

We call your attention to the situation of the imprisoned believer Grigori Ivanovich Petrenko, born 1939, residing in the Kirghiz SSR in he city of Frunze, 131 Pensinsh Street. He was sentenced in December, 1966, to five years in a camp with general regulations in the Novosibirsk region.

On 6 January 1969, as he was in the camp 36/I in the village of Kairsha in the Kirghiz SSR in custody, he was called to the superintendent of the colony, Lt. Col. Dronov, who said to him: "The Baptist Petrenko died today, from now on he is not in this region." From that time Petrenko's bond with his relatives was ruptured. After a long time it was possible to obtain information from the Ministry for Internal Affairs concerning his place of residence in the camp named

above. In this camp he was denied the opportunity of visits or (
receiving things sent to him. Because of that he is completely exhauste
and lies in the hospital as one seriously ill, according to the lettei
from his relatives. It is absolutely necessary that you take action a
once so that such things not happen elsewhere to other prisoners wh
believe in God.

(2) Pressure Against the Christian Faith

The believing prisoner from the city of Krivoi Rog, 27 Korolenk
Street, 66-year-old Thedor Ilyich Petrakov, is serving a five-year tern
under strict regulations on account of his belief in God in a camp i
the Dnepropetrovsk district in the village Makartovo. He is an invali
of the second class and is in poor health. He was waylaid in the cam
because of his belief in God. As his illness grew worse, he was denie
the packages of food sent from home. The acting superintendent c
the colony, who is also the Political Instructor, Major Shcheglov, said
"I am a person who does not want to do evil to anyone; reject you
faith, reject God — and eat for your health." The packages of foo
are sent back, even in this time that is difficult for him. His conditio
is worsening. It is absolutely necessary that he be released. Thi
honorable old man, Petrakov, has been slandered in the press as
robber. But his real guilt is indicated clearly by the words quoted from
Major Shcheglov above.

Jesus Christ said: "Blessed are you when men revile you and pei
secute you and utter all kinds of evil against you falsely on my account
(Matt. 5:11).

(3) Hatred and Scorn

In the Kiev district, region Volodarsk, village Lovachevo, the believe
Sergei Prokofyevich Kravets was humiliated. We reproduce his letter:

"To the Attorney General of the USSR Rudenko (and a cop!
to the Council of Churches of ECBs in the USSR).

"Notice! We are calling your attention to the misconduct anc
the illegal act which happened to me at the hands of the loca
militia. On 29 September 1968, the Captain of the militia, Kono
valov, and the Lieutenant, Vasilkovski, appeared in my apartmen
with burning cigarettes in their mouths. The first asked whethe
I had already eaten that noon. I answered: 'No.' Then he dashec
through the apartment. First he grabbed a letter addressed to the
VS ECB, next the Bible, then the hymnal *Guzli*. When I askec

if he had authorization from the procurator for confiscating books and letters, he answered: 'I have the right to turn your house upside down,' and he shouted with a piercing, threatening voice: 'Take all pictures off the wall.' I asked, what kind of suspicion existed. He answered me only with evil, vulgar insults without considering that the children were present. My wife took the hymnal back and said it was a gift from her deceased father which she had preserved for forty years. The two officers began to tear the book away from her and to wrench her hands. They battered her nose, her face was bloodied, and they gained possession of the book. Then Konovalov grabbed me violently by the neck and threw me into the militia car which then drove off. On the way, there was no end to the vile, vulgar insults. It was as if I was not flanked by officers but rather surrounded by wild beasts. Konovalov's fists danced before my eyes and touched my face. Lieutenant Vasilkovski regretted that they had found no one who would burn my house to the ground. The car stopped, and they led me into the militia quarters. Capt. Konovalov cried: "Lie down!' I lay down. He cried again: 'Kiss the floor!' I refused. After a few minutes I was picked up and put in jail. Next day I was taken to the People's Court. This body declined to take my case. Then they released me."

This letter was sent to Attorney General Rudenko. We have the hope that you will return the Bible, the hymnal, and the other religious writings, even though the militia called it forbidden literature. There needs to be no further commentary on that which happened. God sees it.

f) Terror

On 10 April 1969, the following occurred in the city of Kopeisk, in the Chelyabinsk region. During the worship service a group of atheists came in, led by the local official Belousov, and disturbed the worship service. They pulled out a number of empty bottles, put them on the table, and photographed them with the people. The believer L. Ushakova was taken out of this service and brought to the militia where she was interrogated and afterward told: We will sick the hoodlums on you in order to mess you up. On April 11, as the believers came from the worship service at 8:30 P.M., a gang of young people fell upon them, knocked a few of them down, and went on their way. We do not know if that was just an unruly band or a "special group."

(5)   *Heavy Fines*

Fines for attending worship services are multiplying. They a assessed to pensioners who receive a minimal pension, the families prisoners, and families with many children. In this it is recognizab that by your material oppression of believers, you create the conditior of their physical destruction for the sake of their faith. The situatic of believers in the city Nizhniy Tagil in the Sverdlovsk district go beyond all norms of decency. These turned to you with a letter whic we cite here:

"To the Chairman of the Supreme Soviet, Podgorny.

"With copies to: The Chairman of the Ministry for Religio Kurogdov;

The Attorney General of the USSR, Rudenko;

The Committee for Human Rights;

The Council of Relatives of the Imprisoned in the USSR;

The Council of Churches of Evangelical Christians and Ba tists;

All Evangelical Christian and Baptist believers in the USSI

"From the believers among the Evangelical Christians an Baptists of the city Nizhniy Tagil, Sverdlovsk district.

"An open letter.

"Romans 12:12, 13: 'Rejoice in your hope, be patient in tribu lation, be constant in prayer. Contribute to the needs of th saints.'

"We, the believing ECBs of the city Nizhniy Tagil, turn to a who love God. Support us before God with fasts and prayers; w need it, for the persecution has been growing of late in our city We ask God to help us remain true in the faith under all circum stances. In 1966 four of our brothers were sentenced for the faith: A. Y. Sholl (for three years with strenuous regulations I. G. Arbusov (for four years with strenuous regulations), N. Y Skvortsov (for three years with strenuous regulations), B. Y. Prol horov (for three years with normal regulations).

"They are presently in the camp in the Sverdlovsk district. I the house in which Sholl lived with his family, four person between 60 and 80 years of age are staying with his wife. Thes four have been fined a total of 1,100 rubles in 1968 and 1969. Tw hundred and ninety-seven rubles were withheld from their per sions. Their possessions were confiscated and sold for a trifling sum on June 11. The confiscated possessions: 3 sewing machines, 1 washing machine, 2 wardrobes, 2 sofas, 1 table — all that was sold for 205 rubles. The family still has 598 rubles to pay. This sum has now been laid upon the house. The fines have reached such a level that some pensioners can from their pensions discharge barely 20 per cent of that which is laid upon them in the course of certain years. Consequently the property belonging to many of them has been confiscated. Sister A. Kushnir was assessed a fine of 450 rubles. Of this, 130 rubles were withheld from her pension. Her radio was taken from her. Sister P. Tyurikova has to pay a 300-ruble fine. Of this, 180 rubles were withheld from her pension. It is the practice to seize personal possessions to pay for the complete fine if the sum is not paid within five days. The total of all fines which have been laid on the congregation is 4,945 rubles. Of this 3,242 rubles have been paid in the ways described above. 1,703 rubles remain to be paid. Our congregation consists of twenty-three members. All of the fines on believers are levied for carrying out worship services. The total amount is divided among the members as follows:

	Name, Occupation	Fine	Paid	Remaining
1.	P. Tyurikova, housewife	400R.	180R.	220R.
2.	B. Blinova, worker	250R.	250R.	—
3.	D. Pisareva, pensioner	155	155	—
4.	A. Kushnir, pensioner	450	130	320R.
5.	A. Vorobyev, worker	300	300	—
6.	K. Printz, pensioner	550	120	430
7.	F. Printz, pensioner	450	312	138
8.	N. Yeremina, worker	300	150	150
9.	M. Gorbova, pensioner	210	90	120
10.	N. Lump, worker	250	100	150
11.	E. Shcherbina, worker	150	150	—
12.	B. Kilina, worker	250	250	—
13.	N. Porkhacheva, pensioner	75	75	—
14.	N. Posokhova, pensioner	250	200	50
15.	E. Kraeva, worker	200	200	—
16.	E. Kostina, pensioner	160	160	—
17.	T. Yachmeneva, pensioner	200	200	—
18.	D. Danilova, pensioner	50	25	25

	Name, Occupation	Fine	Paid	Remaining
19.	V. Vorobyev, worker	50	50	—
20.	O. Lupp, pensioner	75	55	20
21.	V. Martinova, pensioner	20	20	—
22.	T. Arbusova, housewife	50	—	50
23.	L. Sholl, father	100	70	30
		4,945R.	3,242R.	1,703R.

"All this notwithstanding, do not despise the believers, but pra
for them that God might illuminate them and give them com
pensation. To suffer for Christ is the right of believers and thei
happiness. But the tears flow involuntarily as silent accusers o
those who hate the truth and who persecute the innocent."

(6)   New Persecutions

The persecution and arrests increase in number and severity. Th
persecutions and arrests of believing ECBs are like a devastating hur
ricane. Convictions are taking place in many cities. In September o
this year the following believers from the city of Kislovodsk wer
sentenced to several years of imprisonment: M. A. Ivanov, A. I. Sinitza
A. I. Paleni, V. M. Khrilupov, V. J. Malishkin. In Moscow on Sep
tember 11 of this year V. F. Rishuk and J. Bogdanov were sentencec
to three years in prison. In Karachayevsk, Anna Gudaseyev and Khari
ton Chekhov were seized. Alexander Bichek and Yakov Morosov wer
also under house arrest there. In the city Cherkasske the ECB believe
Adam Dubitzki was seized. In the region Ust-Dzhegutinskaya, D. Shin
ganov is under detention. In the city of Timoshevsk, Tatyana Voro
shilova. In Rostov on September 13 of this year the presbyter D. R
Rogoshin, an old man, was seized again just after he had finishec
serving a sentence. In Kharkov the 19-year-old believer Vladimir Sim
renko was arrested in December of this year. In Prikumsk the believe
D. T. Kusnetsov was sentenced. In Dnepropetrovsk the same happene
to K. J. Smirinski. In Odessa in July of this year the believer S. Misen
ruk was sentenced to four years in prison and five years in exile. O
March 8 of this year the young believers Nadezhda Osokina an
Nadezhda Klipova were arrested, and they are still languishing in priso
in detention pending investigation. In Timoshevsk, V. M. Kusnetsov
V. Chepikov, and V. Droshin are in detention pending investigation
In Riazan on September 10 of this year the following believers wer

sentenced: A. V. Bikov, E. N. Kudreshov, L. I. Belikh, Sergei Terentyevich Golev, the old man of 74 years who has spent 19 years of his life in prisons for his belief in God. They led him, a sick man, who could hardly drag his legs along, into court, leading him by the hand, and sentenced him again to three years in camp with a strict regime. We have sent you a telegram that his sentence under these circumstances is equivalent to homicide. But the court was not suspended and the sentence came to pass. In response to our telegram came a form letter indicating that our petition for revision will be passed on to the state prosecutor of the Riazan region, who is the very individual who arranged to have him sentenced. It is still absolutely necessary to point out that in the new trials and sentencing the exact same charges were made against Bikov, Kudreshov, and Golev for which they had just served prison terms. According to the sentence the Bibles taken from them must be destroyed. There have been still many other actions taken against believers in many other cities of the land, as for example in Briansk, Piatigorsk, Chelyabinsk, and others.

(7) Even the Very Ill Are Taken

The situation of believers in the camps: On the basis of facts which the relatives of the imprisoned have communicated to us, we direct to you again the question of the very poor health of Petr Prokofyevich Popov, 81 years old. He is in the hospital of the camp of the city of Omsk. He has been sentenced to three years of camp with strict regulation. His term began on 21 July 1967. He has undergone two operations in the camps. Dmitri Vasilyevich Minyakov contracted open lung TB while in prison. According to the law he should be released. He has been in the Barnaul hospital since last year. Kornei Korneyevich Kröker fell from the fourth floor during farm labor in May of this year. He has very severe fractures and is in the hospital in the city Kemerovo in the Kemerov district.

N. P. Savchenko is serving his sentence in the camp of the Sverdovsk district, village Novoselevo, and he had been refused, illegally, gifts of food from home. He has a wife and seven children. The imprisoned old man, B. N. Gulyuk, languishes in a camp with severe regulations in the city Shakhty in the Rostov district. He is very weak physically. Because of his belief in God he has been sentenced with strict regulations. He still has a full two years to serve.

It is incredible that all these are imprisoned! We regard your indifference and your continued incitement of the prison camp superintendents to such measures as tantamount to a purposeful physica destruction of the prisoners.

(8) *Freed Ones Are Further Oppressed*

The situation of believers who are returning from imprisonment According to the letters which the believers of Prokopyevsk hav written to you and us, this is the situation of those who have bee freed from prison:

From the first day of their return they must allow themselves to b threatened by the local authorities and constantly watched, that is, b the state security forces and the agents for religious affairs. They a urged to give up their religious practice under threat of an immediat return to prison.

The servants of the church, who are appointed to their posts o spiritual service by vote and the laying on of hands by a congregatio are forced to take public work and to stop their leadership in th church. They are threatened with immediate arrest and sentencing a indolents. It is not necessary to cite all the names. Yet we must nam one case. When the chairman of the Council of Churches of ECB Gennadi Konstantinovich Kryuchkov, preached his first sermon in worship service after his release from prison, he was fined 50 rubles an was threatened with the confiscation of furniture, such as his sofa an bed, if he did not pay. At the same time he was warned that if h preached repeatedly, he would again be arrested and sentenced. A other released members of the Council of Churches have also bee menaced in this way. That is, however, a direct violation of the la of separation between church and state. It is virtually the case that a the released are under home arrest due to all the spying that goes o From the first day of their release you force them to choose: eith remain true to God and go to jail, or deny God. That is the wa things really are.

(9) *Christian Radio Broadcasts Forbidden*

Concerning the confiscation of radio receivers because of the recep tion of religious broadcasts: We give excerpts from a decision in th Vitebsk region of the judicial proceedings, 12 December 1968, und the chairmanship of V. A. Kononov and with associates M. E. Es penko and A. S. Kachalova, Secretary Orlova, the assistance of state attorney M. D. Rizo, and the prosecutor V. H. Koslovski, concerni the defendents N. S. Sloboda, V. F. Sloboda, and P. S. Kurash:

"Besides this, the college of judges considers it absolutely necessary, according to Part I, Article 222 of the Criminal Code BSSR, to apply an additional measure of punishment, the confiscation and transference to government property of the radios belonging to the accused N. S. Sloboda and V. F. Sloboda ('Latvia' brand) and to the accused P. S. Kurash ('Belarus' brand), from which they received broadcasts of a religious nature from foreign parts on the pretext of tuning in to religious instruction and practicing their religious cult. Conformable with the indictment of 3 March 1969, the sheriff of the People's Court of the Verkhnedvinsk region, M. I. Ganos, accomplished the confiscation of the radio on the basis of the above-standing judgment."

There are no words for this perfect illegality. Of course if the believers do not have the right to receive religious broadcasts, then it is not surprising that you decide against them from the first for their testimony to the faith.

FREEDOM FOR THE GOSPEL

Taking all this together, we must time after time remind you that God's delay is not really delay, but patience. Yet He is powerful and great and does not let things go with impunity. Do not fill the cup of this patience too full. Repent while there is still time and give the so grievously tested Russian people the opportunity to hear the message of salvation in full measure. Give everyone the legal right to believe, as his conscience and conviction command him on the basis of the Word of God. You have increased the threats against us. But can one see the suffering of his nearest ones and stand by indifferently? When we see it taken all together, we cannot be silent. May God the Lord enlighten you and make it clear to you. We have this comfort: Psalm 103:6: "The LORD works vindication and justice for all who are oppressed."

September, 1969. On behalf of the Council of Relatives of Imprisoned Evangelical Christians and Baptists who are sentenced for the Word of God in the USSR. Signed: Vins, Vilchinskaya, Koslova.

The Extent of the Persecution

[1970: The persecution continues. During the efforts by Western and Eastern governments to relax tensions the Relatives' Council of Imprisoned ECBs reported in a letter to the government and the Supreme Court and at the same time "to all believers" of the ECBs.]

To the Prime Minister of the USSR, Comrade A. N. Kosygin.

To the Chairman of the Supreme Coviet of the USSR, Comrade N. V. Podgorny.

To the Attorney General of the USSR, Comrade Rudenko.

To the Chairman of the Supreme Soviet of the USSR, Comrade Gorkin.

Copies: To the various public Agencies of the USSR.

To the Council of Churches of Evangelical Christians and Baptists.

To all Evangelical Christian and Baptist Believers.

From the Council of Relatives of Imprisoned Evangelical Christians and Baptists who have been sentenced for the sake of the Word of God.

"Blessed is he who considers the poor!" (Ps. 41:1).

"When justice is done, it is a joy to the righteous, but dismay to evildoers" (Prov. 21:15).

URGENT INFORMATION

In November, 1969, the First All-Union Conference of the Council gave you in its explanation a thorough analysis of the condition of believing ECBs in the land, in which you have the honor of being the leaders, and it set out the conclusions of the analysis in seven points.

It seems that this should have been enough to direct your full attention to the suffering of Christians who live in the territory of the USSR. The proofs and conclusions which the congress exhibited are really conclusive. Yet in the three months that have passed since then, certain things have happened in various places in the land which can simply not be passed over in silence — namely, new, strengthened persecutions and repressions. In fulfilling the commission of the congress to which we have referred we are informing you of the following facts:

I. New Arrests and Trials

On 18 December 1969, in Kishinev, the elder of the church, Michail Ivanovich Khorev, was sentenced again. In January, 1969, he had returned home from the places of isolation after completing a different sentence. His arrest took place under extraordinary circumstances: on December 12 his wife was taken to the hospital in serious condition; on the next day he was arrested. Three children remain at home, the oldest is seven years old. Michail Ivanovich has six percent vision in one eye; with the other eye he can see nothing.

A moving letter from Mrs. Khorev was sent to you. You have, however, given it no answer.

In Dedovsk, a city in the Moscow region, a member of the Council of Churches of ECBs, Peter Vassilyevich Rumachik, was again arrested. He had only recently returned home from prison.

This family has already suffered three times from reprisals. The first time the whole family was exiled in the far north, the second time prison camp, and then prison again. The family's father, Vassili Smirnov, is already in prison; Rumachik is his son-in-law; the second son-in-law, Nikolai Kruchinin, is also in prison. The whole family of thirteen people is without its provider. All this has happened because they obey the commands of the Word of God. In the city of Gomel on 31 December 1969, the believer Vladimir Michailovich Beloussov was arrested.

On 21 January 1970, in Kiev, the Secretary of the Council of Churches of ECBs, Georgi Petrovich Vins, was sentenced to a year of forced labor by the People's Court of the Podolish region. The court gave him this sentence without acknowledging the explanation of the church concerning his spiritual office to which the congregation at Kiev had elected him.

A series of judicial proceedings have recently been carried out throughout White Russia. Contrary to the law, the following were sentenced in the village Borodichy: Nikolai Vassilyevich Shulago and Nikolai Nikolaevich Lasuta; both received five years according to Article 222 of the criminal code of the White Russian SSR.

In the village Rogosno, Brest region, the presbyter Artem Alexandrovich Khivuk was sentenced to five years without restricted regulations. He is an old man, born in 1904, and is ill.

In Ossipovichy, Mogilev region of the BSSR, the Evangelical Christian and Baptist believers, Vassili Cheryopka, born 1902, and Roman Chudakov, born 1919, were sentenced to five and three years, respectively, in a camp without restricted measures, according to Article 222 of the BSSR criminal code.

In Briansk, V. V. Verbitin was sentenced, and Mrs. Senyushchonkova, a mother of six children, received one year of restrictions.

On 10 February 1970, in Pavlodar, the ECB believers, Stepan Moisseyevich Moisseyenko and Ivan Nikolaevich Rudenko, were sentenced.

These have all been sentenced for their confession of faith in Jesus Christ.

II. *Trials Begun*

In a series of places spread throughout the whole country preliminary investigations have been put in motion, as for example in the little village Uti, in the Gomel region of the BSSR, against Fedor Kolenko.

In the village Lobachevo, Kiev region, the preliminary investigations have begun against the presbyter of the church and the believer Kravets. We have already reported to you about this case. In Kravets' case, his house was searched illegally, and the police chief forced him to kiss the floor time after time at this investigation. Against both of these presbyters and Kravets, all requirements for a trial have already been prepared and sentences of three years have been demanded by the state's attorney for each. The accusations, however, have found no confirmation in the judicial processes. Instead of now ceasing the persecution Kravets was sent to further investigations.

III. *Persecutions*

The young believers, Peter Peters, Grigori Kostyuchenko, and many others not named here have been exposed to a persecution which has arrest as its final step. They have been deprived of the right of living at home and thus are forced to wander about in the countryside.

IV. *Brutality at the Dispersing of Meetings*

In many places in the land prayer meetings are periodically dispersed; in many places it is done systematically. The brutality associated with the dispersing of the meeting on January 10 of this year in Krivoi Rog, Saporoshye region of the Ukranian SSR, demands special attention.

On January 4 of this year that church submitted its documents for registration, and the believers considered the onslaught of the police which followed this application as the answer to their proposal for registration. From the petition of the church, which lies before you, it is evident what lawlessness the believing ECBs in the country are subject to. They are like the dust which all walk over with their feet.

After they had thrown old and young believers into a specially ordered bus — it was the middle of winter and the believers were without overcoats — they then opened the upper hatches in the vehicle to make drafts; only when they got to the police station were the charges shown for the first time, and then the people were ordered to go home dressed as they were. Is that not murder? The benches in the house where the gathering had taken place were smashed to pieces and thrown in the yard on the command of Police Lt. Radshenko. That is, a regular pogrom was carried out. We are enclosing a picture of the shattered benches. The young people and the grown children were subjected to a search of their persons during which New Testaments were confiscated. The house was also searched and the Bibles were taken from the homeowner. During the house search some volunteer police helpers stuck a number of the mandarin oranges in their pockets which the homeowners had laid in the cellar for their children; there had been two kilograms of the oranges in all.

At the police station children and young people were put into rank and file. They were then commanded to tune the musical instruments and forced to play and sing while at the same time being photographed. Were not the feelings of believers mocked and scorned there? [Note of the editor: This fact is raised because the official orders for conduct toward believers contain the regulation that "feelings of believers are not to be injured," and this is constantly being repeated, particularly in materials for use in foreign countries.] The upshot of the whole affair was that a few days later the believers were ordered to the city executive committee and fined 50 rubles each, pursuant to the March, 1966, decree. The believers pointed out that applying this decree according to its own wording, at the very most only the homeowner and the organizer of the meeting could be fined. But here, as everywhere, they levied this fine on all participants. The brutality evidenced in the disruption of this meeting is quite typical and not at all a random occurrence.

A police assault of the same kind, under the support of the authorities for Religious Affairs, was carried out on 18 January 1970, in the city of Gomel in the White Russian SSR. The believers were detained until 1 p.m. and entered into official records; then they were taken to the police station. They were released only toward evening. In the same city on 20 June 1969, the homes of eighteen believers were searched simultaneously under the auspices of the state's attorney "in order to confiscate religious literature." In the course of the searches Bibles, New Testaments, wall plaques, and hundreds of writings of other religious literature were confiscated. In Kishinev and other cities the same kind of searches were carried out. In Dedovsk, Piotr Rumachik's apartment was searched nine times, during which even the underwear of his six children was examined. Rumachik is now under arrest.

The believers ask us to explain to you in our petition that they regard such events as pure mockery of the feelings of believing ECBs. They request us to write to all believers to participate in intercession for them.

In the same congregation — in contradiction of all norms of humanity — a member of the church, Vladimir Michailovich Beloussov, was seized on New Year's Eve, 31 December 1969, and he is still in jail. Many believers there, including also children of minor age at school, were summoned to appear by the investigating judge.

We are of the opinion that your intervention could force the local authorities to return promptly the spiritual literature, Bibles, Testaments, and other materials and also arrange to restore the fines which have been paid.

As you were informed by means of a telegram which the believers at Brest sent to you, a surprise attack was perpetrated by the police during the New Year's Eve celebration 1969/1970. The believers were gathered together at 15 Chernyanskaya Street. The homeowner, Luka-zhnik, and his son, were later sentenced to 15 days in jail because they had placed their apartment at their disposal for the New Year's Eve celebration. Besides this, the lady of the house, his wife, had to pay a 50-ruble fine. For the whole family the fine amounted to 150 rubles for this one act. This means that they may not eat anything for two months, but only pay their fines.

Arrest and fines for a New Year's celebration are an unheard of violation of elementary rights of freedom of Soviet citizens. Believers have the right to hope that the fine will be refunded and that such occurrences will not be repeated.

In the city Pavlodar houses have been searched and spiritual literature has been confiscated, including Bibles and New Testaments. The believers have taken the effort to seek justice with your help; their answer was the court action against the two above-named believers: S. M. Moisseyenko and Y. N. Rudenko, who were sentenced to three and two years in a camp.

V. Treatment in the Camps

Many of our relatives who have suffered at the various places of imprisonment and who are suffering now have forfeited their health. Now, however, since the penal measures in the camp were sharpened after November, 1969, the situation of our prisoners has become even more difficult: the period between visits has been extended and the parcels of nourishment cannot be accepted as often as before. In great uneasiness we have been forced to remind you that the health of believers, who undergo prison terms, is subjected to the most difficult trials.

As we have written to you formerly in concern for the Uzlovaya presbyter, we again write on behalf of the sick and the elderly. Postponing their release could have a tragic end and will lay as a heavy burden on your conscience:

(1) Sergei Terentyevich Golev from Riazan, servant of the church and a member of the Council of Churches of ECBs, is spending his twenty-first year in imprisonment for his faithfulness to the truth of the Gospel. He is very ill with diabetes, he has diseased feet, he is 74 years old; if he was taken to court while he was barely still alive, is it right, then, to hold him behind bars as he awaits his death day by day?

(2) Vassili Nikolaevich Gulyuk from the city of Batais, Rostov region, born 1902, is an invalid of the second group. Since October, 1966, he has been serving a five-year sentence in a camp with sharpened measures.

(3) Axel Fedorovich Iskovskich, elder of the church in Dedovsk, Moscow region, is an elderly man, 78 years old; he is very ill. On 8 August 1968, he was sentenced to three years in a camp.

(4) The presbyter of the ECB church in Rostov on the Don, Dimitri Stepanovich Rogoshin, a 70-year-old man who has a heart condition, has languished in a camp with heightened regulations since 13 September 1969.

(5) The presbyter of the church of ECBs from Omsk, Popov, an old man of 83 years, is already in his third year in prison camp hospitals with heightened regulations. His feet have already been operated on twice — he should be released immediately.

(6) Dimitri Vassilyevich Minyakov, 49, from Barnaul, member of the Council of Churches, has contracted open lung TB in the camps, where he has heightened regulations, due to the harsh conditions which were laid directly upon him. He has been in detention since 25 September 1967, and needs to be released from prison very soon.

(7) Vladimir Yefimovich Chepikov from Timochevsk, Krasnodar region, has been in prison since 1969. He has chronic eczema. Residence in the camp is unbearable and a torture for this smitten one.

(8) Vladimir Petrovich Sinchenko is a young man, 19 years old, from Kharkov; he has a very weak constitution and is suffering from a liver complaint. For his activity as a choir director and orchestra leader in the congregation he has been in the camps since 2 September 1969. He was sentenced to three years. He is exploited in his forced labor in a harsh way — in breaking up stones. He receives no hot food

from morning to evening. His young, weak body is not able to meet an adult work quota. To exploit him further at this work is inadmissable since that will damage his health irrevocably and could have a fatal consequence.

VI. *Dying in the Camps*

On 22 November 1969, Ivan Alexeievich Afonin, the presbyter of the ECB church in Uzlovaya, died. His death took place in the camps of the Tula region near the city Donskoi (pos. Komsomolsk p./ya U Yu 400/I "Ch"). He was 44 years old, an invalid of the second class, had a heart disease, and suffered from rheumatism. He was illegally exploited at labor and died also at his work station. We and his relatives wrote to you earnestly about his condition and pointed out the possibly fatal consequences. On the basis of that information we asked you to free him. But these warnings were in vain. You ignored them and delivered up the corpse to his widow and his nine children. Six of the children are still very small. We are forced to take note of the fact that the circumstances which surrounded this death are too questionable to allow his end to be seen as a natural one. The diet which was his by right as a second-class invalid was taken away, and the camp superintendent threatened continually to let him rot in prison. The death of Ivan Alexeievich will rise with an accusing voice before the face of the everlasting God and before all mankind through the tears of the orphans and the sighs of his widow.

May the Lord forgive you for disregarding our warnings which sought to protect the life of an innocent man.

Now, after we have told you of this casualty, we are forced to repeat ourselves in order to remind you with all seriousness and concern that you must immediately release the people who are ill and aged.

VII. *Severity of Sentences*

We remind you that it has been a long time that we have been deeply distressed about the terrible sentences of the trial in Odessa. This judgment sentenced believers to terms of nine and ten years (including exile). We are of the opinion that the agencies of the attorney general and the courts of the land have transgressed in that they have directed Article 227 of the penal code of the RSFSR and the corresponding Articles of the Union Republic against believers of the ECB confession.

It is still necessary to let justice rule. Revise these sentences!

VII. *The situation of Believers in Dubravy, Verkhnedvinsk District, Vitebsk Region, White Russian SSR*

We have described this situation extensively in the earlier reports. The answer of the Attorney General of the White Russian Republic passed over the situation of the believing families in silence, particularly the situation of the prisoner Nadezhda Sloboda, and took no steps to see that the local authorities — Secretary Soltan of the Party Organization and Chairman Bykov of the collective farm — stop terrorizing the family. On February 13 of this year a new act of unprecedented arbitrariness occurred: in the family of Ivan Sloboda and the prisoner Nadezhda, from whom two daughters had been taken away four years ago, they have now taken away the remaining children, aged 10, 7, and 5. We are not able to describe the tears of the children during the separation from their father and from their suffering — human words are too weak to picture what has happened. The cause for all this, responds the State Attorney of the White Russian SSR, is the religious education in the family. We telegraphed you when this happened and now ask you to give much attention to our telegram.

IX. *Interrogations of Children and Reprisals Directed Against Them*

(1) A letter from Christian ladies, mothers in the Baptist churches, has been sent to you, which told of the deep suffering occasioned by various reprisals including interrogation, which are directed at the children of believing parents. There were 1,453 mothers from 43 cities of our land who signed this letter. Disregarding that letter, such interrogations have now begun anew.

In the city of Kishinev school children were subjected to interrogations on religious themes by agents of the state security police and by the state's attorney general. State security police agent Skortsa offered a cigarette to the student, Volodya Burlak, at his interrogation; the same officer gave his brother a blank sheet of paper to sign. Later he wrote on it what he wanted.

The children of believers Dubchak, Chornykh, and Fedorenko were also interrogated. A letter from these parents has been forwarded to you with an extensive description of what happened. Interrogations took place also in Gomel, Pavlograd, Barnaul, and other places.

It must be taken with complete seriousness that a repetition of such events will result in a refusal by the children to attend school and also a refusal by the parents to hand their children over to derision there.

The Christians who live in the territory of the USSR have been presented with this problem again.

(2)   In contradiction to the prohibition of a fundamental law of the land, Lenin's decree concerning the separation of state and church of 23 January 1918, and even against the March order of 1966, the earlier practice of recording religion and membership in a believing family has again been practiced in filling out children's documents. As an example we enclose a photograph of such a comment, issued on 14 June 1969, for the student of the eighth class, Maya Nikolaevna Kobysh, School No. 4 of the city Sholtye Vody, Dnepropetrovsk region.

In this letter we have touched on different aspects of the situation of ECB believers in the USSR and have done so only on the basis of facts and in abbreviated form. All these examples of persecutions, such as house searches, violent dispersal of meetings, public defamation, and others, have as their ultimate aim the arrest of believers. As a consequence of all this, children and families are brought into distress.

We cannot let you forget that God's will directs you and that which you have done. All the believers that you are persecuting are bearers of God's light in the world, His life-creating Word, which will be taken from the earth if the church of Christ is removed. With deep confidence of meeting soon with God the church says: "Even so, come Lord Jesus!" But at the same time the moment will come when every brave soul who rejects Him will shout to the hills and the mountains: "Fall on us and hide us from the face of him who is seated on the throne, and from the wrath of the Lamb; for the great day of their wrath has come, and who can stand before it?" (Rev. 6:16, 17).

We summon you once again to pay closest attention to the events referred to above and to do all that is in your power. "For it is a joy to the righteous when justice is done, but to evil doers it is terror." May God Himself grant you to see matters clearly.

16 March 1970. On behalf of the Council of Relatives of Imprisoned Evangelical Christians and Baptists who suffer in the USSR for the Word of God. Signed: M. Yu. Rytikova, S. E. Petlyukha, M. S. Butkova, S. Ya. Vilchinskaya, L. M. Vins.

For 21 Years Fruitless Petitions for Official Registration

[Soviet propaganda maintains constantly that many congregations are not ready to submit to the laws of the state and let themselves be registered. As proof of the exact opposite, we publish an extract from a petition to the government by believers of the city Yoshkar-Ola of

December 1970. The statements contained in it can be corroborated by the experiences of many other congregations.]

As you know, the ECBs of our land have had for many years to exist outside the law. All complaints and petitions to the various courts and authorities remain unanswered, and that in contradiction to the pertinent laws. Believers are subjected to ever more severe persecutions and repressions.

Our congregation of believing ECBs in the city Yoshkar-Ola was registered until 1949 (from 1942) and held worship services without hindrance. But the local authorities then removed the registration under the pretext that the Christians had no appropriate hall for worship. From then on the congregation was regarded as "unregistered" and they began to persecute the believers.

The believers, however, continued to meet for worship services and at the same time prepared a request for a return of the registered status to the congregation. This unsuccessful request has been pursued now for 21 years.

Dozens of letters and petitions have been addressed to the various jurisdictions with the request for registration. At the same time we requested that every type of persecution cease. Within the last year alone believers have turned to the agencies which are responsible for registration three times with the request to register the congregation of Yoshkar-Ola. Among other agencies to which the congregation appealed, it sent the request for registration to you, honored government. But since all our requests to you are directed back to the authorities about whom we have complained, these therefore persecute us and oppress us with even greater spite.

There is a constitution in our land and all other laws rest upon it: freedom of conscience, the inviolability of residences, the inviolability of personality, the laws on human rights, and the moral code — but these are all transgressed by the authorities.

Obviously these laws do not apply to believers and consequently are not valid for them. For us a different set of standards evidently applies: damage, humiliation, oppression, and persecution. Instead of giving us the legal right to live as citizens of a free land with human laws, we believers are horribly persecuted.

Soldiers and militia have broken into our houses where worship services take place more than thirty times. On more than thirty occasions believers have been fined — a total of 1,055 rubles. And these fines are usually levied on pensioners and families with many children

Under these conditions we are constrained to turn again to you. In response to our last request to you for registration we were forced to suffer outrages from the local authorities which went beyond anything that had previously occurred.

Honor for the Government Even During Persecution

[The following is an extract from "A Proclamation on the Question of Unity" by the Council of independent ECBs of 6 December 1970.

Rumors have spread that we violate the laws of the government This is not true for the following reasons:

(1)　On the basis of the Word of God we recognize that the government is ordained by God and that we are to behave respectfully toward it. The duties of citizens are heeded honorably.

(2)　According to the Word of God church and state are divided from each other.

(3)　The official work of the Council of Churches of ECBs bears an internal, ecclesiastical character. As confirmation of the fact that the Council of Churches of ECBs recognizes the government and does not go around it, we point to the matter of registration; almost all congregations have sent a request to the government with this kind of information:

1. the number of congregational members,
2. the signatures of all leaders (at least 20),
3. the addresses of the places of employment of the committee members,
4. the addresses of residence,
5. the addresses of the places of meeting,
6. the names of all committe members, and
7. the list of the leaders with signatures, etc.

Is there still something illegal that the Council of Churches of ECBs does?

The efforts of the Soviet government are currently directed against the spiritual leadership of the Council of Churches of ECBs. These honorable officers are vilified, dishonorably treated, and then opposed Thus the Council of Churches of ECBs is not a law-breaker but a sacrifice to lawlessness. We hope that all true children of God will stand by us in spite of the persecution until we become one and the Lord reigns in our brotherhood.

MOSCOW REPORT: AGAINST SUCH, NO LAW

David E. Kucharsky*

"Do you see any signs of a religious revival in the Soviet Union?

A tourist guide must tire of answering the same questions, even when the guide works for the Soviet government and considers rote replies a professional asset. This one, a seemingly imperturbable woman approaching middle age had obviously been challenged with similar queries many times before.

"Especially Americans want to know," she said.

We had just been through the complex of cathedrals that dominate the Kremlin. Looking up from Cathedral Square, the sightseer can hardly help wondering the extent to which the Christian heritage of the Soviet peoples might be recoverable. To the amazement of virtually every newcomer, there are many more crosses than red stars rising above the Kremlin walls. Left over from the czars are a cluster of magnificent cathedrals casting their shadow over the great power center of international Communism. Even though the churches are not "active," the best architecture, murals, the frescoes within the seventy-acre walled area called the Kremlin continue to speak of a great Christian culture of the past — and perhaps of a potential for the future.

The guide said, as expected, that she did not sense any religious revival going on among the nearly 250 million inhabitants of the Soviet Union. She went on to concede indirectly the existence of certain signs that are interpreted in the West as indications of a spiritual awakening, but for each she gave an alternative explanation.

"On Sunday," she said, "you can hardly get into the Kremlin cathe-

* Taken from the June 23, 1972 issue of *Christianity Today*. © 1972 and used by permission of *Christianity Today*.

drals because of the large crowds." Oh? "Well, yes, but now icons are very fashionable. It is not a religious feeling that brings the people to the cathedrals. It is a renewed sense of appreciation for ancient art."

As for actual church services, the guide said they attract mostly old people — "you can go and see for yourself."

Then, backing up a little, she suggested that when the younger people do attend they go out of curiosity. Her sixteen-year-old son, for example. "He never prays," as she put it, but he went once just to see what it was like. The "once" turned out to be this past Easter Sunday.

One does not draw sweeping conclusions from a conversation with an Intourist guide. But the little interview conducted as we were leaving the Kremlin did little to disprove reports of revival. The guide was clearly defensive, and one can only wonder why.

Another guide was telling some of the several hundred newsmen covering the summit meetings in Moscow last month that people are going to church "just to hear the singing." Western correspondents in Moscow confirm that there is a revival of religious interest among the people, as do Soviet intellectuals, though they do not agree on what is behind it.

The visiting newsmen saw no overt signs that Christianity is taking on new life under a system dedicated to atheism. No Jesus people here. No crosses worn as lapel pins or necklaces. No Christian coffee houses. No impressive statistics on Bible sales.

The same question asked of the guide was put to the Reverend Ilia Orlov, a preacher and organist at the Moscow Baptist church. Orlov simply quoted the words of Jesus that the gates of hell would not prevail against the Church.

But what happened in Orlov's church on May 28 suggested that a resurgence of religious interest is occurring. On that rainy Sunday morning, more than 1,000 persons including President and Mrs. Richard Nixon filled all available seats for the first service. The church had been full for two hours before the start of the 9 A.M. service. Security men were keeping the crowds at a distance. When the Nixons departed and the security men followed, hundreds of people who had been standing in the streets getting soaked rushed into the church and took whatever standing room was left.

The Nixons' visit to the church may well have been the best thing that ever happened to it. The visit also gave the Christians of the Soviet Union a measure of recognition they had not had since the start of the

Revolution more than fifty years ago. Although the church is the only Protestant congregation in a capital city of some seven million, no head of state had ever worshiped there before. If there is indeed a spiritual spark among the Soviet people, this gesture could have helped to fuel it. Even Tass, the official Soviet news agency, recognized the church visit with a six-paragraph dispatch.

There had been no public announcement that the Nixons would go to the church. Obviously, however, some word had been dropped to the congregation. A few repairs and some painting had been done, and strings of birch and lilac branches were strung along the sides of the balcony. The clergymen who took part in the service had appropriate remarks, carefully prepared.

The President and his wife had taken leave of their summit conference hosts that morning. The visit to the church was the only time during their thirteen-day journey through four countries — Austria, Iran, and Poland, besides the Soviet Union — that either of them stepped out in public without ranking government representatives at their sides. Only an interpreter and the President's top communications man, Herbert Klein, accompanied the Nixons.

It took only a few minutes for the presidential motorcade to transport them to the church from the Kremlin palace where they had been staying. Although not many people were on the sidewalks at that hour, there were more than one would find in an American city at nine o'clock on a dismal Sunday morning. People glanced up somewhat indifferently as the black cars sped by. The Baptist church, originally built for a German congregation some 150 years ago, is located off Pokrovsky Boulevard, a main artery in the Soviet capital (the main Jewish synagogue and the Catholic cathedral in Moscow also are on side streets). The church is housed in an ordinary-looking building painted a mustardy yellow that seems a standard color in parts of the Soviet Union. The building also houses the national offices of the All-Union Council of Evangelical Christians-Baptists, the government-recognized umbrella for virtually all Soviet Protestants.

The President was greeted at the door by the All-Union Council leaders and signed a guest book in the lobby. Mrs. Nixon was given a bunch of red, pink, and white carnations by one of the women of the church. The group proceeded up the center aisle, and the Nixons were seated in the second row. The interpreter beside them translated simultaneously what was said and sung.

The church has a medium-size sanctuary with a high, wood-beamed ceiling supporting three large silver chandeliers. Walls are in a multi-colored pattern of muted shades. At the front of the church is a large window bearing in Russian the words "God Is Love." Besides the lilac and birch branches festooning the balcony sides, there were hydrangea and tulips in front of the ornate wooden pulpit.

Following an opening prayer by the pastor, the Reverend Michael Y. Zhidkov, forty-four, the congregation stood and sang "All Hail the Power of Jesus' Name." Few times in the history of the Church has the singing of a hymn carried more meaning. The rendition deserves to be remembered more than the *Titanic* passengers' "Nearer My God to Thee." The church's sixty-four-pipe organ was out of order, but perhaps that was just as well under the circumstances.

Then came the Scripture reading, Acts 2:1-18, inasmuch as it was Trinity Sunday, and another prayer, followed by a public welcome to the Nixons by the Reverend Alexei M. Bichkov, also forty-four, who last December was named general secretary of the All-Union Council, Bichkov said, "We cordially greet our esteemed guests on the very Sunday when the Christians of our country celebrate the coming down of the Holy Spirit." He went on to note that Soviet Baptists had established good relations with Baptists and other denominations in the United States, and added: "We as Christians support in our prayers all that promotes peace and friendship among nations, establishes social justice, secures national liberty and economic progress in all countries, and we testify 'that God was in Christ reconciling the world to himself.' "

His reference was to Second Corinthians 5:19, and his statement was the only allusion while the Nixons were in the church to the matters that had brought them to Moscow. American and Soviet leaders had signed a number of agreements the week before, including the Anti-Ballistic Missile Treaty. Following Bichkov's statement, the congregation stood in honor of their special American guests. There were few Americans in the church for the service. Some reporters were allowed in, but all photographers were kept outside. Most of the congregation were people in their thirties and forties.

The choir of about eighty voices sang a Russian sacred composition. About two-thirds of them were women, wearing white blouses. The director and the other men wore black suits. The choir sat in the balcony at the rear of the church, cooled by a small electric fan.

An obviously prearranged program provided for a sermon by the

Reverend Ilia Ivanov, who as president of the All-Union Council is the dean of Soviet Baptists. He is a distinguished-looking white-haired man who took as his text the familiar passage from Galatians 5: "But the fruit of the Spirit is love, joy, peace, longsuffering, gentleness, goodness, faith, meekness, temperance: against such there is no law." He did not dwell on the later point, but the symbolism in the context ought not to be overlooked.

Referring literally to the observance of Pentecost, Ivanov said, "This is a special day for Christ's Church." The hearer was left to draw an inference if he wished about the other sense in which the day was special — as the leader of the free world worshiped in a Christian church at the power center of a world movement that regards the Gospel as a myth no longer needed and destined to oblivion. "It was the springtime of Christ's church on earth," he said.

After the sermon the congregation sang "What a Friend We Have in Jesus," and Mr. Nixon joined in. Zhidkov then explained to the congregation that because of the Nixons' tight schedule they would have to leave. He bade them good-bye and said "God bless you" in English. The President and his wife had been in the church for half an hour. The service — the first of three held there each Sunday — would go on for another hour and a half.

There was an exchange of gifts. The Nixons were given a specially made reproduction of a painting of Jesus at the Sea of Galilee and a wall plaque showing a girl holding a flower. The church was presented with a covered crystal bowl and a Parker pen with the President's signature inscribed on it.

The church is one of about 5,000 Protestant congregations recognized in the Soviet Union; total membership of the congregations is officially reported at about 500,000. The Moscow church had about 100 baptisms last year and courts some 5,000 members.

There is reason to be hopeful about the future of evangelical Christianity in the Soviet Union. That there is fresh, relatively young leadership among the Baptists in the persons of Bichkov and Zhidkov (who besides being pastor of the Moscow church is a vice-president of the All-Union Council) is a distinct plus. (Also added to the council membership recently was Jacov Duchonchenko from the Ukraine.) The bear is not going to become tame in the foreseeable future, but fresh, creative minds can deal with him more effectively than battle-weary veterans.

Bichkov was born near Moscow, was converted in 1949, begaı preaching in 1967, and now is a member of the executive committee of the Baptist World Alliance. Zhidkov is a native of Leningraı whose father was a well-known Baptist leader. The son studied at Spuı geon's College in London and at MacMaster University in Hamiltonı Ontario. He speaks English well.

The challenges these Protestant leaders face, few clergymen in thı West would envy. And, understandably, it is not easy to get them tı talk about problems, or to talk about anything substantive for thaı matter. They are aware that both in the free world and in the Sovieı Union there are those who regard them as having "sold out" to thı government, or worse yet, who think that one or more are puppets oı politicians if not KGB informers. These charges do not stand uı against thoughtful scrutiny, because no one in the Soviet Union gainı anything by being publicly associated with a church. The identificatioı is a social liability in many respects. The only reasonable motivatioı for it is authentically spiritual.

The clergy of the "headquarters" church are sometimes thought to bı favored over other Soviet believers because theirs is the showcası church. But anyone who looks into their situation will learn that thı privileges they are supposed to enjoy are a little short of a joke. Theʏ may have some small advantages for being in the capital, but on thı whole they operate on an austerity program that by American standardı is severe.

Nevertheless, allegations against the Soviet Baptist leaders persist anı undoubtedly exact a psychological toll. They must feel the worst wheı the blows are delivered by their own countrymen, and they have had tı suffer for a number of years now from the *initiativniki*, Protestant dissı dents who want churches of their own free from any connection witı the All-Union Council. The government apparently vows to recogniuı no more than one group, so the *initiativniki* operate illegally as aı underground church with some support from the free world. Whilı such tension may seem like a problem for the government, the Comı munist leadership may be taking advantage of it and not conscientiousl seeking a settlement. The Communists know that as long as thı Protestants are fighting among themselves they pose little threat to thı political status quo.

It should be said for the *initiativniki* that some of them unquestionı ably have very sincere motivations. People in the Soviet Union do noı protest for kicks; they do not demonstrate with the easy abandon of left- and right-wing elements in the United States, where the rights of dissenters are protected by law. As the *Economist* recently put it, in the Soviet Union even the mildest expression of dissent is severely penalized, "so that any outburst of real violence there reveals an acute intensity of desperation."

Two incidents in the weeks just before the summit support the theory that there is a growing religious stirring in the Soviet Union that will be hard to suppress. One occurred right in Moscow, at the American Embassy. About fifteen people came all the way from Barnaul, Siberia, some 2,000 miles distant, to air religious grievances. They were described as couples with children. They said that they were not being permitted to worship as they wanted to, and that they were being discriminated against in schools and employment because of their Christian beliefs. According to one report, they said that their church had been burned and that they held the government responsible. Embassy officials allowed them to stay in the building overnight, and Soviet authorities were asked not to take action against them. The group left a statement of grievances before departing.

The other incident was a youth riot that followed a self-immolation in Kaunas, Lithuania. This involved Catholics, and it had perhaps more nationalistic than religious motivation. But as the *Economist* put it, religious and nationalist grievances in the U.S.S.R. are probably closely intertwined: "Numerous protests have been made to the authorities which show that the protesters speak both as Catholics and Lithunians." The magazine offered this thoughtful analysis:

> The Lithuanian, Ukrainian, and other non-Russian dissenters who are starting to raise their heads represent a special danger to Mr. Brezhnev. They have long resented the fig-leaf of Soviet federalism, which totally fails to conceal a tightly centralized state with a strong bias in favor of Russian interests. But they have been too frightened, and perhaps too resigned to permanent subjection, to act. Now the remarkable achievement of the Russian Jews in making their plight known, and giving their masters so much trouble that many thousands have been allowed to emigrate to Israel, has clearly had a profound impact on the non-Russian peoples of the Soviet Union. For a long time it had only been the Tartars and a few Ukrainians who were prepared to stick their necks out. Now more of the discontented nationalities are stirring.

Unfortunately, much of the free world uses "Russia" and "Soviet Union" interchangeably and is unaware of the extent to which the vestiges of an old religious culture are still visible there. Actually Russians now number less than half the Soviet Union's total population, whose other components have been multiplying faster than the Russians have.

Issues of religious freedom were all but lost in the hard news that enveloped the summit meetings, so it was helpful that the President's trip called attention to spiritual priorities and nationality interests in other ways. In Kiev, the beautiful capital city of Ukraine, the Nixons visited one of the oldest churches in the world, the magnificent Saint Sophia Cathedral, as their last public event before leaving Soviet soil. Among the things they saw there was the famous mosaic of the Oranta — the Virgin Mary with her arms held up in prayer. This is one of the restored mosaics in the church that date back to the eleventh century when Yaroslav the Wise built the first parts of the Orthodox cathedral to commemorate a military victory. The Nixons also saw in the cathedral frescoes of Yaroslav's daughters, four of whom married kings in Europe.

"Those Ukrainian daughters must have been very attractive if they all married kings," the President said to the guide. She answered that one son also married a princess.

"So Ukrainian blood must be all over the world," Nixon responded.

"Yes," she said, "Ukrainian blood is all over the world."

"In America there are also Ukrainians," he went on — "in Chicago, in Pittsburgh, in many, many other places."

The city of Kiev dates back more than 1,400 years. Prince Vladimir introduced Christianity there in the tenth century, and his statue, with cross held high, overlooks the Dnieper River from a picturesque bluff. One prominent historian says there were mass baptisms in the river and the name of the main street in the city, Kreshchatik, derives from the term for Christian baptism.

While in Moscow, Mrs. Nixon toured two of the cathedrals inside the Kremlin in the company of newsmen. The Cathedral of the Annunciation was erected in the fourteenth century. The Archangel Cathedral goes back to the fifteenth and houses the tombs of a number of the czars. A few days after her visit, some correspondents who were taken through came out reporting that the scene was "quite glorious . . . to the Western eye because there are a number of the old churches and these onion domes look as if they were gilded yesterday."

The religious aspects of the summit journey were not entirely limited to cathedral-viewing and church attendance. At least one religious issue came before the summit in a direct way, thanks to persevering Jews. Presidential aide Henry Kissinger assured newsmen that Mr. Nixon broached the plight of Soviet Jewry in the top-level talks. "Soviet leaders are aware of our views on the problem," Kissinger said. He gave no details on how the matter was brought up, or how the Soviet leaders responded. Kissinger called it a "particularly difficult question" and an internal problem" for the U.S.S.R.

The Soviets have become surprisingly sensitive to the allegations that Jews are mistreated in their country and that they find it hard to get permission to emigrate to Israel. Several books just published by the Soviet government that seek to counter the charges were made available to newsmen at the press center. The books deny that Soviet Jews are inhibited, an argument that does not seem convincing to those who visit what might he expected to be the showcase synagogue in Moscow, for the building, on which some work is now being done, has been rather neglected. The Soviet propaganda alleges that Soviet Jews who emigrated to Israel have realized their mistake and have begged to come back.

The Soviet minister of culture, Miss Yekaterina A. Furtseva, appeared at a news conference in the press center and during questioning also denied that the government has deprived Jews of the chance to enrich their own cultural consciousness. She suggested that the Jews themselves have lost interest in that pursuit: "Most Soviet Jews are busy building the Soviet society and economy."

Although some Jews have resorted to violence to attract world opinion and thereby bring pressure on the Kremlin, by and large the campaign has been orderly and conducted within the political process. Would this "establishment approach" or "working within the system" work as well for Protestants?

The answer is not easy, because the problems, though both revolving about religious freedom, are somewhat different. The Jews want primarily to get out; improvement of their opportunities within the country is not the main issue for them as it is for Protestants. Moreover, the problem for Protestants must be worked out through the church leaders who are in office and recognized by the government, and these persons cannot be expected to demand things of the government and attract attention by being vocal. Things have eased up a bit since

the days of Khrushchev and Stalin, but Soviet society still does nc
tolerate open criticism of major government policies. Patience an
perseverance are probably the chief virtues to strive for as things nov
stand.

If, of course, a genuine revival of religious interest and new Christia:
conviction should sweep the country, that would place the whol
situation in a new light.

Hopefully, the summit accord reached in Moscow will encourag
even more of a thaw in relations between the Americans and Soviet
which in turn may indirectly increase the opportunity for Christia:
witness. There seems little doubt, for example, that having more Bible
and Christian literature in the Soviet Union would aid substantially i:
promoting the Gospel. But the Soviets have continued to be very stric
about communication not only from the outside world but within th
country. Very little non-Communist literature, religious or secular, i
allowed into the country. News dissemination among citizens is als
extremely limited.

Some argue that there is no Soviet law forbidding the importatio:
of Bibles or other literature, and that customs officials are simply makin
administrative decisions in confiscating such materials. If true, thi
might provide some room for applying diplomatic leverage, formal an
informal. As cultural exchanges grow between the United States an
the Soviet Union, the prospect of some success will become mor
promising.

A bigger problem is education. Some scholarship help to deservin,
young believers in the Soviet Union that would enable them to go t
colleges in the West ought to be a priority matter. But even mor
crucial is education in the lower age brackets, and among children i:
the Soviet Union the government claims sole responsibility for educa
tion. Perhaps some boarding school arrangements ought to be explored

Meanwhile, American Christians can do no better than to heed th
plea of Ivanov for spiritual fruit, a plea believers regard as embarras
singly familiar but one that has yet to be lived up to even among thos
who regard themselves as theologically orthodox. The harvest of th
Paraclete may be scarce, but truly against such there is no law.

+ Bekannt gewordene Haftorte
von Christen 1968–71